THE MYTH
OF ASIA

by

John M. Steadman

SIMON AND SCHUSTER
NEW YORK

FIRST PRINTING

SBN 671-20223-5
LIBRARY OF CONGRESS CATALOG CARD NUMBER: 70-75867
DESIGNED BY EDITH FOWLER
MANUFACTURED IN THE UNITED STATES OF AMERICA
PRINTED BY THE BOOK PRESS, BRATTLEBORO, VT.

To my sisters
ALICE STEADMAN MCMURPHY
and
ALICE BUNKER KANY

ACKNOWLEDGMENTS

In writing this book, I have been greatly indebted to my friends and colleagues at the Henry E. Huntington Library for encouragement and advice—to Dr. Allan Nevins, Dr. J. E. Pomfret, Dr. Robert Wark, Dr. James Thorpe, Dr. Ray Billington, Dr. Paul Zall, Miss Mary Isabel Fry, Mr. Eric Johnson, Mrs. Winifred Freese, Dr. William Elton, and Mrs. Lillian Bean. To Dr. A. L. Rowse I am especially grateful for detailed criticism of the original manuscript. To my friends at Emory University—Chancellor Goodrich C. White and Professor Thomas H. English—I should like to express my thanks for reading and criticizing earlier versions of the first two chapters of this book. To the editors of *The American Scholar* and *The Emory University Quarterly* I am indebted for permission to reprint in the first two chapters material that appeared earlier in their pages.

J.M.S.

CONTENTS

CONTENTS

FOREWORD
by A. L. ROWSE

This is a book both original and distinguished in itself and important for our time. It shows, from a wealth of knowledge, that the West overestimates the unity of Asia, that indeed to think of Asia as a unity is profoundly mistaken, both in history and today. There are at least three Asias—the cultural complex of China and Japan, that of India and its related cultures, and Islam, which has been closest to the West and has most influenced the West, particularly in earlier science, mathematics and astronomy.

This is one aspect only of the book's main theme. It is extremely illuminating about Asian cultures, about religion and art, no less than science and philosophy.

The book has an important contribution to make in the crucial issue of our time, relations between East and West, and to the understanding of them. It gives the historical background, essential to the comprehension of the greatest political dilemma of today. So much depends upon our getting it right, and this thoughtful and scholarly book offers significant help to all serious minds at this crossroads.

In the end, in showing that the monolithic concept of Asia is untrue, that there is and always has been at least as much variety and diversity in the East as in the West, the implications of the book are hopeful: One sees the unity of mankind under the diversities and conflicts of both East and West.

I can imagine no more urgent theme today, and no more revealing book, brilliantly and wisely written, on so compelling a subject.

PREFACE

If this book has a *raison d'être,* it is the striking re-emergence of Asia and its increasing importance in the life and thought of the West. Developments in India or China—or Vietnam—are no longer merely "Asian affairs"; they have assumed global significance. Asian history has become, in a sense, world history. The political rebirth of the Orient and the cultural convergence of East and West are too obvious to be ignored; and few responsible persons can be—or are—indifferent to them. Western observers greet these signs of the times—as their stargazing ancestors once hailed the approach of a comet or a planetary conjunction—with either jubilation or dismay. And they make prognostications. Erudite journals and popular magazines alike press upon us the imperative need to "understand Asia." Or they urge us to "build bridges between East and West."

These exhortations may be timely, but they are hardly new. For decades, in Europe and Asia alike, writers in more specialized fields (literature and art, religion and philosophy) have been engaged in such feats of engineering—projects scarcely less ambitious than the "stupendous Bridge" over the Abyss in *Paradise Lost.* Some of them have succeeded, imposing order on cultural confusion and erecting a few piers and substantial arches to withstand the general chaos. Others have ended—where they began—in Pandaemonium.

To "understand Asia" one must first remove not only popular

fallacies, but also more learned misconceptions about Asia. These have originated in large part, from a tendency to overgeneralize on the basis of highly specialized knowledge. A writer's very competence in one field of study or his intimate acquaintance with one particular culture sometimes betrays him into making dangerous assumptions about others. An Englishman with (let us say) an intimate knowledge of Indian philosophy fancies that he can speak for Asia as a whole. A French authority on Japanese art lectures on the "Oriental temperament" in general. An American specialist in Southeast Asian politics theorizes about the entire East. Nor are Asians themselves altogether free from this vice. A man admirably qualified to discuss particular aspects of his own national or regional culture—Japanese, Chinese, Persian, Indian—speaks *ex cathedra* for the Orient as a whole; for is he not himself an "Oriental"?

There is a tale, apparently Indian in origin, of the five blind men who tried to describe an elephant.[1] One felt his ear, another his side, the others his trunk, his leg, or his tail. Naturally, their reports conflicted. For the first, the beast was like a winnowing-fan; for the second, like a wall. For the others he resembled a serpent, a tree, or a rope.

The story is not altogether irrelevant to Western—or, for that matter, to Oriental—misconceptions about the East. The specialist in Indian philosophy perceives one Asia, the student of Japanese art another, the authority on Southeast Asian politics a third, the "China hand" a fourth.

Or perhaps (and this is the theme of this book) this particular elephant does not really exist. Perhaps, all the time, there was no elephant there at all—merely a wall, a tree, a rope, a serpent, and a winnowing-fan!

A second difficulty, then, with many specialized discussions of Asia is the tyranny of the word and the concept. Because one talks about "Asia," because one has an idea of "Asia," one assumes that it must actually exist. This bias toward "idealization" (or rather "idolization" in the Baconian sense) is fairly widespread. Many a writer on Asia treats the Orient as though it were a single entity (which it is not)—and thus postulates a unity that has no

real existence outside his own imagination. In the idiom of the
parable, he imagines an elephant that is not really there.

A third difficulty is the tendency to overstress the differences
between Europe and Asia. In such cases the geographical
polarity of "east" and "west" reappears as a cultural antithesis
between spiritual contraries. Affirming the one means denying
the other. If Asia is "spiritual," then Europe must necessarily be
"materialistic." If Europe is "world-affirming," then Asia—to
preserve the contrast—must, surely, be "world-denying." If
Europe emphasizes "theory," then Asia must stress the "aesthetic
component."

For obvious reasons, such antitheses are especially tempting
to exponents of "meta-history," *Kulturgeschichte*, or the philosophy of civilization. These philosophical historians are, by
education as well as professional interests, concerned rather with
ideas than with facts. To the tasks of rationalizing cultural
geography and idealizing cultural history they bring their school-
ing in formal logic. Knowing the advantages of defining a term
by its opposite—that contraries appear more evident by their
dissent—they apply this logical principle to the study of civilizations. To define the Orient, they contrast it with the West. To
elucidate European civilization, they emphasize its opposition to
Asia. In their hands, the terms become mutually exclusive—
what is true of the one cannot be true of the other.

So deep-rooted is this tendency to think in terms of regional
and cultural polarities that, even when a writer has discredited
one pair of antitheses, he often feels obliged to introduce another
in its stead. For the Victorian antithesis of "static" Asia and
"dynamic" Europe he may substitute the theosophist's formula
of "mystic" East and "scientific" West—or, perhaps, the Marxist
opposition between "exploited" and "exploiter." For Schweitzer's
contrast between "world-affirming" and "world-denying" cultures he may substitute the distinction between "humanism" and
"religion" or "thought" and "spirituality." Underlying much of
this speculation is the implicit assumption that there must be
some fundamental contrast—some *essential* difference—between
Eastern and Western cultures; the immediate problem is merely

to pinpoint and define it. If one formula proves inadequate, then one must (of course) search for another.

Even the best kind of guide for the wider public frequently shows the same tendency, but in his case it is, perhaps, more justifiable. In introducing the general public to some particular facet of Oriental culture—philosophy or literature or art—the author naturally attempts to explain those aspects which would seem most strange and unfamiliar to his audience. Realizing the different "structure of expectation" an American (let us say) and a Japanese might bring to an ink painting, a *haiku*, or a Zen *koan*, he points out the relevant differences between the Western artistic or religious traditions (which have shaped the reader's sensibility) and their Sino-Japanese counterparts (with which the reader, presumably, is ill acquainted). The contrasts he draws are slanted toward a particular audience in a particular context—and to this limited extent they are justifiable. He usually intends them more as a semipopular introduction to his subject than as a definitive statement of fact.

Unfortunately, his subject may easily get out of hand, and he may distort both Eastern and Western traditions by oversimplifying them and exaggerating their differences. He may ignore Western analogies, albeit obscure ones, to the very principles he proclaims as distinctively characteristic of an Asian tradition. Or he may forget that he is really discussing a particular facet of a particular culture and begin, instead, to pontificate about Asia as a whole.

In such cases the reader must, if he can, make his own mental reservations. For "Western" he must read "modern American" in one context, "medieval French" in another, and "Attic Greek" in a third. For "Oriental" he must substitute "Kano painting" or "Yellow-Hat Buddhism" or "Advaita philosophy as set forth by Shankaracharya and reinterpreted by recent Indian Vedantists." For, in fact, "Western" and "Eastern" sometimes mean all of these things in different pages of the same work.

The scope of this book is less ambitious than such "introductions to Asian civilization." It attempts less to "understand Asia" (the elusive beast of the Indian parable) than to clear the

ground for understanding, by removing certain widespread misconceptions. Before one can corner the elephant, one must first
cut back the jungle.

Several of the writers whose views I shall re-examine are
giants in their fields, and in writing this book I have found them
indispensable. The critics among them often display an excep-
tional sensitivity to the spirit and values of the Asian culture
they know best—even though their knowledge is sometimes deficient. The scholars in turn possess considerable knowledge
about one or more Eastern civilizations—even though their
sensitivity occasionally fails them.

Their achievement is impressive, and I am greatly indebted
to it. In criticizing it, I am not attempting to undermine it but
to qualify it—to ascertain the extent to which its merit has been
partially obscured by an uncritical acceptance of the myth of
Asia and the antithesis of East and West. I am not challenging
the value of their work; I am merely reassessing it in the light of
an apparent fallacy—just as an astronomer might reappraise the
observations of his predecessors, should he discover that they had
interpreted their data with reference to an imaginary planet—
a phenomenon not unusual in Indian astronomy.

For primary sources, I have relied on standard translations,
most of which are readily accessible. When absolutely necessary,
I have added the Oriental terms in parentheses, as these could
not always be translated in a single word. Nevertheless, I have
used them sparingly. As E. W. F. Tomlin observes, much of the
"attractiveness" of Oriental philosophy "for Western readers
resides . . . in its exotic terminology, and . . . in its apparent . . .
vagueness. Words such as *Nirvana, Karma, Vedanta,* and *Maya*
produce, it seems, an effect very much like hypnosis, above all
perhaps upon those to whom their meaning is unknown."[2]

These observations are, alas, all too true. In certain works this
alien vocabulary seems merely a form of literary ornament—a
stylistic device. In others it serves apparently as a surrogate for
equally traditional Oriental drugs—soma juice and Indian hemp.
Like them it is an opiate.

To anatomize a myth is a difficult operation—especially when it happens to be not only a fabulous creature but also a hybrid. In its present form the myth of Asia is a composite mixture of Indian mysticism, Sino-Japanese art, and that perennial obsession of the West, "Oriental despotism." These topics have, on the whole, determined the central emphasis of this book.

In trying to give them the attention they deserve, I have reluctantly passed over certain other aspects of the Asian scene— aspects equally significant, perhaps, when approached from other points of view, but less relevant to the myth of Asian unity. I should have liked to say more about Chinese science and philosophy, about Indian art and architecture, and about the art and thought of Islam. I should have liked to discuss Oriental literature and aesthetics in greater detail, and to devote more space to contemporary trends in ideology and politics. In these pages, however, I have not attempted to achieve a comprehensive survey of Asian civilization or a systematic comparison between European and Asian values and institutions. Either of these projects would be a task for more than one lifetime. There have been far too many "bird's-eye" surveys of the Orient already, and altogether too many sweeping comparisons of Europe and Asia. Comparisons between different cultures are valid only insofar as they involve detailed analysis of concrete examples—examples that are not only commensurable but truly representative. The critic must be even more cautious in selecting such data than in drawing inferences from them. Few comparative studies of Oriental and Occidental civilization meet these requirements.

Moreover, in the strictest sense, this book is less the history of an idea than the anatomy of an illusion, the dissection of an eidolon. Asia is not (in Arthur O. Lovejoy's phrase) a "unit-idea," the multiform and variegated East cannot be reduced to a "single specific proposition or 'principle' expressly enunciated by . . . philosophers."[3] The Orient is not so much an idea as an association of ideas, a complex of varied and often contradictory meanings.

Thus, the central concern of this book is less the realities of the Orient (though these have occupied our attention) than our own *illusions* about the Orient—not so much Asia per se as the myth of Asia.

In examining this myth, I shall be concerned primarily with three aspects—its influence on our attitudes toward Oriental religion and philosophy, its effect on our understanding of Oriental art and aesthetics, and finally its persistence in our views of the politics and economics of the East.

PART ONE

The Problem

i

THE MYTH

OF ASIA

. .
.

1

When a speaker mentions the Occident in more than a geographical sense, his audience generally knows what he is referring to. It is already thoroughly familiar with "Europe" and "the West" as virtually synonymous terms for the same society—a relatively unified community linked by common religious and intellectual traditions, similar linguistic patterns, and considerable racial homogeneity. Despite its sectarian differences and divergent political and economic ideologies, it possesses a common intellectual and spiritual background in the Judeo-Christian tradition, on the one hand, and secular rationalism, on the other. With minor exceptions, most of its surviving languages belong to three Indo-European groups—Germanic, Latin, Slavic. In its expansion from the European continent to other areas, this community has gradually embraced non-European races and cultures. Geographical limitations have become increasingly irrelevant, and "European society" is no longer peculiar to European soil.

Yet when the same speaker alludes to the Orient, his intent is less obvious. Instead of a single society he may be referring to several societies—all of them characterized by profound differences in language and race and in religious and intellectual traditions. Like "Europe" and "the West," "Asia" and "the East" are near synonyms, but they display a far wider range of meanings.

Precisely how to define and classify these sub-Asian communities remains a bone of contention among anthropologists and historians, and we shall return to this problem later. For the moment we may tentatively follow a modified version of Professor Arnold Toynbee's scheme—a system that tends to disintegrate "Asian society" into three principal civilizations.[1]

First of all, there is a Far Eastern community, consisting chiefly of China, Korea, Japan, and Vietnam. What cultural unity it possesses results largely from the diffusion of Chinese civilization or from such cross influences as the cultural exchanges between Korea and Japan. Mahayana Buddhism and Confucian and Taoist thought have given these countries a religious and philosophical vocabulary that has transcended national boundaries. Despite local variations, Korea, Japan, and Vietnam have all made extensive (though not always exclusive) use of Chinese scripts. Moreover, even though their languages are of diverse origin, all three have borrowed heavily from Chinese.[2]

Secondly, there is an Indian society whose civilization and principal religion derive, like its languages and peoples, from "Aryan" and Dravidian roots. ("Aryan" is, of course, a *linguistic* rather than an ethnic term. It does not apply to all the Indo-European languages, but only to the Indo-Iranian tongues.) It possesses strong cultural ties, however, with several of its neighbors in "Farther India"—notably the Theravada Buddhist countries of Ceylon, Burma, Thailand, and Cambodia, whose religion and civilization are heavily indebted to those of ancient and medieval India. Except for Ceylon, whose languages and peoples most closely resemble those of Hindustan, the populations of these southeastern countries are largely descended from Mongolian peoples from the river valleys of southern China.

Thirdly, there is an Islamic community, extending eastward across Asia from Turkey and Jordan as far as Malaya, Indonesia and the Philippines, and westward across North Africa from Egypt to Morocco. Besides sharing a common religion, it fuses elements from the older cultures of Syria, Arabia, and Iran, embracing a wide variety of peoples and including languages of Indo-European, Semitic, and Mongolian origin. Widely diffused through both continents, it can no longer be regarded as distinctively Asian.

These three communities overlap, particularly in areas where the cultural and religious values of Indian society have encountered those of Islam or China. Moreover, all three have undergone profound transformation through the influence of the modern West.

As labels for analogous but antithetical communities, therefore, the terms "Asia" and "Europe" are patently inaccurate. On the one hand, Western society has outgrown its original association with the European continent, and the designation "European" has become increasingly anachronistic. On the other hand, the classification "Asian" does not sufficiently distinguish the major societies of that continent. Western society is, on the whole, *inter*continental; Eastern societies, with the partial exception of Islam, are for the most part *sub*continental. For none of them is the continental designation appropriate.

The largest significant unit of an Oriental society is, then, not Pan-Asian but "sub-Asian." That is to say, the actual communities of the Orient cover only limited areas of the continent, and there is no single community even roughly coextensive with Asia itself. Except in a strictly geographical sense (and even this has only limited validity), the concept of Asia is largely void of meaning. Unlike Europe, Asia designates no single society. The term "Eastern," unlike "Western," cannot be employed, even loosely, to identify a single community. As the analogue and antithesis of Europe, the Eastern counterpart of Western society, the reality of Asia is largely verbal.

2

Nevertheless, many Europeans and Asians still believe that these concepts distinguish fundamental differences between the civilizations of the Orient and the Occident. East and West, they maintain, are not merely demographic or geographical terms; they are also modes of thinking and feeling—modes so different as to be virtually irreconcilable. Underlying the manifold and obvious diversity of the Orient, there is nevertheless an Eastern psyche distinct from that of the West, a mentality peculiarly and characteristically Asian. The genius of the East, they insist, is static and introspective, while that of the West is dynamic and extroverted. The Orient, passive and contemplative, has displayed this genius in the cultivation of the spirit; the Occident, active and practical, in the amelioration of its environment. The Eastern psyche, resigning itself to physical and social restrictions, attempts not so much to master them as to escape them by self-mastery. The Western mind, confronted by similar obstacles, endeavors rather to harness them in the service of its own desires. The one seeks to transform itself, the other the world about it. The one espouses thought; the other embraces action. Eastern man, in short, renounces the world to cultivate his own soul; Western man subordinates spiritual requirements to material needs. The one looks for happiness in the microcosm, the other in the macrocosm. The gulf between East and West is as profound as the difference between spiritual discipline and scientific technique, nirvana and utopia.[3]

This arbitrary juxtaposition of the mystic and the entrepreneur as the representatives of Orient and Occident would be less unrealistic if it placed adequate stress on other aspects of Asia besides the contemplative. The antithesis of spiritual East and materialistic West eliminates all voices of Asia except those of the bonze and the Brahmin. While it is obviously more applicable to communities professing the Hindu or Buddhist religions than others, even within these it is mostly relevant to the priestly or monastic classes. It neglects the political dynamism of Islam, the practical humanism of Confucianism, and the increasingly secular orientation of most Asian governments.

It also ignores Western history. It has little relevance, for example, to medieval Europe. Before the Renaissance and the industrial revolution (movements significant for the progressively secular orientation and development of Western society) the European solution to the universal problem of reconciling spiritual and material requirements (the respective claims of the cloister and the bazaar) did not differ radically from the solutions evolved by the societies of the Orient. The asceticism of a Christian hermit was not essentially alien to that of the Hindu sannyasi or the Moslem fakir. A European monk or friar might have found in the Buddhist monasteries of East and Southeast Asia even more profound resemblances to his own Order than the tonsure, rosary, or begging-bowl. The really marked divergences between the Eastern and Western solutions did not begin to occur until after the disintegration of medieval society in the West, as secular government and erudition matured and broke their religious ties. The current differences between Europe and Asia are to be measured less in terms of their traditional values than in terms of the changes which the West has experienced in the course of the last four hundred years. For as Asia itself has begun to undergo the same changes, these divergences are becoming less profound; they represent, in many instances, different *stages* of development toward similar goals rather than different *lines* of development or different orientations.

The origin of this antithesis between impractical spirituality and efficient worldliness is to be found primarily in the nature of the European impact on Asia. That this influence has been essentially economic, technical and political—rather than spiritual—is due less to the psychological character of either region than to the nature of Europe's ambitions and Asia's needs.

Both were primarily material, though certainly spiritual and cultural values were also involved. If European merchants sought markets, European missionaries sought converts, and in varying degrees European administrations attempted to transplant French or British, Dutch or Iberian culture. If Oriental societies were first impressed by Western science and technology (or, more concretely, by Western guns!), some of them showed an increasing, albeit critical, admiration for other aspects of European civilization—its political institutions, its philosophy and literature, its music and art. In most of the major Asian societies this response to Western values was marked by bitter internal controversies and by contradictory attitudes not only in the state but also in the individual. No major Oriental society altogether escaped the cultural impact of the West; and in most cases this alien intrusion provoked too severe a soul-searching, too radical a reassessment of traditional values, to be dismissed as merely "material."

Nevertheless, it is the material aspects of Western civilization, rather than its spiritual heritage, that have left the deepest imprint on the East. Asia's heavy debt to European economic and political theory and methods has been in large part an answer to material needs its traditional institutions did not satisfy. The diffusion of Western culture has been, in a sense, an accident—or rather an inevitable and sometimes involuntary consequence of the recognized need to learn (and, if possible, equal) the technological achievements of Europe and America.

When the "Western barbarians" (as the Chinese called them) began to establish their commercial and military outposts in the Orient, they possessed certain undeniable advantages—superior firearms and naval vessels, techniques of mass production, methods that enabled them not only to utilize sources of energy but also to display greater precision in exploiting them. When the West first threatened the security as well as the prosperity of Oriental states, the latter had to acquire the same, or superior, weapons and techniques—and employ them to sustain the old values and the old institutions.

At first they hoped chiefly to "modernize" their technology, but nonetheless to retain the essential values of their societies intact—to become, in a reasonable degree, "modernized" without becoming "Westernized." But as it turned out, this was an impossible compromise. They learned, painfully and gradually, the futility of pouring new wine into old bottles. It was impossible to modernize one aspect of society—even the "material" aspect—without endangering the entire fabric. Western technology, it appeared, was infectious, if not subversive. It could not be dissociated from other aspects of European civilization. Nor was it subject to quarantine. In admitting it (like Pandora's box or the Trojan horse) into their midst, the societies of the

Orient "caught" the contagion of "Westernization." They became vulnerable to a host of subtle, invisible viruses—endemic in the culture of the West—toward which they had no inherited immunity and for which they could find no easy remedy.

The opening wedge for this cultural infiltration, however, was neither cultural nor spiritual. It was the manifest evidence of Western material superiority.

Throughout, the initiative rested with the Occident; and by the very character of this relationship, in which Europe acted and Asia endured, the one necessarily assumed a dynamic part, the other a static role. As Western merchants sought and found trade, and as Western statesmen established dominion, they tended to re-create Orient and Occident alike in terms of their own functions and ends—into complementary images of governor and governed. To the West, Asia appeared as the wax into which Europe was to imprint its own ideas of civilization and order. To the East, Europe seemed a latter-day Procrustes, maiming the Asian societies in the very act of forcing upon them the rigid hospitality of its own convictions. Both views were biased.

The belief, sometimes expressed by Asians, in the antithesis of an inherently imperialistic Europe and a relatively nonaggressive Asia has also originated in the character and magnitude of the Western impact in recent years. It errs in at least three respects. It ignores the empires of ancient and medieval Asia. It overlooks the fact that ethical criticism of the imperial concept has been, on the whole, a comparatively recent development originating largely within the framework of European liberalism rather than of Asian thought. Finally, it misrepresents the causes of Western dominance in the modern period. European empires in the Orient were acquired not by more aggressive intentions but by superior weapons and the ability to exploit existing frictions within Asian societies to the intruder's own advantage. Conversely, the relative quiescence of Asian states was due not to moral compunction against "imperialism" but to the fact that Western competition in the East had left little scope for new Tamerlanes.[4] The only Oriental power to make significant territorial gains during this period—Japan—achieved them after radically modernizing its industry and armed forces. The real basis of this apparent contrast is, then, not the contrasting motivation of East and West but their different stages of technological development.

3

Although there is no objective basis for the dichotomy of East and West either as contrasting communities or as antithetical temperaments, the sense of European or Asian identity is nevertheless strong enough to make this dichotomy convincing to many people on both continents. They continue to believe in the duality of Orient and Occident, primarily because they have become accustomed to regarding themselves as Europeans or Asians.

The geographical distinction between Europe and Asia and the factors primarily responsible for its extension to the cultural plane are Western in origin. The sense of European identity results not only from the tendency of any civilization to regard its own values as absolute, but also from the particular claims advanced by the modern European's predecessors. As the spiritual heir of two of the most self-conscious of cultures—the Hellenic and the Hebraic—Western civilization has, almost from the beginning, retained much of their inherent spiritual exclusiveness. The one thought in terms of the difference between Hellene and barbarian, the other in terms of Jew and Gentile. The Greek city-states were acutely sensitive to the contrast between their own values and those of other societies. Alexander and his successors rationalized their conquests on three continents by professing a mission to propagate Hellenic civilization. Rome claimed a similar right to extend the aegis of its law. Jerusalem believed itself to be the unique repository of the right doctrine and worship of the one true God.

Christian society, in turn, advanced a further claim. Inheriting the learning of Greece, the law of Rome, and the faith of Israel, it declared them all incomplete in the light of its own revelation. What was folly to the Greek and a stumbling block to the Jew became the foundation stone of a new community, exclusive in an entirely different sense from its forebears. Rejecting its predecessors, Christianity retained their claims to authority and utilized them to buttress its own. The wisdom of the Greeks was foolishness in the eyes of God, but it exalted Christian civilization over the barbarian. The law of Rome was secondary to the divine edicts revealed to Judea, but it gave the successors of the Roman Empire an established right to dominion. The religion of Israel was complemented by a new dispensation, but its claim to be the uniquely chosen vessel of the true God was the basis of the spiritual authority of the Christian church. Christian society thus repudiated its temporal and spiritual forebears—the Academy, the Capitol, the synagogue—but it erected its own edifice on the foundations they had left.

The predecessors of the Christian community thus established a frame of reference that shaped its attitude toward all other societies. Like Greece, Rome and Israel before it, European Christendom (both Greek and Latin) tended almost inevitably to look upon the peoples outside its own political and religious structure as barbarians or infidels. As the one veritable "City of God," before which all other temporal or spiritual dominions were doomed ultimately to fall, it regarded the alien groups on its frontiers as a triple danger—to classical civilization, to Roman law, and to true religion. Even the schism between Greek and Latin Christendom meant substantially that analogous claims to intellectual, political and spiritual dominion were advanced by two communities instead of one.

It was easy, therefore, for European Christendom to conceive its relationships with non-Christian societies to the east in terms of a "quarrel of continents."[5] Its Near- or Middle-Eastern neighbors had been traditionally hostile not only to itself but also to its Greek, Roman and Hebrew predecessors. The Far East was virtually unknown. It was from Asia that the Persians invaded Hellas. It was from Asia that Avars, Huns and Bulgars penetrated Europe. It was from Asia that the Turks harassed and eventually overran the Byzantine Empire and ultimately imperiled Vienna. For centuries Christian Europe regarded the regions to the east as an exotic fable or military threat.

Even before the time of Alexander, the Greeks had already begun to think of Asia as the antagonist of Europe. Aeschylus' drama *The Persians* emphasized the intercontinental aspect of the war between European and Asian societies. The supreme act of *hybris* with which Xerxes invited nemesis was bridging the Hellespont—daring to join together what the gods had put asunder—and then scourging the sea for shattering his bridge! Herodotus likewise conceived the Trojan and Persian wars in terms of this larger pattern—the ancient feud between Asia and Europe.

Although Alexander's conquests and the maritime trade of the Roman Empire opened the way for a limited knowledge of India to reach the West, Greek and Latin Christendom found the route to the Orient barred by Islam. China and India were too remote to be known except indirectly, and opinion concerning these countries remained largely myth. In medieval epic and romance they sometimes appeared as Islamic allies against Christendom. The Moslem states of the Near East, on the other hand, constituted a recurring menace to Christian Europe, and it was primarily in terms of this threat that the Western mind conceived Asia. As late as the sixteenth century, Torquato Tasso depicted the First Crusade not merely as a Christian triumph over Islam but also as a European victory over Asia and Africa. Turkish military pressure from the East revived belief in a quarrel of continents.

In this way the original geographical division between Europe and Asia also became the symbol of a cultural and political dichotomy. As Europe had become virtually synonymous with Christian society, Asia became identified with its major adversary. Even before the first Portuguese voyagers set foot on Indian soil, the categories in terms of which Europeans were to interpret the Orient had already been evolved.

In the Orient, on the other hand, the consciousness of Asian identity originated largely in reaction to the colonial system and in the common denominator of anti-Western sentiment. A series of invasions, all within a period of four hundred years, by rival forces from Europe gave new life to the ancient Greek concept of a war of the continents. Standing in analogous relationships to Western powers, Oriental nations experienced for the first time in history the bond of a common interest and a common intent. In this respect at least, Asian consciousness has been the creation—and the instinctive expression—of submerged nationalism.

It was not as Asians that the peoples of Asia responded to the challenge of the West—to the threats of the "Western barbarians" or the promises of Western civilization. Most of them, after all, had never heard of "Asia," and few had any clear idea of Europe. They reacted as Chinese, as Japanese, as Burmese; as Hindus or Moslems, Confucians or Buddhists. For many a Chinese scholar-official there was but one real civilization—his own. Beyond the Great Wall, beyond the mountains and deserts and the sea, there were merely varying degrees of barbarism. When the mandarin first encountered European gunboats, he was not concerned with their danger to *Asia* but with their threat to *China*. Initially he could no more regard his own society as forming a common class with Asian barbarians (India and Japan and Persia) than he could imagine ranking China on the same level as European barbarians (Britain or France). The idea of "Asian identity" would have had as little meaning for him as "Eurasian identity."

Later, when pan-Asian sentiment did develop, the real motivation remained cultural or national—not continental. Though many Oriental leaders—Chinese, Indian, Japanese—voiced eloquent appeals for Asia's liberation and rejuvenation, they were primarily concerned with their own countries—with Mother India, the Way of the Gods (which fortunately coincided with the ways of the Japanese), or with the dignity of China. While it would be unfair to dismiss their exhortations as simply nationalist propaganda in a pan-Asian disguise, they tended nevertheless to picture the regeneration of the Orient largely as an extension of their own distinctive cultures. Pan-Asian sentiment might exist, but not, in actuality, a pan-Asian movement. With few exceptions, each major society imagined such a movement only under its own leadership. India would regenerate Asia through her spiritual and ethical example. Japan would liberate the Orient from "Western imperialism" through her Greater East Asia Co-prosperity Sphere. China would recover the cultural and political hegemony that belonged to her by tradition and by natural law. In their struggle for political independence and material prosperity, the dominant motives of these Eastern peoples have not been "Asian" but communal. Their basic loyalties have been to the tribe or the nation, to political party (Indian Congress or Moslem League, Comintern or Kuomintang), or to religion and culture.

The tendency to conceive the Western impact on the East almost entirely in terms of the colonial relationship has, however, obscured the deeper grounds of Asian consciousness. Although the external relations between European and Asian societies during the modern period have to a considerable extent taken place within the framework of the colonial system, Western influence cannot be regarded simply as political or economic dominance. There is a danger of considering East-West relations purely on the national level and ignoring the more complex encounters between their civilizations.

These deeper roots of Asian consciousness are more profound than frustrated national ambitions or the humiliations of the colonial system, and they have not been eliminated by the termination of overseas government by foreign powers. They consist in the twofold crisis with which the invasion of Western civilization has confronted the civilizations of the East. On the one hand, these cultures face the common peril of disintegration through absorption of Western values and reorientation toward Western norms. On the other hand, they recognize their relative under-development in terms of Western economic and political standards. These factors are interrelated, and both have heightened the sense of Asian identity. The first, by confronting Oriental societies with virtually the entire value system of the Occident, has contributed the common denominator of an awareness of their own non-European character and of their common danger. The second, by emphasizing the gulf between the political and economic development of the East and that of the West, has implanted in Asian communities both a common sense of material inferiority and a common desire to achieve material parity with the Occident.

The continuity of most Asian societies resides in their civilizations rather than in their national structures. Consequently, Oriental governments face the problem of altering deep-rooted traditions often far more ancient than themselves. Native sovereignty has not resolved the tensions created under colonial rule by the conflict of alien and indigenous values.

Introducing these alien concepts into an Oriental environment is, in many respects, a highly artificial solution. In Europe they developed *within* the process of social evolution and were in part molded and defined by it. In Asia, on the other hand, they have been imposed upon this process from without, as external norms for its development and control. In thus attempting to achieve virtually overnight standards that the West evolved over a period of centuries, Eastern governments have intensified the crisis of Asian civilization.

4

Thus in East and West alike the word "Asia" is really an equivoque. It has no fixed meaning—no clear-cut denotation—but it is extraordinarily rich in emotional connotations. Though these may make it the despair of the logician, they enhance its value for the poet, the artist—and the politician.

The problem of the "meaning" of Asia has been complicated, therefore, by the tendency of many Western writers to exploit its ambiguities—to exaggerate the element of mystery and to dwell (consciously or unconsciously) on its more exotic aspects. As a result, the Orient of belief became scarcely distinguishable from the Orient of the imagination. Supposed fact and conscious fiction combined to produce a geographical fantasia as legendary

as the geography of medieval maps and as unreal as the landscape of a dream. And in at least one celebrated instance a
Westerner's highly representative vision of the Orient has been
not only metaphorically but *literally* an opium dream. Thomas
De Quincey's nightmares of "oriental imagery and mythological
tortures" filled him with "unimaginable horror." "Every night,"
confessed the English opium eater, ". . . I have been transported
into Asiatic scenery." In his fantasies he "brought together all
creatures, birds, beasts, reptiles, all trees and plants, usages and
appearances, that are found in all tropical regions, and assembled
them together in China or Hindostan. From kindred feelings, I
soon brought Egypt and her gods under the same law. I was
stared at, hooted at, grinned at, chattered at, by monkeys, by
paroquets, by cockatoos. I ran into pagodas, and was fixed for
centuries at the summit, or in secret rooms; I was the idol; I was
the priest; I was worshipped; I was sacrificed. I fled from the
wrath of Brama through all the forests of Asia: Vishnu hated me:
Seeva lay in wait for me. I came suddenly upon Isis and Osiris.
. . . I was kissed, with cancerous kisses, by crocodiles, and was
laid, confounded with all unutterable abortions, amongst reeds
and Nilotic mud." Toward the Chinese, De Quincey confesses
to "counter-sympathies" deeper than he can analyze. "I could
sooner live with lunatics, with vermin, with crocodiles or snakes."
"A young Chinese seems to me an antediluvian man renewed."
Equally disturbing were the "ancient, monumental, cruel, and
elaborate religions of Hindostan." "Southern Asia, in general,"
he declared, "is the seat of awful images and associations. . . .
The mere antiquity of Asiatic things, of their institutions, histories,—above all, of their mythologies, &c.,—is so impressive,
that to me the vast age of the race and name overpowers the
sense of youth in the individual." "The vast empires" of Asia
". . . give a further sublimity to the feelings associated with all
oriental names or images."[6]

Exoticism and vagueness—these are hallmarks of romanticism,
and the fact is not without relevance for our inquiry. Like most
myths, the myth of Asia evokes romantic echoes, fantastic overtones. The West has always interpreted the East in poetic terms.

Geographical remoteness has given it "aesthetic distance." Unfamiliarity has made it a byword for "the marvelous." We laugh at Don Quixote for peopling La Mancha with the figments of chivalric romance—for perceiving a giant in a windmill and an enchanted princess in a peasant girl. We are amused by the naïveté of his countrymen, who identified the deserts of Baja California with an enchanted island in *Amadis of Gaul*. Yet from ancient to modern times the West has been equally romantic, equally superstitious, in its conceptions of Asia.

Alexander's fictitious letter to Aristotle acquired the prestige of an "authority," and it eventually found an honorable place in medieval encyclopedias, natural histories, and geographies, side by side with Aristotle himself, Ptolemy, and Pliny. The wonders of the East it recounted were accepted as literal truth; several later figured in the tales with which Othello captivated Desdemona. Legends of Eastern paradises were also taken literally; some of them were ascribed to the earliest patriarchs— and thus fell little short of being "gospel truth." The East that the Western scholar encountered in serious treatises was scarcely less fabulous than the Orient which his courtly contemporaries discovered in chivalric romances—or less fanciful than the Asia of the saints' legends which the common man heard preached from the pulpit or saw emblazoned on chapel walls.

The fair enchantresses and exotic princesses of romantic epic are often Orientals. Tasso's Armida is as fabulous as her Celtic cousin, Queen Morgain le Fay. Ariosto's Angelica, the daughter of the Emperor of Cathay, is scarcely less fabulous. Both move in the same realm of fantasy, among the wholly or half-legendary heroes of European romance, Orlando and Ruggiero and Rinaldo. They are as unreal as Circe and Calypso, their classical counterparts—or as Rider Haggard's "She."

Aurangzeb is Dryden's contemporary, but still so remote that he can enter the romantic world of heroic drama with little difficulty—along with Montezuma and Almanzor. Even more romantic is the East of that popular eighteenth-century genre, the Oriental tale. William Beckford's *Vathek* plunges us into the world of the *Arabian Nights* and the *Shah Namah* peopled by jinns and magicians and luxurious sultans. The same romantic sensationalism—an aromatic blend of sensuous and sensual extravagance, magnificence and lust—reappears in Thomas Moore's *Lalla Rookh* and in the Oriental episodes of Byron's *Don Juan.* The finest of the romantic poems on the Orient, Coleridge's *Kubla Khan,* is (or so its author would have us believe) the product of an opium dream.

The modern West has altered its views of Asia, but these are still as romantic as ever. For the East of Puccini and Rimski-Korsakov it has substituted the Orient of Mme. Blavatsky. Scheherazade, Turandot, and Lalla Rookh have been supplanted by the lama, the yogi, and the Zen adept. The *princesse lointaine* has yielded place to the Oriental mystic. In Western eyes, the East is still the home of marvels, and many Occidentals will still believe almost any romantic tale about it—the Indian rope trick; Shangri-la; rishis who are as old and wise as the Taoist Immortals and still haunt the Himalayan ranges; Tibetan lamas who fly on kites, undergo initiation ceremonies for "opening the third eye," and project themselves in space or time at will. More than one volume of deliberate fantasy has passed for literal truth.

We still live in a mythopoeic age. But we still want a Euhemerus to distinguish fact from fiction and history from myth.

5

In exploring the myth of Asia the reader may find it helpful to bear the following points in mind:

1. The habits of mind that distort our views of the East are basically the same as those that, nine times out of ten, have also warped our views of Western society. The "good European" tends, all too frequently, to approach his own society through a technique of systematic exclusion. Analyzing it by the method of contraries, attempting to discover what it actually is by finding out what it is not, he defines it by contrasting it with other

civilizations. He isolates its essential characteristics—and affirms its uniqueness—by emphasizing its differences from other cultures and understressing the values it shares with them. This method often yields a radically oversimplified, vastly overgeneralized picture of the West, but it is even more misleading when applied to an alleged "Oriental society"—the complement and contrary of Western civilization. (There is, after all, some warrant for speaking of the unity of Western society, even though the term is more an obstacle than an aid to clear thinking. But there is, as we shall see, no justification whatever for assuming the unity of Asian civilization. When one uses such a term, one is really talking about India or China or Islam—or else about Central or Southeast Asia or Japan—or perhaps about some incredible witches' brew compounded of all of these.)

2. Though the notion of Asian unity and the dichotomy of East and West are equally illusory, they have nevertheless left their mark on comparative criticism in a wide variety of fields— philosophy and religion, art and literature, economics and politics. The "universal histories" of the eighteenth and nineteenth centuries were strongly influenced by them, and one can still detect their influence in contemporary histories of civilization and philosophies of history. One of the dominant motifs of this essay is the degree to which they have prejudiced, and distorted, comparative criticism in all of these fields.

3. The notion of Asian unity and the dichotomy of East and West are, to a considerable degree, survivals of intellectual systems that once commanded respect but have now been superseded. The notion that geographical differences inevitably involve analogous contrasts in culture can be traced through Montesquieu and Bodin back to Ptolemy and Hippocrates. The tendency to explain the philosophy, religion, and art of a particular culture in terms of the "spirit" of a people or the "mind" of an age is a heritage from transcendental philosophy and *Kulturgeschichte*, with their notions of the *Zeitgeist* ("spirit of the age") and "race ghost," and their theory of a world spirit successively manifesting itself in different modes, different ideas, and different values at different times and places. In such a

context it would not have been altogether illogical to look for the "essence" of European or Asiatic society, to define the "mind" or "spirit" of Orient and Occident, or even to emphasize their contrariety. Such concepts once possessed a certain intellectual respectability, if not validity; for they were supported by the astrology of Ptolemy and Bodin or by the metaphysical assumptions of the transcendentalists. Now that both of these systems are discredited, the notion of a European or Asiatic "spirit" and the search for the "essence" of Eastern or Western civilization no longer have a rational foundation. They are ideological fossils.

4. The terms we commonly evoke in contrasting European and Asian values originally referred (in many cases) to contrasts *within* the European tradition or *within* the Indian or Chinese tradition. Such are the contrasts between "Attic" and "Asiatic" styles in Western rhetoric or between "spirit" and "realism" in Chinese painting. Though such antitheses as these actually developed within the same tradition (whether European, Chinese or Indian) as a result of rivalry among different schools or between different aesthetic or philosophical ideals, they have nevertheless become detached from their original contexts and transformed into cultural differentiae of East and West. Instead of applying them specifically to differences within the same cultural tradition, critics often regard them as distinguishing characteristics of Europe and Asia. (Laurence Binyon, for example, insists that "all" Chinese painters aim at capturing the inner spirit of an object rather than its mere outer appearance— and takes this principle as a criterion for differentiating the art of East and West. Yet many of the Chinese theorists, from whom he ultimately derives his views of Oriental art, deplore the fact that the majority of their contemporaries and many of the ancients as well seek the external likeness rather than the inner reality.)

5. In certain limited contexts the dichotomy of East and West may be significant. In novels where the author is consciously treating the confrontation of European and Asian values, the antithesis would naturally be of fundamental structural and

thematic importance. It would also be significant in cases where a writer or painter or musician is deliberately attempting to "Orientalize" or "Westernize" his content or his style. All the same, one should bear in mind that in many instances the basic opposition in the author's mind is not between Europe and Asia, but between particular countries or cultures. E. M. Forster's *A Passage to India,* for instance, is not concerned with large-scale relations between East and West so much as with *personal* relationships between individual Englishmen, Hindus, and Indian Moslems—individuals divided by culture, nationality and religion. Whistler's style during its Japanese phase was less "Orientalized" than "Nihongized." The "Orientalizing" vogues in modern European architecture and decor would be better described as Chinese or Japanese, Indian or Persian. Despite their flair for the exotic, Europeans of the eighteenth century rarely confused Indian and Chinese styles or motifs.

6. With the exception of a comparatively few instances, where the opposition of Europe and Asia is part of the artist's conscious intent, the dichotomy of East and West tends to obstruct, rather than assist, us in attempting to understand the art and thought of either region. It distracts our attention from problems that faced the particular thinker or artist in a particular situation, and diverts us to more abstract and general problems that can hardly have existed for him at all. For considerations that *were* significant for the creative artist or thinker, it substitutes an arbitrary and largely irrelevant antithesis that can have little or no bearing on the content and style of his work, on the particular technical problems he faced (whether of thought or of expression) and the particular solutions he devised to resolve them. The significant features of a painting, a philosophical treatise, or a devotional work all spring, in fact, from a concrete situation. They arise in response to particular technical problems and within a context that offers certain clearly defined possibilities of development and expression and (equally important) certain significant limitations. These, I would suggest, are the proper concern of the critic, regardless of whether he is dealing with

Oriental or Western materials. The desire to "compare" East and West can, for the most part, only distract him from his true office, his real function.

7. The difficulties that the cultural historian inevitably encounters in defining Europe and Asia, in isolating their essential characteristics, and—if he is rash enough to try—in determining their frontiers are hardly surprising. For he is, in fact, endeavoring to impose geographical boundaries on *ideas,* to fix chronological limits for *values,* and this attempt is almost bound to be unsuccessful. The higher values of both European and Asian civilizations cannot be circumscribed and pinpointed in this way. They belong primarily to the intellect and thus partly transcend the restrictions of time and place.

The effort to establish a cultural watershed—a psychological Continental Divide between Europe and Asia—is, therefore, almost as futile as trying to square the circle. (If the mind is really "its own place," it can just as easily make East of West as Hell of Heaven.) Even if the historian should   succeed—to his own satisfaction and the astonishment of his peers—in drawing such a cultural frontier, it could be valid only when applied to a very limited period. As he well knows, or ought to know, these societies are not static but dynamic. Neither their values nor their boundaries—linguistic, political, and so on—have remained constant. The Europe and Asia of 1000 B.C. are not those of today, nor are their cultural "frontiers" (if one grants such a concept) still the same. When our contemporaries speak of the "interplay" between East and West in the ancient world, the Middle Ages, or modern times, they are using terms that have altered radically in meaning and extension.

8. Most of the alleged "encounters between East and West" would be more accurately described in terms of a broader social context and a wider community of values. Through a gradual diffusion of values and attitudes—by conquests, by alliances, or by ordinary commercial and cultural exchanges—many of these European and Asiatic societies shared a common civilization. Such an "East Mediterranean synthesis" (as Professor Cyrus Gordon terms it) existed during the Minoan and Mycenaean

periods. Similar international and intercontinental civilizations characterized the Mediterranean world during the period of the Hellenistic and Roman empires. In the complex interaction of Hittite and Assyrian, Canaanite and Egyptian, Persian and Hellenic values one finds much more than a series of sporadic "encounters" among different civilizations; one recognizes, on a larger scale, a type of cultural and social exchange that one has already noted in smaller societies. This long-term, continuous cultural dialogue, even if sometimes interrupted, becomes the instrument for gradually creating and diffusing a new and more comprehensive civilization.

9. Finally, our notion of Western civilization is itself a composite mixture of "warring elements"—a complex molecular structure that unites seventeenth-century experimental and mechanical philosophies with legal and political concepts derived from ancient Rome, that combines humanistic and aesthetic values borrowed from ancient Greece with religious values inherited from ancient Israel. This complex image of ourselves we have, in turn, projected backwards in time, reimposing on the ancients themselves a Western identity they would hardly have recognized. As a result of this parochial attitude we tend to confuse Greek civilization with Western European civilization; we overestimate its rationality; we underestimate its strong affinities with the ancient Near East; and we overlook the extent to which it continued to play a constructive role in medieval Islam.

6

There is, then, no objective basis for the dichotomy of Europe and Asia either geographically or culturally. Modern geographers reject the artificial division of what is, in fact, a single land mass. The concept of a "quarrel of continents" actually developed from tensions between individual nations or civilizations—encounters between ancient Greece and Persia, between medieval Christendom and Islam, and between particular communities in modern Europe and Asia. The antithesis of East and West is, therefore, meaningless except as the sense of European or Asian identity has made it seem credible.

Today the alleged unity of Asia seems to mean little more than the sense of belonging to a common economic and political category—of marching in the ranks of the "developing nations" toward some remote but not inaccessible Utopia; of fighting in the same ranks against the rear guard of "Western colonialism" and "imperialism." Such an attitude may account, in part, for the sense of a common cause—and even of identity—that Oriental peoples sometimes share with the "underdeveloped" countries of Africa and Latin America. It provides, however, no foundation at all for the notion of Asian unity.

"Modernization" and "Westernization" are not the same thing, but they are, on occasion, so closely related that it is difficult to dissociate them. In seeking to achieve a sort of "industrialization with honor"—to become modernized without becoming altogether Westernized—the developing countries of the East do, in varying degrees, face a common problem. To modernize their economy means altering their mores; and this in turn means altering (even in a minor degree) the national way of life and the national character. There is a difference between absorbing Western culture and being absorbed by it; but the line is not always easy to draw or, once drawn, to hold to.

The most obvious signs of unity in Asia are, paradoxically, those of Western influence. If a Japanese converses with a Burmese they will probably be speaking English. The only architectural styles common to all parts of Asia are Western styles. The only music one hears almost universally throughout the East is Western music. If one encounters the same volume on bookstalls in Tokyo, Delhi, and Teheran, it is probably a Western book. If there is a gradual *rapprochement* among the numerous subsects of Buddhism, they owe it, in large part, to the labors of Westerners like Colonel H. S. Olcott and Mr. Christmas Humphreys. Even pan-Asian sentiments are really a European legacy—a reaction to colonial rule.

Thus far we have examined in fairly general terms the development of the dichotomy of Europe and Asia. Originally the latter term referred, apparently, only to the northwest coast of Asia Minor.[7] By the time of Herodotus and Euripides, however, the term had been broadened to cover most of what we now call Western Asia; not only the Trojans but also the Persians and Phoenicians were "Asiatic" champions in the "quarrel of continents." The notion of intercontinental rivalry persisted during the Middle Ages, acquiring religious overtones, and gained new vitality during the modern colonial period as a direct result of European commercial, military and cultural expansion throughout the Orient. During the course of nearly three thousand years the *content* of this dichotomy has undergone striking changes, but the dichotomy itself has shown an equally striking capacity for survival. Not only has it obscured some significant differences among the principal Asian cultures ("the three Asias") and some equally significant similarities between European and Asian societies; it has also gravely distorted scholarly criticism of the religion, philosophy, art, and politics of East and West alike.

In recent years one of the most familiar forms of this dichotomy has been the opposition between Asian "other-worldliness" and European "this-worldliness"—the antithesis between Eastern spirituality and Western technique. We shall explore several of its aspects in the next two chapters.

PART TWO

Philosophy and Religion

ii

NIRVANA

AND UTOPIA

. . .

1

Kicking a stone hardly refutes Berkeley—though Dr. Johnson thought it did, regarding a bruised toe as a more forceful argument than a syllogism. Visiting a Kowloon market or an Indian bazaar will not discredit the fallacy of the "mystic East," but it ought to make the visitor himself more skeptical. Though both are more colorful, and perhaps more human, than a Western supermarket, they are scarcely more spiritual. Indeed the idols of the marketplace often become the cult images of the temple. Throughout the Orient, Mammon has his own shrines. In one avatar or another—as Kubera or Jambhala, as Ganesh or Lusing—he presides over altars as though they were counting-tables. For financial benefits Asians can invoke him directly—just as Romans once prayed to Fortuna and Jonson's Volpone to his gold—or command his services through a higher deity. If the method seems spiritual, the intent is clearly secular. It is still the universal profit motive, though partisans may christen it "other-worldliness."

Chronic deprivations produce their own optical marvels, which one may interpret either as illusions or as prophetic visions. Fasting ascetics dream of ambrosia; thirsting caravans behold oases. What wonder that poverty should do the same? What wonder that to many Asians (as to many Europeans) the goods

of the world-to-come should appear larger and more distinct—
equally real and infinitely more attainable—than those of this
world? Yet, even so, neither Asians nor Europeans pray exclusively for eternal rewards. To the gods, Elysium or nirvana may
seem an instant payment, and the lifetime of a world or of infinite worlds may seem shorter than a one-day loan. To men,
however, even one lifetime—much less a cycle of reincarnations!
—is a long time to wait for a return on an uncertain investment.
Small wonder, then, that Asians and Europeans alike attempt to
"cash in" on their celestial investments; that (as Indian legends
assure us) holy ascetics have by their austerities put the gods
in their debt and thus imperiled the solvency of heaven; that
the saints themselves have sometimes drawn prematurely on
their accounts in the treasury of merits. Asians and Europeans
alike implore the blessings of *this* life and, when other expecta-
tions fail, seek material gain by prayer.

The "spiritual" Oriental petitions his gods for the kind of
aid that the crass Westerner has come to expect from his doctor,
banker, or weather forecaster. For commercial advice, he can
consult a fortune stick instead of a stockbroker. To cancel ancestral debts and appease his ghostly creditors, he can literally
consume imitation currency in the temple courtyard instead of
metaphorically "burning" hard cash; in lieu of vaccination he
can solicit the smallpox goddess—the Indian Hariti or the
Chinese Tou-shen.

Thus the alleged antithesis between a worldly Europe and an
otherworldly Asia gives a distorted picture of both East and
West. But it also overlooks the major differences that exist among
the various Oriental religions themselves. If Islam possesses the
severer faith and stricter discipline, Hinduism is the more un-
worldly—though paradoxically the more sensual—of the two.
The chief emphasis of Confucian thought is ethical and political;
its ideal is less the spiritual *dévot*, the rishi, than the "moral
man," the "superior man." It produces practical sages and
philosophical magistrates rather than saints. Buddhism is highly
spiritual; but essentially it is neither theocratic like Islam[1] nor
theocentric like Hinduism. Despite the "living Buddhas" of

lamaism and the deified kings of "Farther India," a pantheon fully as complex as that of ancient Rome or modern Benares, and an eschatology that makes Dante's seem ingenuous by comparison, its central doctrines are agnostic and skeptical. Its stricter sects ignore or deny both God and the soul.

To understand the origins of the antithesis of spiritual Asia and materialistic Europe one must look primarily to the disparity in their economic development—and to its corollary, the nature of the ends that Eastern and Western societies have sought from one another. For cultural and spiritual guidance, Asia still relies on her own traditions. For political and scientific techniques she turns to Europe. It is hardly surprising, therefore, that for many Orientals the conventional opposition of East and West should involve a profounder contrast—the confrontation of matter and spirit.

Henry Adams, commenting on the vicissitudes of Western culture, found symbols of the contrasting aspirations of medieval and modern man in the Virgin of Chartres and the dynamo— spiritual grace and material power. The antithesis of Oriental and Occidental civilizations, as popular opinion conceives it, could be expressed in almost identical terms. One does not need to go outside Japan to find it; it is epitomized for us in the Buddha of Kamakura and the cyclotron. Both represent attempts to come to grips with the underlying reality of the universe—but a universe conceived in radically different modes. For the traditional East, reality is essentially immaterial, impalpable, ineffable —a spiritual ground beyond being and nonbeing and quite incapable of translation into human terms. For the modern West, on the other hand, reality is material, concrete, capable of being analyzed in the laboratory and expressed in mathematical formulas.

Thus, the argument goes, Orient and Occident are diametrically opposed both in their ends and in the methods by which they attempt to achieve them. The one seeks union—or actual identity—with a spiritual reality through self-mastery; the other attempts to master physical nature instead. The one aims at contemplation, the other at action. While the Asian tries to identify himself with a reality beyond the universe, the European endeavors to harness the universe to serve his own needs. The former accomplishes his end through denial, the latter through action. They aim respectively at nirvana and utopia.

Such is the popular conception of East and West, and it must not be left uncriticized. In the first place, it is not absolute but relative; it is not a matter of extremes but of degree. Obviously, the East is not wholly dedicated to God, nor is the West wholly dedicated to Mammon. The *relative* emphasis on spiritual and material values in Oriental and Occidental civilizations is potentially significant; their *absolute* dedication to one or the other end is merely a fiction.[2] While it is true that Western nations have made greater material progress than Eastern countries during the last four hundred years and that this achievement has entailed distinct spiritual disadvantages, one can easily overestimate its importance. More efficient techniques for attaining material ends are not necessarily more vicious than archaic and primitive means to the same ends. Driving laboriously to market in an oxcart does not confer spiritual graces denied to the passenger in a motorcar. The material needs of Eastern man are, and have been, fully as pressing as those of his Western counterpart—while his means for satisfying them have been drastically fewer. Like Europe, Asia has waged its own wars for wealth and empire. In the future it will continue to be increasingly committed to the acquisition of Western techniques and the pursuit of Western standards of prosperity.

Secondly, the dichotomy of spiritual East and materialistic West actually distorts the usual pattern of contacts between different civilizations. In the cultural interchanges between Europe and Asia, the transmission of aesthetic and spiritual values can rarely be dissociated from the pattern of military or commercial expansion. Cyrus Gordon has stressed the importance of mercantile and military colonies or enclaves as channels of cultural transmission during the Amarna Age; the role of merchant guilds and mercenaries in spreading artistic and religious values at this time can be paralleled at a later date by the role of Phoenician merchants in transmitting Asian influences to Greece during the

"Orientalizing period" of Greek art, and at a still later date by
the role of Roman mercenaries in spreading Mithraism, Christianity, and other "Oriental" religions through northern and
western Europe. The overseas trade between China, India, and
Rome indirectly stimulated the expansion of Indian culture into
southeastern Asia and the spread of Mediterranean religions into
southern India. Just as Greco-Roman military and mercantile
enterprise indirectly influenced Indian sculpture, the art and
religion of India reached Central Asia and China over routes
made possible by Kushan conquests and by the enterprise of
merchant caravans. So far as cultural expansion was concerned,
the diffusion of "higher" religious and aesthetic values depended,
in Europe and Asia alike, partly on commerce and conquest; they
followed channels established by the merchant or the soldier.

In the third place, this aspect of the myth applies primarily to
the modern West, rather than to Western civilization as such,
and to the East of tradition rather than of today. The average
intellectual and political leader in modern Asia thinks largely in
terms of utopia rather than of nirvana. Virtually the same relationship exists—though to a lesser extent—between the contemporary Asian and his predecessors as between the contemporary
Westerner and his medieval ancestors. If the Occident has preferred the dynamo to the Virgin, the Orient has elected a similar
alternative—subordinating Buddha to the cyclotron and atomic
energy.

In the fourth place, the assumption of spiritual differences has
greater validity for certain Asian and Western nations than for
others. Nirvana is not a universal Asian ideal, nor is utopia a
universal aspiration in the West. A further distinction is needed
to clarify the difference between those religions, such as Hinduism and Buddhism, which seek felicity in nirvana or its equivalent, and those which seek it through conformity to divine law
in a particular human society, whether the law be natural or
revealed. (Such is the case with Judaism, Christianity, and
Islam.)[3] In the former—which I shall designate hereafter as the
"nirvana religions" or "Indian faiths"—the emphasis is on union
with a higher spiritual reality through contemplation; in the

latter—which may be appropriately designated as the "Abrahamic faiths" or "religions of Law"—it is on conformity to a divine will through obedience. Though both types of spirituality may include aspects of each other—for example, the goal of divine union among Christian, Hebrew, and Moslem mystics, and the significance of Law (or dharma) within Hinduism and Buddhism—they nevertheless place their basic emphasis and found their emotional and intellectual structures on different points and with different orientation.

Since both types of religion are widely current in Asia, one cannot regard either one as the unique representative of Asian spirituality. The nirvana religions, which the Western observer often takes as characteristic of the Oriental mind, are limited largely to East and Southeast Asia. The religions of Law, on the other hand, are predominant in Central and West Asia and constitute a common tie between those regions and Europe, North Africa, and the Americas. There is thus no typical Asian spirituality comparable and antithetical to the spirituality of Europe and America, for the simple reason that no pan-Asian spirituality exists.

2

The dividing line between the two groups of religions is the relationship of the finite to the infinite or of the temporal to the eternal. In the nirvana religions the relationship is generally regarded as a psychological illusion, and the solution is largely epistemological, dependent on one's conception of knowledge. The finite self is the result of false knowledge; with true knowledge the self is reabsorbed into the Infinite Self. In the religions of Law the relationship is a metaphysical reality with an absolute ethical imperative; the finite being is not a mere illusory manifestation of the infinite Being but its creature and vassal, subject to it in all things and obligated to conform to and execute its will. In the religions of nirvana the finite self is a shadow; in the religions of Law it is the clay vessel shaped by the potter's wheel.

"Thy kingdom come, thy will be done"; "Thine is the kingdom, and the power, and the glory"; "Thine, O Lord, is the greatness, and the power, and the glory, and the victory, and the majesty: for all that is in the heaven and in the earth is thine; thine is the kingdom, O Lord, and thou art exalted as head above all"—these prayers may refer to the same spiritual reality as the nirvana religions, but they are radically different in mode from the Hindu mantra: "From the unreal lead me to the Real, from darkness lead me to the Light, from death lead me to Immortality."

The religion of nirvana offers identity with an Absolute Being through contemplation; the religion of Law seeks to accomplish the divine will through obedient action. Neither aims, of course, at a secular utopia, but of the two the religion of Law is the more likely to attempt the transformation of human society in conformity with its own interpretation of divine law. The result is a more spiritualized ideal of utopia as an earthly realization of the Kingdom of God.

The religion of nirvana, accordingly, has a dual significance for the Western observer. It offers the most striking counterpart to the utopian aspirations of the modern West and of the "New Asia." Historically, moreover, it has played a major—though not always dominant—role in most of the cultures of East and Southeast Asia. In spite of the manifest differences between India, Ceylon, Burma, Thailand, Indochina, China, and Japan, the doctrines of Hinduism, Buddhism, and Jainism constitute a major part of the intellectual and spiritual heritage of these countries and have exerted a significant influence on their art, literature, and mores. The common aspiration of all three of these religions is that absorption of the individual in a universal Absolute which the Buddhist terms nirvana.

Underlying all three religions is the conception of the bondage and misery of the finite being, ignorant of its true nature. Through a series of reincarnations the soul must suffer the consequences of its previous actions in accordance with the principle of reciprocal justice (or karma) whereby every good or bad action brings its corresponding reward. Liberation (moksha) can be obtained only through perfecting and transcending the finite self and its desires, achieving thereby its return to its true nature and the renunciation of its erroneous egoism.

The state to which the perfected self returns is beyond intellectual definition and hence beyond definable attributes. The Buddhist writer Nagasena refused to describe it except in such terms as "Nirvana is." The literal meaning of nirvana is "waning out," and in the Theravada Buddhism of Southeast Asia, it refers to the extinction of the fires of greed, anger, and illusion. In its larger significance, however, it refers to the cessation of the desire for separate existence, to the extinction of the individual being in the universal Self. Nirvana is the reward of spiritual enlightenment, and for the Theravada Buddhist it may be achieved within this life through individual effort; for certain schools of Mahayana Buddhism, on the other hand, it is a Paradise lying beyond death, and can be achieved less through individual exertion than through the free acceptance of grace.[4]

Hinduism, similarly, finds its highest good in the individual's surrender of personal identity and his reabsorption in the Absolute Self; atman (the soul) realizes its essential identity with Brahman (absolute reality). For many Vedantists nothing is real except one Being, and apart from this Being the individual soul has no real existence. "Brahma[n] exists truly, the world falsely; the soul is only Brahma[n], and no other." This Being is alone true Existence, Knowledge, and Bliss. As the individual soul recognizes its separate existence as illusory and realizes its identity with this Being, it is freed from the cycle of birth, death, and rebirth. "Verily, even if one performs a great and holy work, but without knowing that the whole world is Brahma[n] or the Self, and that I am Brahma[n] or the Self, that work of his merely perishes in the end. One should worship the Self alone as his true world. The work of him who worships the Self alone as his true world does not perish." Like nirvana, the Self is beyond intellectual expression or logical apprehension. "The Self is to be described by No, No. . . . He is incomprehensible, for He cannot be comprehended."

The ideal of the Jains is similar to the principal ideal of the Buddhists and Hindus—self-liberation through conquest of worldly desires. Jainism recognizes three categories of souls, ranked in order of their degree of liberation from the bonds of worldliness. The lowest are the souls still bound by works and worldly associations. Immediately above them are those souls which have achieved virtual liberation from this bondage. Highest of all are the perfectly enlightened souls who have renounced all worldly desires, achieved perfection, and been raised to the rank of gods.

All three of the nirvana religions seek liberation through spiritual enlightenment. All three bestow peculiar veneration on the contemplative recluse in quest of illumination. All three have evolved distinctive meditative techniques as a principal (though not exclusive) means of achieving deliverance. Though they also stress right action and conformity to the divinely ordained law of nature (dharma), obedience to law does not have precisely the same meaning as in the religions of Law. Nirvana itself differs essentially from the heavenly rewards which the latter generally anticipate. The religions of Law are generally content with one of the first three stages of bliss as defined in Hindu philosophy—residence in the same heaven with God, nearness to God, or assimilation to the likeness of God. The nirvana religions look beyond them to a fourth and final stage—complete union with the divine.

All three nirvana religions derived their intellectual foundations originally from Indian philosophical speculation in the pre-Christian era dealing with the nature of reality and the soul, the cause of suffering, the problem of truth and illusion, and the criteria of true knowledge or gnosis (jnana). For all their subsequent development or accretions, and the proliferation of sects and subsects, they still display the signs of their origin in learned controversy, and still bear the birthmarks of erudite—and sometimes pedantic—debate. Despite its diffusion through East and Southeast Asia and its borrowings from other creeds, Buddhism still shows its Indian genealogy in its hagiology and cosmology, its vocabulary, its scriptures, and—in many respects—its iconology. In varying degrees all three religions have influenced one another, either borrowing concepts or evolving counterconcepts, either assimilating or rejecting aspects of one another. Neither Buddhism nor Jainism accepts in its entirety the Hindu conception of the soul or the self, and Hinduism itself is comprehensive enough to include dualistic conceptions of the relationship of the finite self to the Infinite Self, along with its traditional monism. Despite their differences, however, all three religions remain parallel—or, rather, less parallel than interdependent—systems, which begin with the same human dilemma and arrive, through relatively similar means, at the same spiritual end.

All three are philosophical religions, and despite the fact that the reality they seek is beyond philosophical formulation, despite the importance that all three attach to practice, it is as philosophical systems that they have developed, spread, and survived. They are thus dependent for their continued existence on a relatively small group of initiates and scholars, capable of mastering the basic doctrines and literature and interpreting them to the masses of believers. Thus Hinduism has its priestly castes, and Buddhism has its monastic groups or sanghas. Many of the Jain priests, furthermore, have retained their identification as members of the Brahmin caste.

3

But Buddhism, Hinduism, and Jainism are not merely religious philosophies. They are philosophical religions, and as religions they have had to reach beyond the philosophically adept few who could comprehend them to the illiterate masses who could not. They have been compelled, therefore, to make use of the elements of popular religion, whether indigenous or imported, in order to make themselves personal, concrete, and accessible to the people. They have been forced to avail themselves of various art forms—native and foreign—in order to render sensible an essentially supersensible message. Temples, statues, frescoes, dances, stories, plays had to be utilized in order to accommodate the abstract faith to the popular understanding. It has been primarily through the development and utilization of these media of instruction and worship that these religions have exerted their greatest influence in molding the character and civilization of the peoples with whom they have come in contact.

These two factors—the relatively free philosophical development of the original doctrines, and frequent concessions to the demands of popular religion—are largely responsible for the multiplication of sects and subsects within these three major faiths: the white-robed and naked sects of Jainism; the Red Hat and Yellow Hat sects of Tibetan Buddhism; the Theravada Buddhism of Southeast Asia and the various Mahayana sects of China and Japan; and, finally the Vaishnavite, Shaivite and Shakta sects, the various schools of Vedanta philosophy, and the various forms of Yoga within Hinduism.

The chief concession of the nirvana religions to popular needs has been the concept of personal deities as objects of worship and as a means of salvation to the masses who could not follow the path along the razor's edge to enlightenment. This concept has found expression in the complexity of the Hindu and Buddhist pantheons, in Hindu Bhakti-Yoga, and in the Bodhisattva ideal of Mahayana Buddhism.

To realize the divine through the study of theology (Jnana-Yoga) or through rigid control of the mind in meditation (Raja-Yoga) is clearly beyond the scope of the average Hindu worshiper. Even the approximation of the human to the divine through right action (Karma-Yoga) is a difficult and thorny path. To approach the divine through love is easier; and, therefore, Bhakti-Yoga, which attempts to awaken absolute devotion to a qualified and personal God through conceiving him in terms of human relationships, has the greatest influence among the unlettered Indian public.

Generally this worship of the human manifestations of the god follows five stages: peaceful devotion, servantship, friendship, parental devotion to God as to a child, and adoration of God as spouse. It may also include filial devotion to God as father or mother. In the final stages of bhakti an ecstatic and wholehearted devotion to the god replaces all other attachments. "Where Rama is, there is no room for any desire—where desire is there is no room for Rama."

Bhakti-Yoga is ultimately directed toward Isvara, the Supreme Ruler, who is the highest manifestation of the unqualified and impersonal Absolute. Even Isvara, however, is too abstract for the masses, and he is generally conceived, therefore, in terms of his threefold manifestations as Brahma, Vishnu, and Shiva, the creator, preserver, and destroyer of the universe. With the exception of Brahma (whose cult is now restricted to only one or two minor temples), each of these manifestations has his own sect of devotees, who worship him under a wide variety of forms symbolic of further manifestations of his essential qualities. Vishnu is venerated under the forms of his ten incarnations (or avatars); Shiva, in several forms, such as Mahakala the destroyer, Mahadeva the supreme God, Mahayogi the perfect ascetic, and others. There are also small cults devoted to the sun god Surya or to the elephant-headed god of wisdom, Ganapati. The active or dynamic aspect of each of these gods is symbolized by his female consort (or Shakti), who often has her own sect of worshipers. Especially important for the Bhakti groups are the divine heroes, Krishna and Rama. Much of Hindu literature, art, and music has derived its inspiration from these incarnations of Vishnu the Preserver.

The significance of Bhakti-Yoga for the masses, as contrasted with the Jnana-Yoga accessible only to the erudite, is perhaps most clearly expressed in Krishna's remarks to Arjuna in the *Bhagavad-Gita* regarding the relative merits of the two methods. Arjuna has asked, "Those devotees who, ever steadfast, thus worship Thee and those who worship the Unmanifested Imperishable, which of them are better knowers of Yoga?" Krishna replies, "Those who, fixing their minds on Me, worship Me with perpetual devotion, endowed with supreme faith, . . . they are the best knowers of Yoga. But those who contemplate the Imperishable, the Undefinable, Unmanifested, Omnipresent, Unthinkable, Unchangeable, Immovable and Eternal, having subdued all the senses, even-minded everywhere, and engaged in doing good to all beings, verily they attain unto Me. Greater is their difficulty whose minds are set on the Unmanifested, for the goal of the Unmanifested is very arduous for the embodied to attain. But those who, surrendering all actions to Me and regarding Me as the Supreme Goal, worship Me with single-hearted devotion, for them whose hearts are thus fixed on Me . . . I become ere long the Saviour from the ocean of mortal Samsara (world of birth and death)."

Bhakti and Jnana thus represent the two extremes of Hinduism as a philosophical religion. In Bhakti, the ultimate concessions have been made by an esoteric and caste-conditioned theology to popular cults. Some of these cherished divinities and forms of worship were indigenous to pre-Vedic India. Others evolved later—and some are still developing today. The principal foundation of Bhakti doctrine is practice rather than theory. Utilizing philosophical methods chiefly to serve the ends of devotion, converting reason into the handmaid of emotion, subordinating knowledge to love, it has given theological sanction to modes of worship whose origin and nature were devotional rather than speculative. In the Bhakti cults, accordingly, the devotional aspects of Hinduism outgrew the barriers which the philosophical character of Brahmanism had placed in the path of the unlearned. Emphasis was placed less on the exertions and acquired merit of the individual believer and more on the active role of a divine Saviour in winning to himself those who love him and in accomplishing through his human incarnations the redemption of his creatures from the world. In contrast to the unqualified monism of many Vedantists (Shankara, for instance), Bhakti theologians preached a qualified monism (or at times, dualism) which admitted some sort of reality to the individual soul vis-à-vis the Absolute. "Who cares to become sugar?" Swami Vivekananda quotes a Bhakti devotee as saying; "I want to taste sugar."

The development of Mahayana Buddhism represents a similar evolution in the direction of popular needs. Despite the highly esoteric philosophy of some of its sects, it nevertheless provides a complex mythology of divine persons who manifest and express the inconceivable Absolute which lies beyond all manifestations. Between unenlightened humanity and an ultimate spiritual essence known only as "Suchness" (*Tathata*), Mahayana Buddhism posits a hierarchy of divine beings dedicated to elevating all nature to the attainment of Buddhahood. Viewed from a religious standpoint, "Suchness" is a universal Buddha-Spirit (Dharmakaya), personified as Vairocana Buddha or Adi-Buddha and characterized by infinite wisdom and infinite compassion. This cosmic Buddha in turn manifests himself in seven subordinate Dhyani Buddhas; each of these is manifested in one or more Bodhisattvas, who in turn incarnate themselves in human form. Thus Gautama Siddhartha, the historic Buddha, was an incarnation of the Dhyani Bodhisattva Avalokiteshvara, who in turn manifested the Dhyani Buddha Amitabha.

Cardinal to Mahayana Buddhism is the concept of the Bodhisattvas, who, having attained enlightenment, voluntarily deny themselves the enjoyment of nirvana in order to bring the rest of mankind to salvation. In their unwavering compassion for all life and their free bestowal of their own accumulated merit upon others deficient in good works, they are in a sense antithetical to the Theravada concept of the arhat, who by his own strenuous efforts attains enlightenment for himself alone. Among the most important of the Bodhisattvas is Avalokiteshvara, who was once widely worshiped throughout India and Southeast Asia; he is still revered today in Tibet in the person of the Dalai Lama, and in China and Japan as the goddess Kuan Yin, or Kwannon. Another divinity of paramount importance is Amitabha, who has a wide following in the Pure Land sects of China and Japan, where faith alone and the constant repetition of his name are sufficient to win entrance into his Paradise; in Tibet, he is worshiped in the person of the Panchen Lama.

Jainism has never enjoyed as large and diversified a following as Hinduism and Buddhism, and the cleavage between its esoteric and popular aspects is therefore less apparent than in those religions. A partial parallel exists, however, in the extreme reverence with which the Jains regard their deified saints, the jinas or tirthankaras, who have attained enlightenment.

In all three of these religions there exists a marked distinction between the esoteric and the popular faith with regard to the means of attaining nirvana. In the esoteric faith the attainment of enlightenment and subsequent union of the finite self with the Infinite Self is largely a matter of individual responsibility. In the popular faith the individual does not seek nirvana in and through himself so much as through the enlightened men who have attained it or the gods who have already possessed it.

Thus—in the East as in the West—popular devotion is, on the whole, directed toward personal deities—divinities, who, like their Greek or Egyptian or Assyrian counterparts, can boast a formidable catalogue of epithets and a staggering inventory of attributes; gods and goddesses who were once incarnate as men or beasts and are now manifested in stone; deities who can be propitiated by sacrifices and offerings and prayer. In short, divinities who are much entangled in names and forms, symbols and qualities, and seem far removed indeed from the undifferentiated, unqualified Absolute.

One can rationalize these popular cults as devotions actually directed to the highest God in his various manifestations. Indian thinkers advanced this interpretation at a very early date, and it is still the chief *theoretical* basis for Bhakti-Yoga. But this is essentially a learned sophistication rather than a popular belief. How many of the devotees of Kali or Krishna or Shiva are consciously directing their prayers to the "Highest Self"? How many are aware of the distinction between the higher and lower Brahman—the "unmodified" and "modified" Lord? For the Vedantist, these popular cults are valid, but they fall short of the higher, unqualified Brahman. The gods they honor are, in fact, illusions—the apparitions whereby Brahman, like a conjuror, manifests himself in an illusory world of change. For the Vedantist they are the result—and object—of ignorance; and, though useful for the sake of devotion, they obscure the nature of the only real divinity, the Highest Self.

In contrasting the values of the Orient with those of the Occident, critics frequently take the more philosophical and esoteric aspects of the nirvana religions as their standard of comparison, ignoring the popular cults and the qualities they share with polytheistic religions in other parts of the world. This tendency not only fosters a one-sided conception of Hinduism and Buddhism, but also exaggerates the role of Vedantist and Mahayana Buddhist metaphysics in the societies of East and South Asia. A nirvana religion is not, let us note, precisely the same as a nirvana *culture*. Even when Hinduism or Buddhism faces no major rivals, even when it is the dominant religion in a particular culture, it would be an exaggeration to infer that the *society as a whole* is primarily oriented toward the nirvana ideal. Such a view would be equivalent to inferring, from scholastic treatises on felicity, that medieval Christian society centered upon the Beatific Vision. Certain theologians felt that it *ought* to, but for the vast majority of laymen the *visio Dei* must have been almost as unintelligible as the unmanifested Brahman to the average Indian layman.

4

The term "nirvana religion" can itself degenerate into a myth. Since the ideal of losing personal identity in an impersonal Absolute is not characteristic of the great majority of Hindus and Buddhists and by far the greater part direct their devotions to personalized divinities, in this respect the apparent gulf between the nirvana religions and the religions of Law becomes significantly narrower. Similarly, the striking external parallels between certain forms of Mahayana practice and those of traditional Christianity (parallels in which many European missionaries detected the devil's own sleight of hand) should put us on guard against exaggerating the differences between the Indian and the Abrahamic faiths. Finally, the importance that the ideal of dharma (law or righteousness or duty) has assumed in Hindu and Buddhist thought and practice diminishes still further the gap that separates these Indian "nirvana religions" from Abrahamic "religions of Law."

Though dharma is basically a religious concept, it has had far-reaching social implications. Inasmuch as it involved right

action and the fulfillment of moral law, it inevitably affected
politics and economics, and indeed the whole structure of society.
For Hindus it provided a doctrinal basis for the caste system.
For Buddhists, on the contrary, it entailed the abolition of caste
distinctions. (As Buddhist philosophers used the term, it signified
a variety of related concepts—law, duty, morality; merit and
character; being, substance, or reality.)[5] The Maurya emperor
Ashoka went so far as to establish officers of *Dhamma* (dharma).
If the Indian historian Miss Romila Thapar is correct, Ashoka
interpreted this concept less as "piety resulting from good deeds
inspired by formal religious beliefs" than as "an attitude of social
responsibility." His policy of dharma included "measures which
today are associated with the welfare of citizens."[6]

By neglecting the social and political implications of dharma,
the Western observer tends to exaggerate the otherworldly character of the Indian religions. By understressing the complex
polytheistic structure of popular Hindu and Mahayana beliefs, he
overemphasizes the mystical and philosophical aspects of these
faiths. In some cases, moreover, his own temperamental bias
toward mysticism or his own intellectual predisposition toward
a monistic and idealistic philosophy heightens the exaggeration.
Fascinated by the dazzling obscurity—the luminous darkness—
of Indian mysticism, he confines his attention largely to Vedantist
and Mahayana thought and ignores rival philosophical schools.
The same preoccupation with mystical techniques and "otherworldly" values conditions his interpretation of Indian literature
and art and his attitude toward Far Eastern aesthetics. To the
"this-worldly" aspects of these religions—their implications for
politics and economics—he is, all too often, significantly blind.

Thus, the Western stereotype of "Eastern spirituality" is, we
have seen, based primarily on the nirvana or "Indian" religions—
Hinduism, Buddhism, Jainism. It usually ignores Islam, which as
a religion of Law possesses strong affinities with other "Abrahamic" faiths (Judaism and Christianity) in the West. It also
tends to ignore the polytheistic popular cults in the nirvana religions and hence to overstress the more philosophical aspects of

Vedanta and Mahayana Buddhism, with their emphasis on union with an undifferentiated Absolute.

In the following chapter we shall examine other facets of the same stereotype—first, the tendency to take Mahayana Buddhism as the representative norm of Eastern spirituality; secondly, the tendency to exaggerate the Buddhist element in Chinese and Japanese cultures at the expense of indigenous religions or to reinterpret the latter (Taoism, for instance) primarily on Buddhist grounds; thirdly, the various meanings that the alleged tension between Eastern spirituality and Western technique has held for Asian thinkers in China, Japan, and India over the last hundred years.

iii

TRADITION

AND DEVELOPMENT

. .
.

1

Over the last hundred years, with increased knowledge of the Indian, Tibetan, and Chinese tongues, Westerners have acquired a fuller and more sympathetic understanding of Buddhism and the important cultural role that it has played in East, South, and Central Asia. It is hardly surprising, therefore, that many have come to regard it as the norm or essence of Asian religion—the archetypal spirituality of the East. Thus a distinguished British scholar, Dr. Joseph Jacobs, has taken this "Buddhist stereotype" (if we may call it that) as the basis for the contrast he draws between Europe and Asia. "Buddha and Christ," he declares in his edition of *Barlaam and Josaphat, English Lives of Buddha* (1896), "represent the two highest planes which the religious consciousness of mankind has hitherto reached. *Each in his way represents the Ideal of a whole Continent.* The aim of Asia has always been To Be, the aim of Europe, To Do. The contemplative Sage is the highest ideal of Asia, Europe pins its faith to the beneficient [*sic*] Saint."[1]

In this variant of the East-West antithesis the terms have been slightly altered. In place of the more conventional opposition between spirit and matter—or spirituality and technique—the author has substituted a contrast between two religious modes. He retains the familiar dichotomy of contemplative East and practical West, but with a significant difference—he conceives European practicality in religious rather than in purely secular terms. The essential differences between Europe and Asia are, he maintains, differences in their modes of religious consciousness. The fundamental opposition is between action and contemplation.

This distinction is hardly fair to either continent. The Greek and Roman philosophers who debated the relative merits of the active and contemplative lives often agreed with Aristotle and Plato in preferring the latter. Medieval theologians were almost unanimous in ranking the life of contemplation above the active life. The desert saints would have been as astonished to find their religion equated with activity, however beneficent, as to learn that it was really a European ideal. The caliphs of Baghdad and Damascus would have been equally dismayed by the notion that the "Ideal of [the] whole Continent" of Asia was epitomized in the Buddha. Even Walter Pater would have raised an eyebrow, perhaps, at this application of his aesthetic credo, "Being, not Doing."

The most significant point about this paragraph, however, is its conformity to the stereotype of "Asian" spirituality. The author thinks not in terms of the many Oriental religions and the numerous varieties of "religious consciousness" to be found in the East—but in terms of a single mode, in terms of "the" Oriental religious consciousness. He conceives Asian spirituality in monolithic terms, as a specifically *continental* "Ideal." Moreover, like many other writers on the subject, he derives his stereotype not from Islam, not from Confucianism, but from one of the nirvana faiths, Mahayana Buddhism.

More recent treatments of Oriental religions often exhibit the same characteristic weakness. Some writers base their stereotype on Buddhism, some on Vedanta, others on a combination of the two, with a sprinkling of Jainism thrown in for good measure. But the stereotypes themselves are remarkably similar. They place central emphasis on techniques of contemplation, on the ideal of nirvana, or on mystical identification with an undifferentiated Absolute. Almost without exception, they foster an unbalanced conception of Asian religions—an exaggerated view that not only underplays the non-Indian faiths of the Orient but sometimes distorts the Indian religions as well.

This stereotype is largely inapplicable to Islamic and Confucian principles; neither of these creeds, in fact, lends itself very readily to the East-West dichotomy. However different they may be from each other, both possess too many values in common with the West to present a clear-cut antithesis to Western thought. In origin an "Abrahamic" faith like Christianity and Judaism, Islam has not only assimilated many of their basic insights but has also—like both of these creeds—drawn heavily on Greek thought in developing and systematizing its theology. Indeed it was this dual affinity—a Semitic foundation and a Hellenized logical structure—that permitted theologians of all three faiths to engage in intelligible controversy, to understand their opponents' arguments (even though they challenged their validity), and occasionally to borrow significantly from them.

Confucianism, in turn, commanded widespread respect in seventeenth- and eighteenth-century Europe. To many Britons and Frenchmen it seemed neither alien nor exotic, but strikingly familiar. In its ethical and political principles they recognized a humanistic orientation and a system of natural theology not dissimilar to those of the "noble pagans" of classical antiquity. For more than one Western observer, Chinese philosophy equaled, if it did not actually surpass, that of ancient Greece. Confucius could hold his own in the company of Plato and Aristotle. He could also achieve the more difficult distinction of winning equal approval from Jesuit missionaries and skeptical philosophers. The admiration that Erasmus had expressed for the teacher of Plato, La Mothe le Vayer felt for the Chinese sage. *Sancte Confuci, ora pro nobis!*[2] A prayer to St. Confucius is only one step beyond the invocation of St. Socrates.

Though these Western writers undoubtedly exaggerated the resemblances between Confucian and European thought and though they never fully understood the former, the similarity was nevertheless great enough to make the Chinese system *seem* intelligible to them, to convince them that they really understood it, and to persuade them that its ethical precepts and natural theology were, on fundamental issues, comparable to their own.

The tendency to take one or more of the nirvana faiths as the chief, and sometimes the exclusive, representative of Asian religion usually results in ignoring Islamic and Confucian values altogether, or in minimizing their differences from the Indian creeds. Not a few Western writers—and some Eastern authors as well—overstress the mystical elements in Islam. Emphasizing its Sufi mystics, its fakirs and its dervishes, they pointedly stress precisely those facets of Islamic religion which display the greatest affinities with Hindu or Buddhist mysticism. In large part this bias is probably due to the fact that writers on the subject often take India as their starting point, and then work outwards toward Persia and China. In approaching Islam, they are primarily concerned with its relationship to Hinduism—with the confrontation of these two religions in India and Indonesia, their mutual rivalry, and (in many instances) their mutual enrichment. This approach places maximum emphasis on the cross-influences between these faiths and the spiritual harvests that attended this process of cross-fertilization—Akbar's synthetic faith Din-i-Ilahi, the non-sectarian mysticism of the Moslem weaver Kabir, and the Sikh religion founded by Guru Nanak and his successors.

Not unnaturally, the writer who takes an Indian religion—whether Hindu or Buddhist or Jain—as his point of departure tends to view Islam largely in terms of its relation to the Indian faiths. He sees it primarily in one of two lights—as their persecutor or as their disciple—and he evaluates India's Moslem rulers accordingly. Either they were sacrilegious zealots who plundered her shrines and massacred her holy men, or else they themselves were partial converts and sat devoutly at the feet of her gurus.

Of the three principal religions of Indian origin—the three "nirvana faiths"—only Jainism has remained confined to Indian soil. In one form or another, both Hinduism and Buddhism have left their mark on most of the countries of Southeast Asia. In

Cambodia they were once rivals. In Indonesia and Malaya both faced the rivalry of Islam. In Ceylon they contended not only with each other and with Islam, but also with Anglo-Dutch Protestantism and Portuguese Catholicism. In Thailand and Burma, Theravada Buddhism triumphed, but even today the Thai court still avails itself of the ceremonial offices of Brahmins. In East Asia, Mahayana Buddhism not only faced the rivalry of indigenous creeds—Confucianism, Taoism, and Shinto—but has left its own influence on all three, and in turn been influenced by them.

The fact that an "Indian" religion has been so widely diffused throughout East and Southeast Asia has tempted many observers to exaggerate its contribution to the alleged unity of Asia. Regarding Buddhism as the lowest common denominator of many East and South Asian cultures, they find in it the key to the spiritual mysteries of the Orient. Accordingly they overstress the mystical "Indian" elements in the cultures of China and Japan and underemphasize the rational Confucian contribution to both societies.

In China, Korea and Japan, Buddhism made its appearance relatively late, when many of the essential features of their national cultures were already well established. The Far East assimilated this foreign ideology, integrating it into its own traditional patterns, just as it would later adapt the alien ideas of modern Europe. Buddhist philosophy and iconology—already considerably modified in transit through Central Asia—underwent still further transformation in their new environments. Though all three countries would have been unimaginably different without this Indian legacy, they still retained their individuality and diversity in spite of the common bond. Shinto in Japan and Confucian and Taoist traditions in China played equal, if not greater, roles in shaping national character.

In all three cases, the original Indian elements have become so altered—so transmuted by indigenous beliefs and by influences from Central Asia—that it would be misleading to insist too firmly on their alien origin. In crossing the Himalayas some of the Mahayana divinities have experienced Ovidian metamorphoses that rival those of the Greek and Roman pantheon. The Bodhisattva Avalokiteshvara (the Lord Who Looks Down; the Lord Who Sees—or Is Seen) has become Kuan Yin, the Lady in White who confers the boon of children.[3] The future Buddha Maitreya has become the potbellied Mi-lo, a god of fecundity and prosperity. The Hindu monkey-god Hanuman, who formerly assisted Rama in rescuing his bride from the demon-king of Lanka, has become Hanumoy, the simian convert to Mahayana beliefs, who brought the sutras to China.

The principal Mahayana sects in these countries—the Ch'an (or Zen) disciplines and the cult of Amida (Amitabha) and his Pure Land—developed primarily on Chinese soil. The label "Indian religion" has become, therefore, increasingly anachronistic. Except in the strictest genetic sense, it has become largely another myth of origin.

It has, in fact, attracted an impressive variety of etiological myths, ranging from simian transmission of the scriptures to Bodhidharma's crossing the waters on a sword blade and Kuan Yin's voyage on a single lotus leaf. This mythic embellishment of a historic fact that has itself become a myth is, in a quite literal sense, poetic justice.

2

With its passage from South Asia to East Asia, Buddhism faced a new ideological challenge, and this greatly modified its character.[4] Hitherto its chief rivals had been other "Indian" religions—Hinduism and Jainism—or local polytheistic cults. In East Asia it now had to contend with the indigenous Chinese religions (or philosophies, as some observers would prefer to call them)—Taoism and Confucianism.

In these we must recognize a third category of faiths, distinct from the Indian "nirvana religions" and the Abrahamic "religions of Law." Though both of these native traditions were rivals of one another and of Buddhism, neither of them succeeded in remaining independent, and it was precisely this mixture of the three (like sweet and sour vinegar) that made them acceptable to so wide a variety of palates. The Chinese themselves linked Confucius, Gautama, and Lao-tse together as the Three Founders. Neo-Confucian careerists proverbially, though not always factually, embraced Taoism in retirement. Taoism, in turn, remodeled its pantheon after the Mahayana arhats and bodhisattvas, and left its own imprint on Ch'an mysticism and art. Neo-Confucian philosophers drew on Taoist and Buddhist metaphysics for their cosmology and ontology. Indeed, as Fung Yu-lan (a leading historian of Chinese philosophy) observes, the "Neo-Confucianists more consistently adhere to the fundamental ideas of Taoism and Buddhism than do the Taoists themselves. They are more Taoistic than the Taoists, and more Buddhistic than the Buddhists."[5]

Though Taoist and Confucian principles have undergone many changes in the course of their development, they have always shared many basic concepts and often employed a similar philosophical vocabulary, even though they have ascribed different meanings to their terms. Common to both ideologies are the ideal of the beneficent sage (the perfect—or in any event the superior—man who benefits society by his example) and such associated ideas as the principles of harmony or identification with the universe, conformity to the pattern of cosmic change, the beauty of the natural order (as opposed to artifice), and obedience to natural law. Both schools emphasize the Tao (or "way") of the universe and the Tao of the sage who attempts to make his own way conform to that of the cosmos. Both stress, although in very different ways, the sage's relationship to the universe or macrocosm and his role in, or apart from, human society.

Since each tradition has borrowed, sometimes involuntarily, from the other, it is not always easy to draw a sharp distinction between them. Not a few Taoists have claimed Confucius himself for their school, and conversely many a Confucian scholar has been accused by his fellows of crypto-Taoism. Generally

speaking, the Confucian has tended to emphasize active partici-
pation in the government, the Taoist the merit of abstaining
from action—the value of inaction or *wu-wei.*

The former has stressed clearly defined moral or social ideals
and codes of behavior. It has affirmed the value of rites and
principles (*li*) and, in particular, the duties resulting from the
five primary social relationships—"sovereign and subject, father
and son, elder and younger brother, husband and wife, and
friend and friend."[6] The latter has usually preferred to leave
duties undefined and responsibilities unspecified, and to avoid
distinctions between good and evil.

For the former, the basic natural laws—the laws of Heaven or
the ways of Tao—are rational principles. They can be cognized
as ideas, taught by words, apprehended as "names." For the
latter, the true Tao is unnameable, inconceivable, inexpressible.
It can be neither apprehended as an idea nor taught by words.
To know it one must transcend reason and language. It can be
experienced mystically, it can be realized intuitively—but it cannot be talked about. When asked the secret of nirvana, the
Buddha (according to one Mahayana legend) refused to reply
in words; he merely looked at a golden flower and smiled. In
their conversations the Taoist Sages of the Bamboo Grove pointedly avoided naming the Unnameable. When their discourse
touched on the Great Tao, they followed Gautama's precedent;
they fell silent and signified their meaning by smiling.[7]

Both the Confucian sage and the Taoist hermit benefit society,
their followers insisted, but in different ways—the former directly, the latter indirectly; the former by action, the latter by
inaction; the former by teaching and advising the ruler or accepting an official position in the state bureaucracy, the latter
by remaining in retirement and seeking to perfect himself. "Confucianism," declares Fung Yu-lan, "is the philosophy of social
organization, . . . the philosophy of daily life." It emphasizes the
"social responsibilities of man," whereas Taoism emphasizes
"what is natural and spontaneous in him." The Confucians "roam
within the bounds of society, while the Taoists roam beyond it."
The former esteem *ming chiao* ("the teaching of names denoting

the social relationships"); the latter value *tzu jan* ("spontaneity or naturalness").

The interaction of these two traditions, Dr. Fung suggests, enabled the Chinese to achieve a healthy balance between "this-worldliness" and "other-worldliness." Like Sir Thomas Browne's "great Amphibian," the Chinese sage is at home in both worlds. Seeking "sageliness within and kingliness without," he pursues his own "spiritual cultivation" but also "functions in society." Chinese philosophy is ultimately inseparable from political theory, for "regardless of the differences between the schools of Chinese philosophy, the philosophy of every school represents . . . its political thought."[8]

It is easy to exaggerate the "otherworldly" character of Taoism and to overstress its affinities with the Indian faiths. Despite obvious similarities—eremitism, techniques of contemplation, breathing exercises, an insistence on the ineffable character of ultimate reality and a tendency to approach it by a method of negation —the differences are greater, and go deeper. The Tao is by no means equivalent with nirvana; and even though the Taoists did borrow the latter term from Buddhism, it never acquired the central importance it had possessed in the Indian religions. (As Dr. Holmes Welch points out in his historical survey of Taoism, "one of the nine compartments which composed the Field of Cinnabar in the head was called the Palace of Ni Huan" by the Taoists.)[9] Nor is the Tao equivalent to Brahman or to Suchness (*Tathata*)—even though all three terms denote an unqualified Absolute, with which the sage identifies himself. The Taoist does not, as a rule, seek a complete loss of personal identity or an end to personal existence; on the contrary, he usually seeks to prolong existence; he desires personal immortality. The Tao, as he conceives it, is not only the ground of being and nonbeing; it is also the master key to the mysteries of cosmic change. By identifying himself with it, by following the basic laws of the universe and the principles elaborated in the *Book of Changes,* he hopes not only to survive the vicissitudes of fortune but also to make the maximal and most efficient use of them.

In Taoism, as in Confucianism and as in the philosophies of

the West, there is a notable mixture of practical and theoretical objectives, a fusion of knowledge and action. Holmes Welch finds in Taoist experimental science "a Chinese counterpart of Western science," and in Fung Yu-lan's opinion the Taoist religion (as distinct from Taoist philosophy) possesses the "spirit of science, which is the conquering of nature."[10]

Like the West, with its speculative and practical philosophy and its theoretical and applied sciences, China possesses its "applied" Taoism as well as its Taoist mysticism. Like Western science, it too pursues practical objectives on occasion—the prolongation of life, the cure of disease, the increase of material wealth. Like Western science, it too possesses an experimental method—though admittedly in a more rudimentary form, less systematic, more adventitious, and often smothered in superstitions.

For all its mystical character, Taoism sometimes seeks ends that we are accustomed to associate with Western science, with its emphasis on knowledge as the precondition of action and its insistence on the dependence of applied sciences on "pure" science. Knowing the Tao is not unlike knowing a scientific formula that will enable one to make the maximum use of natural forces by following natural laws. (The chief difference is, of course, that the Tao cannot be reduced to formula.) Like the scientist, the Taoist endeavors to tap sources of energy that are natural, though hidden; what the one seeks in the mysteries of the atom, the other seeks in the Great Mystery (*miao*). Both recognize, in effect, that "knowledge is power," and both find the ultimate source of power in the laws of nature, the "ways" of the universe. In this respect Taoist nature mysticism tends to approach the "natural magic" of Renaissance Europe; and on occasion its ends and methods come fairly close to those of Western pseudosciences. Like Orphism and Hermeticism in Renaissance Europe, Taoism in China became closely associated with alchemy, with the quest for the universal panacea or the elixir of immortality, and with bizarre methods of hygiene.

Western accounts of Taoism often show the same tendency we have encountered in Western surveys of the Indian religions.

In attempting to interpret an Oriental ideology to Occidental readers, the author not only simplifies its doctrines but also emphasizes its mystical and metaphysical elements at the expense of its popular and more practical aspects. To a certain extent this is inevitable; and we may regret, rather than censure, the fact. Any interpretation is in a sense a falsification of the system it attempts to interpret, just as any summary or abstract is, to a degree, untrue to the work it tries to summarize. An outline of a book is no substitute for the book itself, and a schema of "essentials" abstracted from a religion or philosophy is actually a new credo, a fresh synthesis or restatement of traditional doctrines and practices. The distillate of Taoism that we encounter in histories of philosophy or religion may be said to "represent" or "interpret" Taoist beliefs—but only in the sense that a vial of attar of roses "represents" or "interprets" a rose garden. The anatomy of Hindu philosophy that we peruse in textbooks may be said to "explain" Hinduism—but only in the sense that the skeleton, stripped of flesh and blood and life, "explains" the man. In trying to explain an ideology or a culture, the interpreter can only abstract the values that he believes to be essential, and try to fit them into a coherent and reasonably consistent system. Unless he is very much on his guard, he is apt not only to oversimplify but also to overrationalize his original.

It is small wonder, therefore, that textbook Taoism should bear so strong a family resemblance to textbook Hinduism and Buddhism. They are, after all, siblings—offspring of the same Western imagination. The similarities that the Western observer finds in them result in part from his own frame of reference, his own search for a common formula underlying them all, and the common vocabulary in which he attempts to interpret them. In making these religious and philosophical traditions intelligible to the West, he has not only treated them as "systems" (and thus made them appear more coherent and consistent than they have usually been) but has also imposed upon them the characteristic idioms of the European philosophical tradition. Though such concepts as Tao, Brahman, nirvana, and *Tathata* (Suchness) do not really have the same meaning, Western discussions of Orien-

tal thought frequently give the misleading impression that they
do. A commentator who translates or "interprets" all four terms
as signifying "the undifferentiated aesthetic continuum" can
hardly resist the inference that they are actually the same, and
that all three religions are merely variants of the same perennial
philosophy.

In all three religions, however, the monistic philosophical element is incomplete without the complex pantheons of popular
polytheistic devotion. Taoism alone possesses 36,000 gods, who
administer the universe in a celestial bureaucracy under the
scepter of the Jade Emperor, yet have also established official
residences in various parts of the human body. Gods of walls and
moats, gods of hearth and bed and latrines, gods of doors, gods
of soil and crops, gods of diseases and healing, gods of riches
and literature and war, kitchen gods, gods of the department of
thunder, gods of heaven and hell, deified ancestors and elemental
spirits[11]—these are for the most part practical divinities, invoked
for practical and worldly ends. In diversity of function they surpass even the departmental gods of the Romans—practical but
superstitious administrators who ascribed different tutelary deities to most stages of agriculture and to many aspects of urban
life—and who even invented a special goddess (Cloacina) to
preside over the public sewers.

The polytheistic beliefs of the Taoist religion must complement
the monistic orientation of Taoist philosophy. Our knowledge of
Taoist mysticism is incomplete without Taoist practicality, even
though we may regard the basis of both as largely superstitious.

3

Thus the differences between the Chinese and Indian religions
appear to be just as marked as their similarities. The contrasts
between them seem as significant as their parallels. Asian "spirituality" is too varied, too diverse, to be reduced to a single stereotype. To seek in Buddhism a comprehensive formula for the

"Oriental mind"—or even the mind of East Asia—scarcely does justice to the rich diversity of the Buddhist religion, and the attempt usually results in obscuring or distorting the essential features of Taoism and Confucianism. It is equally misleading to look for the norm of "Asian mentality" in a single ideal figure— the Buddhist arhat or sage.

"The contemplative Sage"—to return to the quotation cited at the beginning of this chapter—"is the highest ideal of Asia." Yet this is not a simple ideal. For the author of this sentence the "ideal" was exemplified most fully by the Buddha. Other writers, however, would surely substitute Mahavira or Shankara, Confucius or Lao-tse. No single formula can do justice to the variety of Asia's contemplatives or to the significant differences between the religious or philosophical ideals of India and China.

Chinese and Indian ideals of the sage were, in fact, as different as Plato's philosopher-kings and Byzantine monks. (The latter at least shared a common language.) India's holy men are too diverse to be comprehended in a single category, nor can China's sages be reduced to a single type. Both traditions include a wide range of contemplatives—recluses eremitic and recluses cenobitic; recluses fasting and recluses feasting; recluses peripatetic and recluses stationary. They include learned scholars and holy idiots, magistrates and vagabonds; ascetics who seek enlightenment through self-torture and holy epicures who seek it through refined pleasure. Some pursue self-perfection through books, others through mindlessness; some through painting and poetry, others through philosophy; some through sensation, some through ideation, others through withdrawal from both; some through metaphysical discourse, some through ethical discourse, others through no discourse at all; some through making logical distinctions, some through transcending distinctions; some through dialogue, some through monologue, some through trance; some through syllogisms, some through witty epigrams, some through silence; some through fasting, some through drinking wine, some through sipping tea.

Though China's contemplatives—Buddhist, Taoist, Confucian —differed among themselves, the contrast with India is still greater. Few yogis or sannyasis have sought samadhi through drinking bouts, or, following ancestral example, imbibed spiritual exaltation from soma juice. The Seven Sages of the Bamboo Grove—convivial recluses who enjoyed the leisure afforded by wealth, devoted themselves to the gentlemanly arts of poetry, music, chess, and witty conversation, and tippled themselves periodically into a state of identification with the Tao—would hardly have commanded respect from the hermits of the Himalayan foothills. A patriarch of the Ch'an (Zen) sect tore up the sutras; a Zen monk chopped up a statue of the Buddha for firewood— and both of these actions became popular themes for Zen artists. It is hard to picture a Brahmin performing the same acts, destroying the Vedas, smashing an image of Vishnu or Shiva, and thereby winning widespread respect as a saint. It is equally difficult to imagine a Jain artist or an Indian Buddhist glorifying a wandering hermit for living on crawfish; yet both Japanese and Chinese painters found inspiration in this theme.

Conversely one finds it just as hard to conceive of a Chinese sage voluntarily inflicting on himself the severe penances that Indian and medieval European ascetics have undergone for the sake of acquiring merit and in the cause of devotion. Though Japanese have submitted to icy purification rites under waterfalls and Chinese have committed suicide on holy mountains, they have not as a rule demonstrated their piety by scourging themselves (as have Western saints), nor have they (like the holy men of India) blinded themselves by gazing at the sun, lacerated themselves on beds of nails, or cast themselves under the chariot of Jagannath. Such religious excesses would have seemed repellent to most Far Eastern contemplatives.

Unlike India, China was rather a pragmatic than a God-intoxicated society. The greater majority of her sages eschewed the *farouche* extravagances of India's sadhus. With brush in hand and fresh ink before them, they might on occasion paint idealized portraits of wandering eccentrics like Han-shan and Shih-te—but without attempting to take to the road themselves. They were, as some of them would have hastened to point out, scholars and gentlemen—not unkempt vagrants. Many of them were retired magistrates with a taste for the arts of leisure. Some of them affected eccentricity, behaving as temperament prompted or emotion inspired, rather than as reason advised or convention dictated. Such impulsiveness, however, came very close at times to calculated unpredictability. As in the West, a certain degree of unconventionality could be regarded as conventional behavior among literary men. China's literati or *wên-jên* might provoke a raised eyebrow or delight with a "fine surprise"—but their eccentric behavior rarely exceeded the license that Western Europe allows its "temperamental" artist, its eccentric country gentleman, or its absent-minded scholar.

With such men, the moderate and urbane Epicurus would have felt thoroughly at ease. So would Izaak Walton, for these too were "compleat anglers," who combined the pleasures of the classics with those of field and stream.

Nor was their approach to nature so very far removed from the sensibility of eighteenth-century Europe. They too found refuge from the restrictions of an artificial and overrefined civilization in the simpler society of lake and forest. They too believed in the natural benevolence of humanity and the humane spirit of the wilderness. Seeking communion with the visible forms of nature, finding moral significance and emotional force in her varying moods and aspects, they too cultivated the sublime, the romantic, the picturesque. They too idealized the humbler folk of the unspoiled countryside—the peasant, the woodcutter, the fisherman—and they too idolized the genteel, scholarly (and somewhat eccentric) recluse. They would have understood the vogue of Scotland's "Plowboy Poet (Robert Burns)," even though they never quite produced one themselves. And they would have sympathized with the basic attitudes—the theme and the stance —of Wordsworth's unfinished epic *The Recluse,* whatever misgiving they might have felt about its style.

If Wordsworth regarded poetry as the "spontaneous overflow of powerful feelings," so did many Taoist writers and painters, and not a few Zen Buddhists and Neo-Confucians. The parallel between the Chinese cult of nature and the nature connoisseurship of the English romantics has not, in fact, passed unnoticed

by the Chinese themselves. In Fung Yu-lan's opinion, the Confucian and Taoist traditions in China are roughly "equivalent to
the classical and romantic traditions in the West." The quality of
feng liu cultivated by Taoist "sentimentalists" and eccentrics can,
in his view, best be translated as "romanticism." Though the
term literally meant "wind and stream," it suggested the qualities
of freedom, ease, and elegance; and Chinese poets and sages
often applied it to the man who transcended the "distinctions of
things" and lived "according to himself" instead of "according
to others." The Neo-Taoists of the Chin dynasty and their Buddhist friends cultivated the art of "pure or fine conversation"
(*ch'ing t'an*), which consisted in "expressing the best thought"
(usually Taoistic) in the "best language and tersest phraseology."
Living according to impulse, they emphasized spontaneity and
naturalness (*tzu-jan*) in contrast to classical Confucianism's
concern with morals and institutions (*ming chiao*).[12]

Nevertheless, in China as in Europe the quest for nature often
terminated in artifice; the notion of the original genius who
transcended conventions also became conventional. In their approach to nature the Chinese literati became at times as artificial, as mannered, and as precious as neoclassical pastoralists
in the West. Instead of pretending to be shepherds like their
European counterparts, they masqueraded as fishermen and
composed paintings and poems that were, in effect, piscatory
eclogues. Many of these cultivated recluses were hermits only
in name. In retirement they still enjoyed polite amusements and
polished conversation. Amateurs and connoisseurs, retired officials and men of letters, they affected rusticity but generally remained urbane to their fingertips—which were sometimes very
long.

The genteel humanism of China's literary men and the careless abandon of some of her Taoist eccentrics and drunken sages
are both poles apart from the penances and ecstasies and
pedantries of India's contemplatives. Too commonsense for logic-
chopping and too sane for morbid self-torments, China normally
shunned excess in devotion as in conduct. In her milder climate
the "Middle Way" of Buddhism became hardly distinguishable

from Confucian moderation, the "median" virtue of Aristotle, or
the golden mean of Horace. Even her mystical tradition often
excelled rather in aesthetic than in ascetic values. It became at
times rather a social than a spiritual grace—an ornament of the
well-rounded gentleman rather than the obsession of the saint.
On occasion contemplation came dangerously close to connoisseurship. On occasion the theological virtues became scarcely
distinguishable from the liberal arts.

India's sages often mortified the flesh in painful austerities,
emptying their minds of all except the Infinite and Ineffable.
China's wise men often sat comfortably in bamboo groves, devoting their leisure to more sensuous pastimes—poetry, painting,
and music. They refused as a rule to make any sharp distinction
between nature and the spiritual power that produced and animated it. They found the ineffable Tao in and through nature
and art and literature, in and through the ordinary phenomena
of daily life, in and through the realm of sensory experience that
the Indian regarded as maya (the world-illusion).

Where the Indian contemplative sought union (or identification) with an ultimate reality *beyond* the world process, the
Chinese sage generally sought harmony with nature. He found
the Eternal in time and the Infinite in the finite, resigning himself to the Law of Change and the cycle of "divine transforma-
tions." In the world process he saw a manifestation of the Tao
rather than a tissue of illusions. He was usually content to accept
the Infinite as an incomprehensible and elusive mystery rather
than to theorize about it or seek to annihilate himself in it.
Whether he called it the Tao or the Law of Heaven and Earth,
he saw in it the spiritual force or principle by which the world
was governed; he sought to live by it, to give it expression in his
life and art. He saw transcendent reality as immanent, expressing
itself in the finite, the transient, the temporal. Though both the
Indian and the Chinese contemplative professed to seek "identification" with the ultimate reality, the modes whereby they
sought it were diverse, nor did the terms themselves mean the
same. Neither "identity" nor "reality" had precisely the same
significance for them.

4

Thus, both in orientation and methods, China's intellectual tradition diverged widely from India's. Less skeptical of the reality of this world and more skeptical of the next, it placed greater emphasis on values that India sometimes dismissed as illusory. The life and character of particular men, the rise and fall of particular societies, the concrete details of the historical process itself—all of these possessed greater intrinsic interest, more immediate value, than in the civilization to the south. In spite of China's rich and varied philosophical tradition, she regarded history as no less important—and in fact often combined them. But even her philosophy differed markedly from Indian thought. It was less systematic, less technical, and less abstract. Instead of metaphysics, it stressed ethics and politics. Instead of scholastic hairsplitting, it employed more graceful, less rebarbative techniques not dissimilar to those of a Renaissance humanist—dialogues, historical examples, illustrative anecdotes, fables and similes. Even though Chinese scholars translated a large part of the Buddhist canon from Sanskrit and Pali into their own tongue, the intricacies of Indian logic usually remained alien to them.

Although Buddhism profoundly influenced Chinese art, it never achieved a position comparable to that of Hinduism in India. Although it acquired a temporary pre-eminence under particular emperors, it always had to face the competition of the two principal native religions—Confucianism and Taoism. Except for brief interludes when a Son of Heaven favored some rival cult, the former came closest to being the official philosophy of the civil service and government. The latter enjoyed a wide vogue among the people, though its prestige in higher circles varied considerably. Buddhism never succeeded in monopolizing Chinese culture. The complex, metaphysical faith imported from India had, all along, to compete with well-established native traditions—the practical ethics of Confucius and the practical mysticism of Lao-tse.

In Japan, Buddhism underwent further alterations comparable to those it had undergone in China. It modified the national culture but never completely transformed it. An alien element, like the grain of sand in an oyster shell, it might stimulate the latent creativity of the Japanese spirit, but it must leave to the oyster the responsibility for producing the pearl. Shinto, a complex blend of nature- and ancestor-worship, has been a dominant tradition in Japanese civilization. It has formed the core of the national character, even when overlaid like a lacquered image with the veneers of other religions—Buddhist, Confucian, or Christian. In fact, it has played a role comparable to that of Taoism and Confucianism in China. Fostering a spirit of "natural piety"—inspiring veneration for the forces of nature on the one hand and consolidating family, clan, and national loyalties on the other—it has also molded the Japanese aesthetic sense. The taste for radical simplicity apparent in the severely functional architecture of the Ise shrines; the trenchant austerity of a Tokugawa sword; the sensitivity to texture and to the inherent beauty of natural materials, clay or metal, wood or stone—all of these facets of the national culture can be traced to attitudes already well-established before the first importation of Buddhist art and religion from Korea. However much the Japanese intuition of what is *shibui* ("good taste" or "subtlety") may owe to Zen Buddhism, its origin is to be found much earlier in the indigenous tradition. In fact, just as the native culture of China (and Taoist thought and feeling, in particular) helped to mold the character of Zen (Ch'an) Buddhism on the mainland, so the indigenous culture of Japan (and the Shinto feeling for nature, in particular) helped to shape its influence in the islands. In both cases the imported religion from India adapted itself to local nature religions.

One must also trace to Shinto much of the folklore of Japan, the tales of fox spirits and ghosts and the legends associated with particular mountains or waterfalls. Even apart from the state Shinto that constituted the "established religion" between the Meiji Restoration and the Allied Occupation, the political effects of Shinto piety were far-reaching. It inspired that peculiar reverence for the emperor which preserved the same dynasty on the throne through all the civil wars, the struggles of contending clans, and the rise and fall of shogunates.

Nevertheless, Shinto was less a system of doctrine than of worship, and Buddhism supplied what was patently lacking in the national culture—a systematic philosophy and coherent world view. It contributed a structure of ideas. Yet, even though Japanese civilization acquired its intellect largely from Buddhism, it inherited its spirit primarily from Shinto and many of its ethical and social ideals from Neo-Confucianism. A hierarchic society, strongly molded by personal and social loyalties, it emphasized codes of conduct rather than philosophies—*Bushido,* the code of the warrior, and *Kodo,* the system of family and social obligations culminating in fealty to nation and crown. After the Meiji Restoration both became closely identified with state Shinto, but this was a late and in some respects artificial innovation. Actually both codes sprang in large part from a fusion of native and Confucian traditions; they reflected the feudal structure of Japanese society, the nature of clan organization, and the spirit of the native religion.

Indian modes of "spirituality" are essentially as alien to the courtly and feudal culture of Japan as to the humanistic and bureaucratic civilization of China. Just as the Chinese mystical tradition was rooted in Taoism, that of Japan developed out of her indigenous animism and spirit-worship. In both cases the continuity and dominance of the native traditions do not obscure the profound impact of Buddhism, but they do challenge the widespread assumption that the inner core of both cultures is essentially Indian—that the common bond of a faith that India herself has long since renounced still links East and South Asia, still unites the Sumida and the Yangtze with the Godavari and the Ganges.

Though Japanese culture would doubtless have been radically different without Zen Buddhism, the latter's role has often been seriously exaggerated. So has its Indian character. Only in a very limited sense can it be regarded as a common psychological bond between these northern islands and the remote Indian

subcontinent. Far from being a distinctively Indian contribution
to the Far East, it was largely a Chinese development; and it
subsequently experienced significant modification after its introduction into Japan.

Whatever techniques of meditation (dhyana) the patriarch
Bodhidharma may have brought from India were transmuted, if
not transformed, by contact with Taoism. The Buddhist concept
of enlightenment (bodhi) or "spiritual insight" (satori) still remained the fundamental goal, and the terminology—"perception
of one's Buddha-nature," and the like—also remained essentially
Buddhist. But the distrust of logical method and systematic
philosophy; the emphasis on intuition and immediate experience;
the stress on the "elusive" and "ineffable" nature of reality and
consequently on the necessity for approaching it by indirection,
nuance, and suggestion; the apprehension of the infinite and
eternal through the finite and temporal; the pursuit of art as a
means of spiritual insight—these were characteristic of Taoist
mysticism. Though Zen traced its own discipline—"a special
transmission outside the scriptures"—to the Buddha himself, it
was (as most authorities agree) profoundly influenced by Taoism
in China. That it entrenched itself so firmly in Japan was due, in
large part, to its affinities with the older native traditions. Its
austerity and discipline attracted the warrior class. Its aesthetic
aspects—poetry and painting, the art of flower arrangement,
landscape gardening, the tea ceremony—appealed to a refined
society weary of florid and overornate magnificence. It provided
a moral and aesthetic discipline as well as spiritual training. It
served to educate a class of warriors and gentlemen as well as a
spiritual aristocracy. In art as in society it reinforced the taste for
severe simplicity and elegant austerity already implicit in the
native tradition.

5

Viewed from almost any angle, the traditional opposition between East and West tends to vanish. For Renaissance and nine-

teenth-century Europe it meant the confrontation of Christian truth and pagan error. Yet this conception has become either irrelevant or anachronistic. The "Western" faith has established itself in the Philippines and retains more than a foothold in most other Asian states. If Europe has not entirely lost her evangelic zeal, she has at least tempered it by greater understanding of the merits of Oriental faiths. Critical and often skeptical toward her own traditional creeds, she has not hesitated on occasion to seek illumination from the "Light of Asia."

More valid is the contrast between modern European technology and the underdeveloped East. Yet this antithesis is hardly fundamental. A few centuries ago the situation was reversed. The West had to recover its knowledge of Greek mathematics and the physical sciences largely from Islam, to learn the concept of zero indirectly from India,[13] and to derive from China many of the inventions that would transform Western civilization—gunpowder and the mariner's compass, printing and porcelain. Moreover, the opposition is fast disappearing as Asia becomes increasingly industrialized. It is patently inapplicable to modern Japan.

"In Asia today," observed Jawaharlal Nehru, "industrialization is a myth as powerful as independence used to be."[14] "The transition which India is making," declared a Marxist compatriot, "is from the age of cow-dung to the age of the atom."[15] For the Japanese liberal socialist, Kawai Eijiro, "socialist society is the *ideal* society which should succeed contemporary capitalism."[16]

Implicit in each of these statements is the germ of utopian aspirations. Each contains in embryo the potential form of an ideal society, even though—as Nehru sadly, but wisely, recognized—this may prove to be little more than a myth.

All three speakers were Asian socialists—but only in the broadest sense of the term; all three differed widely in ideology and in party affiliation. Their views are, in fact, representative of a much wider political spectrum; similar opinions have been expressed by other Asians much farther to the left or to the right. More significant are the Western elements in their social thought. Their visions of an Asian utopia have been strongly conditioned by European ideals, and it is precisely this alien coloration that most notably differentiates their views of the ideal society from the beliefs of their ancestors. However sharply divided among themselves they may be, the political leaders of East and South Asia have been deeply influenced by Western economic and social principles. Their ideal commonwealths bear a closer resemblance to Western utopias—to Butler's Erewhon and Bacon's New Atlantis—than to native political theory.

For earlier generations of Asian statesmen, the ideal society was closely associated with traditional religious or ethical concepts—with dharma or Tao or *li*, with world harmony or with natural or divine law. For their descendants it is linked, just as closely, with the victories of technology and the triumphs of political economy. Utopia has become synonymous with modernization and, not infrequently, Westernization. It has come to mean, among other things, a systematic exploitation of nature and a rational reorganization of society under "enlightened" state leadership. It has come to denote the transformation of the physical and social environment through the natural and social sciences. Subordinating mysticism to logic and metaphysics to politics, the idealist of the New Asia transfers to the scientist the authority his ancestors attributed to the seer and the sage. Seeking useful information rather than mystical gnosis, and verifiable facts rather than esoteric mysteries, the modern utopian desires knowledge primarily to alter the world about him rather than to escape it. Substituting Baconian ideas of wisdom for Vedic formulas, he regards knowledge as "power" over nature rather than as "liberation" from nature.

In its present forms (and these are many and varied) Asian utopianism is, in large part, an import from the West. Like other imports, however—Buddhism in China, Chinese culture in Japan, the Spanish language and Roman Catholicism in the Philippines —it has been assimilated and acclimatized. Just as Asia's exports to the West no longer seem alien—just as afternoon tea has become an inalienable part of the British "way of life" and coffee a national beverage in the United States—utopianism, in one form or another, is rapidly becoming as characteristic of the Orient as of the Occident. As a French diplomat recently suggested, "each of the great Asian and African cultures touched by the Western spirit will sooner or later give it a new form. . . ."[17]

An impressive variety of these "new forms" has, indeed, already made its appearance, and several of these have already proved abortive. In the last century the reformer K'ang Yu-wei endeavored to establish "a native Confucian religion to counteract the growing impact of the West." Elaborating the old Confucian theory of the three ages of the world (or three "stages of progress"), he argued that "the growing communications between East and West, and the political and social reforms in Europe and America, show that men are progressing from the stage of disorder"—the first phase of social evolution—"to the second higher stage, that of approaching peace. And this in turn will be followed by the unity of the whole world," a "utopia" to be realized in the third and final "stage of human progress."[18]

The followers of Mao Tse-tung, in turn, have praised him for achieving a distinctively Asian—or, more specifically, Chinese—version of the ideal Communist society. Yet, for many Western observers, this claim is largely illusory. The Maoist state, they would argue, is really a national socialist dictatorship, disguising its nationalist character under a Marxist-Leninist veneer and heavily dependent (like the governments of dynastic China) on the loyalty of its military commanders and the efficiency of its official bureaucracy.

In a *Foreign Affairs* article, "What Is Left of Communism,"[19] George Lichtheim comments on Maoist China's "three-cornered struggle between the bureaucracy, the juvenile Red Guards and the army." In his opinion, the Chinese goal is not truly Marxist but nationalist. In attempting to sacrifice "immediate satisfactions for the sake of building up the wealth-creating apparatus of industrial civilization," the Chinese Communist government is pursuing "the goal of virtually every dictatorship in a backward country, be its ideology Communist, fascist or simply nationalist. The originality of Maoism lies in the methods employed to mobilize the masses in the name of communism for the achievement of aims proper to any national-revolutionary movement: the industrialization of China and the acquisition of military means . . . adequate to the pursuit of great-power politics." In "China's Next Phase" in the same issue of *Foreign Affairs*, Robert S. Elegant sees the Maoist polity as one of "a wide range of substitutes" whereby modern China has attempted to replace the "spiritual world of Confucianism." Throughout the present century "the politically engaged vanguard of China has deliberately sought to destroy both traditional society and the moral values on which it rested." With their slogan "Wipe out the old civilization!" the Red Guards "were bringing to its ultimate expression the overriding political and cultural preoccupation of twentieth-century China."

Now that China's Communist leaders have fallen out among themselves, the Maoist version of the ideal society seems increasingly remote and unrealizable. Ironically it was Liu Shao-ch'i—now the Maoists' *bête noire*—who once hailed Mao's "stroke of genius" in transposing the European character of Marxism-Leninism into its Asiatic form.[20]

The "new forms" resulting from the interaction of Eastern and Western values have, for the most part, proved notably unstable. They are constantly breaking down like radioactive compounds into their component elements or forming new, unforeseen combinations. Japan's Greater East Asia Co-prosperity Sphere, the national socialism of Subhas Chandra Bose, and Sukarno's "guided democracy" belong to the past. Pakistan has not yet succeeded in reconciling the principles of Islamic law with those of modern parliamentary democracy; there is still, in theory and in practice, an unresolved tension between the ideals of a secular utopia and those of a City of God. In Japan and India, parliamentary democracy and the common goal of industrialization have helped to shape the concept of the ideal society, but they have not determined its character. Capitalists and communists, socialists and religious reactionaries—all have their own cherished

notions of what the ideal commonwealth ought to be. Which—
if any—of these several utopias will command the greatest al-
legiance is still uncertain.

In their reactions to Western civilization, the societies of the
Orient have usually been sharply divided. In H. G. Creel's
opinion, the Chinese met the challenge in three ways. "Some have
insisted that China's traditional patterns of life and thought are
superior to all others, and that the Chinese have found themselves in difficulty not because they have been too conservative
but because they have not lived up to the traditional ideals. . . .
Others have . . . [also] believed that Chinese culture provided
the soundest basis of China's development, [but have] wished
to modify it to meet the conditions of the modern world, and to
take over such Western techniques as appeared to be advanta-
geous. A third group has insisted that China's entire traditional
pattern of political, social, and economic organization is unsuited
to the world of today, and that the whole manner of life and
thought must be revolutionized."[21] Creel cites the view of Sun
Yat-sen: "What we need to learn from Europe is science, not
political philosophy. As for the true principles of political philosophy, the Europeans need to learn them from China."

Though this account may be oversimplified, it effectively
counters the tendency to treat Oriental reactions to Western
values as a single formula, and thus indirectly perpetuate the
continental stereotype. To speak of "Asia's response" is to re-
affirm the myth of Asia. "China's response" disintegrates, upon
examination, into a variety of attitudes, and similar internal
contradictions characterize the "responses" of other Oriental
societies—India, Turkey, Japan.

In their controversies over Western values, all of these groups
made use of the dichotomy between Oriental spirituality and
Western technique—but gave it very different interpretations.
For some, these contrasting ideals were literally antithetical; they
were too incompatible to coexist, and the attempt to reconcile
them (to have one's cake and eat it too) could only vitiate both.
For others, they were less antithetical than complementary.
Asian societies might safely borrow the scientific—and even the

political—techniques of the West without seriously endangering their traditional cultural values. Indeed, by a judicious exploitation of modern technology, they might actually reinforce their historic civilizations.

After the Opium War (as J. R. Levenson has observed), "European industrialism and commercial enterprise" challenged the "usefulness of Chinese thought, and, when the question of its usefulness could be raised, the question of its truth became alive." Once the West had "forced revision of Chinese judgments on the older contending philosophies," minor "distinctions and conflicts between Chinese schools paled into insignificance before the glaring contrast of Western culture to everything Chinese. . . . The question 'New or old?' as a test of value continued to be asked, but the question was removed from a Chinese world to the larger world of the West and China."[22]

Throughout the latter part of the nineteenth century, various Chinese officials urged the study of Western science as a means of "self-strengthening." Feng Kuei-fen advised his compatriots to learn the "natural sciences" from "the barbarians and surpass them." Tseng Kuo-fan exhorted China to "adopt Western ideas and excel in Western methods" by sending promising youths "to study in foreign countries." Hsüeh Fu-ch'eng argued that importing the Occident's methods and techniques for utilizing "the forces of nature for the benefit of the people" was quite consistent with following the Way of the ancient sages. China ought to "take over the Westerners' knowledge of machinery and mathematics in order to protect the Way of our sage-kings Yao and Shun . . . and Confucius. . . ."[23]

For the Chinese "Westernizers" of the latter part of the nineteenth century, the solution to the problem of adapting Western to Chinese values (or vice versa) would be summed up in the formula *chung-hsüeh wei t'i, hsi-hsüeh wei yung*—that is, "Chinese learning to provide the [moral] basis, Western learning to provide the [technical] means."[24] The Confucian Way (or Tao) could best be preserved, they believed, through the use of Western "instruments" (*ch'i*) or "methods" (*fa*).[25] Believing that the "only alternative to outright destruction of Chinese civilization by foreign conquerors was selective innovation by dedicated Chinese traditionalists," these "cautious eclectics" (as Levenson terms them) sought to "justify their proposal historically" by insisting that "these areas of innovation were areas of only *practical* value, not of essential value."[26]

The Confucian scholar-official Chang Chih-tung thus "advocated Chinese learning for *t'i* ('substance,' 'essence') and Western learning for *yung* ('function,' 'utility')."[27] "Chinese learning is moral," he maintained, whereas "Western learning is practical. Chinese learning concerns itself with moral conduct, Western learning with the affairs of the world."[28] For traditionalists such as Wo-jen, on the other hand, even the limited introduction of Western scientific thought threatened to undermine Chinese traditional culture. Emphasizing "the distinction, the incompatibility, between the Chinese ideal of the 'human heart' and the Western ideal of 'techniques,'" he and other literati maintained that "ancient China had known the prototypes of that scientific learning which the Westernizers so uncritically admired"—but had wisely "let them go."[29]

In the thought of Liang Ch'i-ch'ao, Professor Levenson distinguishes three principal phases. In the 1890's he argued that "Western and Chinese ideals were really the same" and that European scientific and political goals were quite consistent with Confucius' "real intentions." Over the next twenty years Liang "dispensed with the Confucian sugar-coating and covered his Westernism with a new non-culturalistic Chinese nationalism." In his last phase, after the First World War had brought disillusionment with European civilization, he believed that "Western and Chinese ideals were really opposed. The West was materialistic, the East was spiritual."

In Liang's opinion, Chinese thought (or "Asian civilization") could provide a much-needed *via media* for the Occident. Because "Western civilization" had divided "the ideal and the practical" too sharply, both idealism and materialism had gone to extremes. The Chinese, on the other hand, had traditionally sought to embrace "the ideal in the practical" and thus to harmonize mind and matter. Ch'an Buddhism, for instance, is characteristically Chinese in reconciling "the way of renouncing the world and the way of remaining in the world."[30]

With Hu Shih, the proverbial terms of the dichotomy are completely reversed. Decrying the tendency to "ridicule Western civilization as materialistic and worship Eastern civilization as spiritual," he insists that the former, with its Faustian inability to "know content," is paradoxically the more spiritual of the two. Content with its restrictive "material environment," Oriental civilization is the truly "materialistic civilization" and can "only obstruct . . . the spiritual demands of mankind."[31]

Japanese attitudes show similar diversity, with Sakuma Shozan's slogan "Eastern ethics and Western science" corresponding to the *t'i-yung* formula in China. In the late 1930's, Japanese conservatives conceived their national mission as one of "adopting and sublimating Western cultures" with Japanese "national polity," and thus uniting the "intuitive and aesthetic qualities" of the Orient with the Occident's "analytical and intellectual qualities." On the very eve of war with the United States and Britain, Japanese nationalists regarded their country as the champion of Asia in an inevitable "East-West struggle." As the outcome of this conflict between Orient and Occident, the characteristic values of both societies would be combined. Asia's "spiritual values" would be superadded to "Europe's honest and rigorous speculative thought": "the way of Asia" and the "way of Europe" would be finally united.[32]

Another Japanese observer challenged the traditional views that "Oriental culture is doctrinal in character, Occidental culture scientific." In his opinion, this dichotomy might be valid for China but not for Japan. One postwar critic complained that his country's view of "European and American culture" had been too narrow; "we ignored the ethical and religious basis of that culture, and sought only to adopt its natural science, its material technology, and its external institutions." In his opinion, Japanese nationalists had mistaken "individualism and materialism for Western culture, and opposed to it a Japanese culture stressing collectivism and national spirit." "We believed," declared another postwar observer, "that we could triumph over

scientific weapons and tactics by means of our mystic will. . . ."
This "characteristic reliance on intuition" had blocked "objective
cognition of the modern world" and thereby hastened Japan's
military defeat. Still another critic advocated a "return to the
East" and a fresh attempt to explore the possibilities of "Eastern
spirit." He was, however, skeptical of the conventional dichotomy
of East and West, and explicitly rejected "the simple schematiza-
tion formerly in vogue here, according to which the East stood
for the spirit and the West for material things."[33]

During the latter part of the nineteenth century, the same
dichotomy became fashionable in India—often in terms of the
imagery of foreign commerce. India should trade her own
"priceless treasures"—the "literature of Vedism and Buddhism"
—for more tangible benefits from the West, and thus fulfill the
"Divine economy." While "we learn modern science from England," declared Keshub Chunder Sen, "England learns ancient
wisdom from India. . . . Let modern England teach hard science
and fact; let ancient India teach sweet poetry and sentiment."
Though modern Europe has excelled "on the material plane,"
asserted Swami Vivekananda, India has always been supreme on
"the spiritual plane." Both the "Oriental type" and the "Occidental type" have their distinctive merits, but the present age
requires "the harmonizing, the mingling of these two ideals. . . .
Up, India, and conquer the world with your spirituality!"[34]

For one Bengali nationalist, India should renew her "spiritual
knowledge" by acquiring "physical knowledge" from Britain.
"Once the people of India have acquired knowledge of the
physical world from the English, they will be able to comprehend the nature of the spiritual," and "there will then be no
obstacle to the true Faith"—Hinduism.[35]

For Mahatma Gandhi, on the other hand, modern Western
civilization was a disease that had already depraved Europe and
partly infected Asia. India must avoid it at all cost. To "Euro-
peanize" her by equipping her with European arms and industry would only make her condition as "pitiable as that of
Europe." Ethically, the two civilizations were as contrary as
virtue and vice, piety and atheism. Whereas the "tendency of

the Indian civilization is to elevate the moral being, that of the Western civilization is to propagate immorality. The latter is godless, the former is based on a belief in God."[36]

Gandhi's strategy of passive resistance, his emphasis on "soul force" rather than violence as a political weapon, and—above all, perhaps—his personal example heightened the tendency to equate Indian civilization with "moral force." Indeed he himself ultimately became a symbol of his own ideals, a personification of his cultural tradition. In Indian eyes he has become (as Malraux suggests) *"un Grand Renonçant traditionnel"*—another characteristic example of the sage who triumphs through re-nunciation.[37]

With Gandhi's example in mind, Tagore contrasted the Oc-cident's "faith in material strength and prosperity" with India's "disinterested faith in ideals, in the moral greatness of man," and in the "truth that moral force is a higher power than brute force. . . ."[38]

Muhammad Iqbal was less sympathetic to Gandhi's ideals—partly because they seemed to him thoroughly and typically Oriental. Distinguishing sharply between "two opposing types of world-consciousness, Western and Eastern," Iqbal regarded the former as "chronological in character" and the latter "non-historical." Because Islam "sees in the time-movement a symbol of reality," it has always seemed "an intruder in the static world-pictures of Asia." For the same reason, the British and Mahatma Gandhi could not really understand each other.[39]

For many of India's recent leaders, Gandhi's example has proved an embarrassing commentary on the disparity between ethical idealism and political necessity. Few would care to turn their backs on modern civilization and its industrial and military techniques. Few would care to stake their country's defense on "soul-force" instead of aircraft or to base their Five Year Plans on spinning wheels rather than hydroelectric plants. "I fear," remarked Nehru shortly before his death, "that the spinning wheel is *not* stronger than the machine."

"The real conflict," as he saw it, "which has begun since our independence, is the conflict between Hinduism and the cult of the machine. . . . Science is not, perhaps, completely opposite to religious metaphysics. . . . But how may we reconcile a civilization of the machine with a civilization that was [traditionally] a civilization of the soul?"[40]

In India, as in China and Japan, the ideal of Asian spirituality was bound to clash with Marxist notions of dialectical materialism. To many Asian Marxists, accordingly, Gandhi has seemed not so much the "great renouncer" as the "great reactionary." Thus to M. N. Roy, Gandhi's "moralizing mysticism" appeared little better than the "transcendental fantasies" of Western monks. A "mass of platitudes and hopeless self-contradictions," its "social basis [was] cultural-backwardness; its intellectual mainstay, superstition."

"Indian spiritualism is not different from the Western kind," Roy insisted, nor was India's idealist philosophy fundamentally "different from Western idealism." In contrast to the "materialist philosophy" of the Marxists, "India's spiritual message" could only lead the West back into "medieval barbarism."[41]

In the preceding pages we have examined the origins of the dichotomy of Europe and Asia and its development from a limited (but nonetheless misleading) geographical distinction into a psychological and cultural antithesis. We have noted a trend over the last hundred years to conceive this antithesis in terms of the polarity of Asian spirituality and European technique—largely as a reflection of the character of the Western impact on the Orient in modern times—and a tendency on the part of many critics to seek a comprehensive formula for "Eastern spirituality" in the absolute idealism (or mystical monism) of one or more of the "Indian" faiths. This bias scarcely does justice to Islam on the one hand, or to Taoism, Confucianism, and Shinto on the other. Accordingly, we have stressed some of the fundamental differences among three major religious groups— the "Indian" nirvana religions, the "Abrahamic" religions of Law, and the indigenous religions of China and Japan. We have emphasized the differences between the popular and esoteric aspects of the principal Oriental faiths, and we have pointed out the variety and diversity that invalidate the Western stereotype of the Oriental sage. Finally, we have examined the uses that various Oriental authors—Indian or Pakistani, Chinese or Japanese—have made of the dichotomy of Eastern spirituality and Western technique in attempting to meet the crises that have confronted their respective cultures.

As we have observed, this dichotomy has meant very different things to different Asians. Though the cliché itself has shown a remarkable capacity for survival, it has (like Darwin's biological species) demonstrated its fitness through an impressive variety of mutations. The same diversity characterizes its development in all three of the societies we have examined—Islamic, Far Eastern, and Indian. In China and Japan, in Hindustan and Pakistan, native spokesmen could appeal to the same commonplace for very different arguments—as grounds for wholesale imitation of the West, for wholesale rejection of Western values, or (more frequently) for a judicious and selective compromise between Asian and European civilizations.

Though almost as widespread in Europe and America as in Asia, this cliché has not, moreover, consistently possessed the same meaning for Occidentals and Orientals. In most instances it has served as a partial, even if unsatisfactory, answer to a specific cultural crisis; but the crisis has not been precisely the same for European civilization as for the civilization of Asia. For more than a few Westerners, the dichotomy reflects a deep-rooted dissatisfaction with their own traditional creeds and a desperate, but not illaudable, effort to salvage some element of "spirituality" in a world increasingly dominated by the natural sciences. Unwilling to jettison religious values altogether yet unable to accept their ancestral faiths, they seek in the East the "spiritual principle" they can no longer find in the Western Churches. In some cases this amounts to grotesque credulity; one strains at a Western gnat only to swallow an Oriental camel. In other instances it amounts to an aesthetic mysticism, a "willing suspension of disbelief" that rarely exceeds the limits of poetic faith.

Nevertheless, among the disciples of "Eastern spirituality" one must number more than a few Western intellectuals. Some sought to transcend the limits of sectarianism by adding the insights of the Orient to those of the West. Some, like Aldous Huxley, were looking for a *prisca theologia,* a perennial philosophy. Some, like Paul Valéry and (to a degree) Martin Heidegger, admired the negative methodology of certain Eastern philosophies and their concern with Nonbeing. Some, like Dr. C. G. Jung, found their approach to the unconscious significant for European depth psychology. Some found in Buddhism a congenial reconciliation of skepticism and mysticism that enabled them to stress the value of religious experience without committing themselves to religious dogmas. Some found in the impersonal, undifferentiated Absolute of some of the "Indian" religions a substitute for the personal divinities in whom they could no longer believe. These, in effect, tried to bypass the religious crisis of the West—the long, unresolved conflict between reason and dogmatic faith— by positing an ultimate spiritual reality which transcended logical demonstration and religious dogmas alike, which could not be grasped through words or apprehended through concepts, and about which nothing could be positively affirmed or denied.

In the next three chapters we shall consider three aspects of these current views of Asia—first, the tendency to underestimate the Orient's contribution to logic and science; second, the tendency to overestimate the Orient's influence on Western religions; and third, the tendency to reduce Oriental mysticism to a single stereotype.

iv

LOGIC, RATIONAL THEOLOGY,
AND SCIENCE

. .
.

1

For Maurice Maeterlinck, Belgian poet, critic and dramatist, the opposition between East and West was essentially psychological, and he expressed it through the metaphor of cerebral anatomy. The "Western lobe" of the brain "produces reason, science, consciousness"; the "Eastern lobe," on the other hand, "secretes intuition, religion, the subconscious."[1] Dr. Sarvepalli Radhakrishnan, the eminent Indian philosopher, formerly Spalding Professor of Eastern Religions and Ethics at the University of Oxford and second President of India, opposes "Eastern religion" to "Western thought."

F. S. C. Northrop, professor of philosophy at Yale University and author of *The Meeting of East and West,* contrasts the "intuitive aesthetic character" of Eastern culture with Western rationalism. *"The Orient, for the most part, has investigated things in their aesthetic component; the Occident has investigated these things in their theoretic component."* "Confronted with himself and nature, Western man arrives by observation and scientific hypothesis at a theoretical conception of the character of these two factors"; "Eastern man," on the contrary, stresses the "undifferentiated" or "indeterminate aesthetic continuum." Or—to put it more lucidly—"jen in Confucianism, Tao in Taoism, nirvana in Buddhism, and Brahman or Atman or Chit in Hinduism and Jainism are all to be identified with the immediately apprehended aesthetic component in the nature of things, and with this in its all-embracing indeterminateness, after all sensed distinctions are abstracted."[2]

If there is a partial truth in this, it has been distorted by overstatement. None of these writers has entirely escaped the unfortunate "Western" tendency to bandy abstractions and logical distinctions. Though they all are, in effect, apologists for Oriental culture, none has seriously observed Sakyamuni's warning against the "vanity of theorizing."

All three, moreover, do a manifest injustice to the subtleties of the Indian mind and, in particular, to the refinements of Buddhist logic. Both as a weapon in debate and a tool for doctrinal exegesis, logical studies held an important place in the curriculum of Buddhist universities and monastic schools. In India and subsequently in Tibet, the manual of dialectics rapidly entrenched itself in the canon of Buddhist literary genres. Logic underwent extensive development, as later dialecticians wrote their own explanatory comments on the standard texts—amplifying, clarifying or criticizing unresolved or ambiguous points. In this respect, Indian and Tibetan learning provides a striking parallel to the development of Aristotelian logic in Western civilization. Like the latter, it has its formal syllogisms, its theories of inference and logical proof, its analysis of causality and other "predicaments," its isolation of logical fallacies and sophisms. Like the West, the Orient had its "Alexandrian" scholiasts and its medieval scholasticism.

One can scarcely dismiss this development as an unfortunate excrescence on the Indian intellectual tradition—as mere academic hairsplitting and pedantic logic-chopping. For the disputants themselves the issues seemed vital. Like their Western counterparts at the Sorbonne, they multiplied logical distinctions chiefly in the interest of "right knowledge." As in the West, dialectic could serve a variety of purposes—negatively, to refute an opponent or demonstrate the inadequacy of reason in comparison with intuition and faith; positively, to provide the basis for a coherent and self-consistent statement of religious doctrine and belief.

As an example, let us look at a characteristic syllogism in Dharmakirti's logical treatise, the *Nyaya-bindu*. As the "formula of a reason representing effect" the author presents a syllogism in four parts—major premise, example, minor premise, and conclusion:

1. "Where there is no fire, there neither is smoke."[3]
2. "(As e.g., on the water of a lake, etc.)"
3. "But there is here some smoke."
4. "Hence there must be some fire."

Except for the second term, which involves inductive rather than deductive reasoning, Dharmakirti's syllogism is much the same as Aristotle's. In other Indian systems the resemblance is sometimes closer. Though the Nyaya-Vaiseshika school employed a five-membered syllogism (thesis, reason, example, application, conclusion), both the Buddhist and the Mimamsa schools regarded three members as "sufficient to establish the conclusion." "In the last three," as a leading Russian Indologist Theodore Stcherbatsky observes, "if we drop the example, we will have a strictly Aristotelian syllogism, its first figure."[4] Thus, in Dignaga's logic the syllogism would read as follows:[5]

Wherever there is smoke, there is fire, as in the kitchen.
Here there is smoke,
There must be some fire.

Not only the syllogism of three members but also the syllogism in four or five parts occur in both Indian and Greco-Roman logic or rhetoric. Cicero, for instance, describes a five-part syllogism consisting of 1) statement of the major premise, 2) proof of the major premise, 3) statement of the minor premise, 4) proof of the minor premise, and 5) conclusion. Similarly the anonymous *Rhetoric to Herennius* describes a five-part syllogism composed of "the Proposition, the Reason, the Proof of the Reason, the Embellishment, and the Résumé."[6]

One should not, of course, overemphasize these parallels between Greek and Indian thought. As Stcherbatsky himself points out, there is "a great difference between the European and the Buddhist syllogistic theory," and this difference is "conditioned," in part at least, "by the general philosophic outlook. The Greek philosopher surveys the world as an ordered system of realized concepts whose total and partial connections and disconnections are laid down in Syllogisms. The Indian philosopher surveys the world as a running stream of point-instants out of which some points are illuminated by stabilized concepts and reached . . . in [man's] purposive actions."

Nevertheless "both theories are groping after one and the same central problem, the problem, namely, of the principles of human knowledge." Moreover, the very divergences between Indian and Greek logic actually bring the former into closer harmony with *modern* Western thought. "The solution proposed by Dignaga and Dharmakirti is, in some respects, nearer to Kant and Sigwart than to Aristotle."[7]

Logic is by no means the essence of Buddhism; it can hardly lead to nirvana, and Zen dispenses with it altogether—partly (as Dr. D. T. Suzuki suggests) because the intricacies of Indian theory eluded the practical Chinese mind. Yet it played a substantial part in the development of certain Mahayana doctrines and indeed of Vedanta. The very fact that rival Buddhist and Hindu schools had to defend their doctrines in public debate compelled them, like patristic and scholastic theologians in the West, to justify their beliefs on a rational basis, to argue from reason rather than authority. In formal disputations, neither the authority of scripture nor the testimony of personal experience could establish a case. If one contestant claimed to have experienced samadhi, so could his opponent. If one cited scripture, his antagonist could dismiss it as irrelevant. Like the Jains, the Buddhists rejected the supreme authority of the Vedas. To refute them, a Vedantist could not simply quote mantras and Upanishads; instead, he must advance logical proof for his opinions or convict his opponents of logical fallacies. Like al-Ghazali or St. Thomas Aquinas, he must make philosophy the handmaid of theology. Logical discipline—the "theoretic component"—is no more a stranger in "mystic" India than in "theocratic" Islam and the "rationalistic" West.

And what of the "aesthetic component"—the "undifferentiated aesthetic continuum"—which the Oriental allegedly takes as the primary object of his "investigation"? Is this really so basic, so all-pervasive, in Eastern culture, so notably deficient in the West, as Professor Northrop assumes? Is it, in either Europe or Asia, altogether dissociated from reason and theory? Perhaps another glance at the Buddhist theory of knowledge can clarify this point.

"Right knowledge," declared Dharmakirti, "is twofold—direct and indirect." The former, as his commentator explained, "means knowledge dependent upon the senses," the latter "subsequent measure" or "inference." For the Buddhist logician, accordingly, "there are only two sources of knowledge, sensation and inference," and these (as Stcherbatsky explains) cognize "two kinds of reality . . . , an ultimate or empirical one, reflected in an objectivized image." Thus one encounters "a double world, in India just as in Europe, a sensible one and an intelligible one, . . . a *kosmos aisthetos* and a *kosmos noetos*."[8]

To a limited degree this passage offers support for Professor Northrop's distinction between the "aesthetic" and "theoretic" approaches of East and West. For the distinction between the "sensible" and "intelligible" worlds is also basic to Platonism, yet their relative importance is dramatically reversed. For Plato, the latter offers the more valid knowledge; the realm of ideas is the "real" world, and the realm of the senses thus stands at one remove from reality—a cave haunted by shadows. For Dignaga and Dharmakirti, the more valid knowledge is the "direct" knowledge achieved through the senses; ideas are "constructs," inferences posterior to perception and often subject to error. For Buddhist logic, the basic doctrines of Platonism—God, matter, soul, the independent or "real" existence of ideas—lack logical foundation; as they can be justified neither by perception nor by inference, they are mere hypotheses, incapable of rational proof.

Yet one should not overstress this point. For all their emphasis on the "direct" knowledge of the senses, Buddhist logicians relied heavily on the "indirect" knowledge of inference, both in setting forth their own doctrines and in refuting those of their opponents. Nor did Western thinkers, as a whole, share Plato's distrust of the senses. Before the ink on his parchment was dry, Aristotle opened his attack on the theory of ideas. The atomists gave priority to sense-experience in their own theory of knowledge. And, long before Bacon, Western scientists were recognizing the inadequacies of theory and turning instead to the senses as channels of truth—to controlled observation and experiment.

In fact, the Eastern and Western intellectual traditions show similar tensions between the "aesthetic" and "theoretic" components (to retain Northrop's terminology). Just as Buddhist scholars assailed other schools who asserted the "real" existence of ideas or the "inherence" of concepts in perception, nominalists battled with realists in medieval schools over the "real" existence of universals. Like the Buddhists, they regarded the abstract idea with distrust and affirmed the superior validity of the particular.

Indeed, in stressing the limitations of logical discipline, yet simultaneously elaborating it as a tool for exegesis and controversy, Indian scholars of the "sutra period" show striking similarities with medieval schoolmen in the West. Whereas the Buddhists denied the authority of the Vedas and sought for "right knowledge" in perception and inference, the Vedantists ascribed the highest validity to revelation (sruti) as manifested in the Vedas and a secondary value to philosophical tradition (smriti) as expressed in such works as the *Bhagavad-Gita* and the teachings of the various Brahmanist schools. In arguing their points, accordingly, they gave priority to scriptural authority, but when this seemed ambiguous they looked for support to smriti and to reason. In his commentary on Badarayana's *Vedanta Sutras,* the great Hindu apologist, Shankaracharya, based his arguments on all three. Despite his hostility to the doctrines of rival schools—Buddhist, Sankhya, Nyaya-Vaiseshika, and others —his controversial methods were strongly influenced by their dialectics. Nor could he entirely escape their terminology; he applied their epistemological categories—"perception" and "inference"—specifically to scripture and philosophical tradition (sruti and smriti).

2

Shankara's philosophy brings us to a problem that, in different ways, has confronted Eastern and Western thinkers alike—the role of logic in elucidating and defending religious beliefs. The mystical aspects of his thought will concern us in a later chapter. For the present we shall consider his views of the relative validity of logical method and scriptural authority and the use he makes of both in constructing a more or less coherent system of rational theology. The problems he faced, the types of authority that he recognized, and the methods he employed in establishing his system are not unlike those that one encounters among rational theologians in the medieval West.

As the major Indian theologian, Shankara has frequently been compared to St. Thomas Aquinas—the great Dominican spokesman of medieval European scholasticism. The analogy is not unapt. Both attempted (like al-Ghazali in Islam) to rationalize revealed truth. Both endeavored to give logical coherence to the disjointed and apparently contradictory dogmatic statements found in scripture. Both, for all their originality, were consciously writing within the framework of an established tradition; for the formal structure of their major works they depended on the "classics" composed by their predecessors—Shankara on Badarayana's Sutras, Aquinas on the *Sentences* of Peter Lombard. Both gave primary authority to the scriptures, but supported this "divine witness" with human testimony and with logic. Shankara buttressed his quotations from the Vedas (sruti) with the opinions of Indian philosophers (smriti); Aquinas supplemented Biblical texts with the views of classical philosophers and Christian theologians. Both usually began by stating the opponent's argument and then systematically refuting it, anticipating and answering a multitude of possible objections. Both, in accepted logical procedure, distinguished the several possible meanings of a term, resolved potential ambiguities, weighed the relative value of traditional authorities, and exposed the logical fallacies of their predecessors and contemporaries. Though less systematic and less comprehensive than Aquinas' encyclopedic treatise, Shankara's commentary is, in effect, the *Summa Theologiae* of the Vedanta school.

The complex architecture of Aquinas' *Summa* has reminded many a reader of a Gothic cathedral. Shankara's commentary may, equally well, suggest a Hindu temple, whose sculptured diversity—the teeming multiplicity of *samsara,* the realm of illusion—is merely a façade, a figured screen that obscures the monolithic unity of the single sanctuary.

Both sacred edifices claimed irrefutable authority for their foundations, and revealed truth for their cornerstones. Both architects ransacked the scriptures for building materials. But the structure and masonry were those of the professional craftsman—consistently logical and competent to a fault. These may be temples to the One God, composed *ad majorem Dei gloriam* and in "reverence to the Highest Self." But they are also memorials to human ingenuity and subtlety. In their dialectical cunning they are, if anything, monuments to discursive reason. Both are enduring shrines to that "theoretic component" which is scarcely less evident in "spiritual" India than in the "rationalistic" West.

Admittedly, theory is subject to strict limitations, and in both systems philosophy is the handmaid of theology. Philosophical tradition (smriti) is valid only so far as it does not contradict revealed truth (sruti). The higher truths that logic cannot discover are accessible only through revelation. "The true nature of the cause of the world," Shankara declares, ". . . cannot, on account of its excessive abstruseness, even be thought of without the help of the holy texts; for . . . it cannot become the object of perception, because it does not possess qualities such as form and the like, and as it is devoid of characteristic signs, it does not lend itself to inference and the other means of right knowledge." "The transcendent highest Brahman can be fathomed by means of scripture only, not by mere reasoning." Unlike logicians, who disagree among themselves, "the Veda, . . . which is eternal and the source of knowledge, may be allowed to have for its object firmly established things, and hence the perfection of that knowledge which is founded on the Veda cannot be denied by any of the logicians of the past, present, or future."[9]

Shankara's primary purpose is ostensibly exegetical rather than theoretical. The "object of this system" (he asserts) is "to define the true meaning of the Vedanta-texts and not, like the science of Logic, to establish or refute some tenet by mere ratiocination. . . ." Since "Brahman is not an object of the senses, it has no connection with those other means of knowledge. For the senses have, according to their nature, only external things for their objects, not Brahman. If Brahman were an object of the senses, we might perceive that the world is connected with Brahman as its effect; but as the effect only (i.e., the world) is perceived, it is impossible to decide (through perception) whether it is connected with Brahman or something else. Therefore the Sutra [or collection of aphorisms] under discussion is not meant to propound inference (as the means of knowing Brahman), but rather to set forth a Vedanta-text."[10]

Nevertheless, for all its ostensible distrust of reason, the commentary remains, from start to finish, a masterpiece of dialectical argument. Shankara employs all the resources of logic to resolve the ambiguities of scripture, to urge his own interpretation, and to refute the views of his opponents. Though sruti (revelation) serves as his principal proof, he reinforces it with "subordinate" authorities, smriti (philosophical doctrine) and "reasoning." It is "incumbent," he maintains, "on thorough students of the Vedanta to refute the Sankhya and other systems which are obstacles in the way of perfect knowledge." "The reasoning of the Vaiseshikas and others is, as contradicting scripture, merely fallacious. . . ."[11]

Even in denying the supremacy of logic, Shankara remains a

subtle logician. As philosopher and theologian he does not lack parallels in the West. If his method shows affinities with that of the medieval schoolmen, his doctrines are not altogether alien to those of transcendental idealism in Europe and America. With Kant and Hegel, Fichte and Schleiermacher, Western thought evolved—independently—along lines that brought it at times fairly close to Indian philosophy.

3

The subtleties of Buddhist logic and Hindu dialectics lend scant support to the myth of an Orient indifferent to philosophy and unsympathetic to theory. On the contrary, one finds syllogistic reasoning reminiscent of the classical philosophers, a logical method in theological exegesis or debate that reminds one of the medieval schoolmen, and a critical analysis of perception that, in certain respects, anticipates recent developments in epistemology and psychology.

But, though their methods were rational, such men as Shankara and Dignaga were not *primarily* interested in logic and theory. These were, for the most part, mere tools for ascertaining or defending the right doctrines. Frequently but not invariably, they were preparatory exercises; they laid the foundation, or pointed the way, for higher modes of knowledge. In such cases—as in the medieval West—they assumed the modest role of handmaid to theology. Like fideist skeptics in the Occident, Oriental thinkers could exploit reason to demonstrate the limitations of reason and to point beyond it to direct spiritual experience.

In this respect there is some justification for Professor Northrop's insistence on the importance of the "undifferentiated aesthetic continuum" in Asian culture. But it is not distinctively "Asiatic." Surely it underlies the experience of many Western mystics. Nor is it very widespread in the Orient. It is limited primarily to Hindu and Buddhist societies, and even there it is rather an esoteric goal than a popular possession. Indeed, in Shankara's view, the polytheistic religion of the popular cults may actually obscure the nature of the only true divinity, the Highest Self. The cornerstone of his rigidly monistic system is the distinction between a lower and a higher Brahman, who is the object of two different modes of knowledge, a lower and a higher cognition. The first—properly known as "the Lord" (Isvara)—is *saguna,* i.e., qualified by various attributes. The latter—the true Brahman—is a pure intelligence of which nothing can be predicated except its existence. It is *nirguna,* unqualified by attributes and accidents.

Only the latter can be the object of the true and highest knowledge. The former is merely an illusory appearance, devoid of real existence.

"Brahman," Shankara explains, "is apprehended under two forms: in the first place as qualified by limiting conditions owing to the multiformity of the evolutions of name and form (i.e., the multiformity of the created world; in the second place as being the opposite of this, i.e., free from all limiting conditions whatever." The Vedas "declare Brahman to possess a double nature, according as it is the object either of Knowledge or of Nescience. As long as it is the object of Nescience, there are applied to it the categories of devotee, object of devotion, and the like. The different modes of devotion lead to different results, some to exaltation, some to gradual emancipation, some to success in works; these modes are distinct on account of the distinction of the different qualities and limiting conditions." The "Vedanta-texts teach, on the one hand, Brahman as connected with limiting conditions and forming an object of devotion, and, on the other hand, as being free from the connexion with such conditions and constituting an object of knowledge."[12]

The Vedic texts concerning Brahman fall into two classes ("according as Brahman is represented as possessing form or as devoid of it"), and have two entirely different purposes. The former "do not aim at setting forth the nature of Brahman, but rather at enjoining the worship of Brahman." "Where the texts, negativing all distinctions founded on name, form, and the like, designate Brahman by such terms as that which is not coarse and so on, the higher Brahman is spoken of. Where, again, for the purpose of pious meditation, the texts teach Brahman as qualified by some distinction depending on name, form, and so on . . . , that is the lower Brahman."[13]

For "name and form, the adjuncts (of the one real Brahman) are due to Nescience." Ultimately "there is only one highest Lord ever changing, whose substance is cognition, and who, by means of Nescience, manifests himself in various ways, just as a thaumaturge appears in different shapes by means of his magical power."[14]

Shankara exerted a decisive influence on the subsequent development of Vedanta doctrines. As these have been, for centuries, the dominant tradition in Hindu philosophy, his distinctions between a higher and a lower Brahman and a higher and a lower knowledge of him have achieved an important, if not central, position in Indian thought. By affirming the sole existence of an undifferentiated Absolute (the *nirguna* Brahman) they have indeed—in *philosophical* circles—tended to foster a corresponding emphasis on what Professor Northrop has called the "undifferentiated aesthetic continuum."

But one must not take them as representative of Vedanta as a whole. Badarayana's Sutras do not make these distinctions, nor does Ramanuja in his own commentary on this work. Whereas Shankara's personal God is unreal and his real Brahman impersonal, Ramanuja's real deity is a personal God. For him there is "no room for the distinction between a param nirgunam and an aparam sagunam" Brahman—between the higher Brahman without attributes and the lower, qualified Brahman.[15]

Modern Hindu thought is predominantly Vedantist and usually follows Shankara's lead in its interpretation of the Vedas. It espouses a radical monism (Advaita or "nonduality"), stresses both the unreality of the individual soul and its essential identity with the Absolute, and regards the phenomenal world as a deceptive illusion (maya), a magical show.[16] Hence it is difficult for many Hindu scholars to approach the history of Indian philosophy objectively; in evaluating the past they tend to overstress the elements that confirm contemporary beliefs and convictions. In actuality Shankara appears to have imposed his own philosophical views on Badarayana, wrested scriptural texts to his own purpose, and forced upon the Vedas a doctrinal consistency that seems at times extraneous and arbitrary—a systematic unity that the texts themselves fail to justify. In short, he handled his own scriptures much like Catholic or Protestant exegetes in the West.

In the same sutras, however, other Vedantists, such as Ramanuja, found warrant for very different doctrines—a personal god and a plurality of souls—grounds for a system not altogether different from Leibniz's monadology. Moreover, the Vedas themselves—composed over a period of centuries, unsystematic in organization and method, and often inconsistent in terminology and doctrine—lent themselves to a variety of interpretations. Unlike the Buddhists and Jains, most philosophical schools gave at least lip service to the scriptures but disagreed profoundly as to their meaning. Between the absolute extremes of spiritual and materialist monism, Indian thought displayed a striking diversity that comprehended every shade of opinion—fideism and skepticism, personal monotheism and atheism, dualism and pluralism, ceremonial rigidity and moral relativity, mysticism and logic. Like Shankara's absolute idealism, most of these systems have parallels in Western thought—the idealism of Vasubandhu in that of Bishop Berkeley, the skeptical empiricism of the Buddhists in Locke and Hume, the Sankhya dualism of matter and spirit in Cartesianism, and Sankhya atomism in the philosophy of Democritus and Leucippus. With its denial of the soul and God, its negation of any eternal moral law or existence after death, its emphasis on sense-perception as the only source of knowledge and expediency as the chief rule in politics, Carvaka materialism is not too far removed from the systems of Lucretius and Epicurus in antiquity, Thomas Hobbes in the seventeenth century, and the pragmatic and positivist schools of the modern West.

Indian philosophy displays, in brief, much the same range and diversity as Western thought. The problems that engaged Brahmins and gymnosophists also challenged disputants in the schools of Greece and France and Germany—the "mind-body" problem and the relationship of mind to matter, the nature and origin of the universe, the analysis of causality, the ideality of space and time, the definition of the *summum bonum* and the best way to achieve it, and—though they did not always frame the question in these terms—the relative validity of philosophy. Intellectuals in almost every society have had to face the problem of the relationship between reason and revelation; the solutions of Indian thinkers are scarcely less varied than those of their Islamic, Judaic and Christian colleagues in Western Asia and Europe.

To refute the dichotomy of spiritual East and materialistic West one scarcely needs to look beyond the contrast between Carvaka materialism and the idealism of Berkeley and Plato and Hegel. By such arbitrary selection of data one could argue, not implausibly, that the real antithesis is the opposition between the spiritual Occident and a materialistic Orient! Though patently absurd, such an inference would be scarcely less ridiculous than the contrary view—a belief still so widely held that it is almost proverbial. Both rest on a highly subjective choice of evidence.

4

Thus, instead of a contrast between Eastern religion and Western thought, one encounters two distinct logical traditions, Indian and Greek, and two major religious groups, "Indian" and "Abrahamic,"[17] besides the indigenous religions of China and Japan. The logic of Islam and medieval Europe derives from Greece. That of Tibet and China stems from India. (Though China can boast an indigenous "logical school," most of her treatises on this subject were translations from Pali or Sanskrit.) In logic, as in religion, Islam is much closer to Europe than to the rest of Asia. If there is such a thing as an Asian personality, it is a split personality, for the mind of Asia is as divided as its spirituality.

Eastern and Western cultures have passed through similar crises of soul and intellect and similar tensions between religion and reason, or science and faith. The Greeks themselves experienced this conflict; in the opinion of one observer, it was largely on religious grounds that the ancients rejected the theory of the earth's movement in favor of a geocentric universe. "Astronomy in antiquity was as thorny a subject as biblical criticism in modern times."[18]

Like Western thought, Eastern philosophy passed through a scholastic phase. Like the Abrahamic faiths, the Indian religions met the challenge by reconciling reason and revelation on logical as well as scriptural grounds. The problem that confronted the Indian theologian Shankara was comparable to that which challenged the Moslem thinker al-Ash'ari, the Hebrew philosopher Maimonides, and such Christian schoolmen as Abélard, St. Albertus Magnus, and St. Thomas Aquinas.

In all of these cultures the exact bounds of philosophy and religion remained an undefined, but bitterly contested frontier. If al-Ghazali challenged the philosophers, Averroës sprang to their defense and attacked their adversary. In one generation the Church anathematized the champions of scholastic method; in the next she canonized them. A few generations later, Protestants and humanists would join forces against the schoolmen. Both deplored the tyranny of Aristotle but on rather different grounds; the former denounced the corruption of religion, the latter the degeneration of learning.

In philosophy and logic medieval Europe was heavily dependent on Islam. In science her debt was even greater. In mechanics, in astronomy, in medicine, and in several other branches of natural philosophy, Greek science reached the Latin West primarily through an "Islamic detour."[19] Greek texts originally translated by Nestorian Christians at Baghdad now became accessible in Latin through the labors of Jewish and Christian translators at Toledo and of Arabic and European scholars in Sicily. Though a few translations were made directly from Greek manuscripts, late medieval science was largely Arabic in character. Rhazes, al-Farabi, and Avicenna ranked little below the ancients in authority, and students usually approached Aristotle through Averroës' commentary. The Hellenic tradition, as scientists of the late Middle Ages knew it, was really a Greco-Arabic tradition.

The humanist reaction against Arabic learning may (as George Sarton has suggested) have been partly motivated by hostility to Islam. Yet one cannot attribute it entirely—or even primarily—to bigotry. Its real roots lay elsewhere—in the reaction against scholastic method, against the overemphasis on logic at the expense of rhetoric, and against the tendency to subordinate eloquence to jejune subtlety. Equally significant, however, was the philologist's concern for the integrity and purity of the original text. In seeking to eliminate the Arabic detour, in rejecting the Latin translation from the Arabic in favor of the original Greek text, the humanist was not displaying a sectarian bias. He was exercising judicious scholarship.

He conceived his mission, in fact, as a scholar's crusade, directed not against the infidel abroad but against the barbarian at home. Its objective was not Jerusalem but Athens or Rome. It aimed not at liberating the Holy Sepulcher but at restoring the Lyceum and the Academy, the Acropolis and the Forum.

Like all zealots, however, the humanist was blinded by the dogmas of his faith. In displacing other superstitions, he substituted his own—the idol of the Renaissance and the myth of Europe. The former is too familiar to require comment: the flowering of the arts in ancient Greece, their transplantation to Rome, their degeneration during the barbarous ages and their eventual rebirth in thirteenth- and fourteenth-century Italy. The myth of Europe is less obvious but more deeply entrenched. In reorienting Renaissance Europe toward classical civilization, the humanist helped to foster an illusion that his disciples accepted uncritically, and still accept—the integrity and continuity of the Western tradition. By a curious distortion of the principle of primogeniture, we assume that our own Western civilization is the sole residual heir of the classical legacy. Because our own European culture derives from that of classical Greece, we infer that the latter is purely a European achievement and that we are its unique legatee. This is a magnificent obsession, but it will hardly bear examination.

Neither Greek science nor that of the medieval and modern West is entirely a European achievement. Both built partly on Asiatic or African foundations. Classical astronomy and algebra showed strong Mesopotamian influence, just as ours still bear the imprint of Arabic speculation. Many of the pseudosciences that flourished in classical or medieval Europe—astrology, haruspicy, and alchemy—had developed on African and Asian soil. The scientific tradition of ancient Greece was partly "barbarian" in origin; the learning of Christian Europe was strongly indebted to Islam.

In science as in art and religion, continental labels and geographical categories are misleading. If Greek and Roman artists imported motifs from the Near and Middle East, the latter received them back—transformed—from Greece or Rome. If Rome opened her gates to the Oriental gods, the Orient in turn learned to worship Rome's tutelary deities—her transplanted Olympus, her deified emperors, and her Christian saints. The same cosmopolitanism is evident in classical science. Though it is essentially Greek, it is not essentially European; many of the leading scientists were Africans or Asians, and in several fields Alexandria was more influential than Athens. Hellenistic and Roman civilization was neither Eastern nor Western, neither European nor Asian nor African. It was all of these, and none. It was ecumenical—in science, in religion, and in art. The Pax Romana had imposed a truce on the War of Continents, and in all of these fields the continental labels became increasingly irrelevant.

In the Middle Ages, of course, the picture was radically different. The classical world had disintegrated into rival theocracies: Rome, Byzantium, and Islam—the Latin West; the Greek East, with its shifting frontiers in Europe and Asia; the Arabic domains to the east and south, stretching from Persia to the Maghreb and Moorish Spain. Yet, for all their hostility, these had more in common than they cared to admit—"the cultural legacy of the heathen world around the Mediterranean and Judeo-Christian monotheism."[20] Though the older ecumenical society had been shattered and its heirs divided by language and religion, they still bestowed sporadic, if grudging, admiration on the glory that had been Greece, and—more significantly—they still felt the need of the secular wisdom, the sciences and technical skills, of the ancients. Athens might still seem incredibly remote from Jerusalem, and Alexandria from Mecca; but theologians in Christendom and Islam alike needed logic to defend and rationalize their dogmas. When sick, they required the ministrations of a qualified physician. The physician, in turn, needed botany, anatomy, and astrology. The astrologer, for his part, required skill in mathematics.

"The two scientific bibles of the Middle Ages and the Renaissance," as a leading historian of science, George Sarton, points out, "were known under names of Arabic affiliation, the *Canon* of Avicenna and the *Almagest* of Ptolemy."[21] The former dealt with medicine, the latter with astronomy. The medical classics of Hippocrates and Galen, the mathematical works of Euclid and Apollonius, Archimedes and Menelaus of Alexandria, the botanical treatises of Theophrastus and Dioscorides reached Europe "via two sets of translations—Greek-Arabic and Arabic-Latin."[22] The astrolabe clocks and other automata that delighted the later Middle Ages and the Renaissance represented another Hellenistic legacy inherited through Islam.[23] "There appears to be no longer any question . . . that the mechanical clock and fine instrumentation evolved in a direct line without substantial change from the mechanical water clocks of the Alexandrian civilization, transmitted through Islam and Byzantium from a tradition that may have originated in China, that reached Europe in the twelfth and thirteenth centuries."[24] The West derived its knowledge of statics, astronomy, and the impetus theory of projectiles—an important doctrine in mechanics—largely from Greek science via "the Islamic detour."[25]

Modern chemistry evolved from the pseudoscience of alchemy, which Islam had transmitted to the West. Hindu mathematics and theories of perpetual motion, Chinese innovations in artillery and magnetism, likewise penetrated Europe via Islam. So did algebra; passing in succession from Babylonian to Greek to Arab, it flourished in Islam. One of its leading exponents was the poet Omar Khayyám. The author of the *Rubáiyát* devoted his leisure to cubic equations as well as wine, women, and verses. What was more, he managed to "solve many of them."[26]

In optics "the Arabs clearly surpassed their Greek masters,"[27] and in this field the West owes an immeasurable debt to them. They laid the foundations for the major triumphs of European optics—scientific perspective in art and architecture, the invention of the telescope, the microscope—and spectacles.

In Islam as in Europe, historiography had to struggle against personal and sectarian bias. Nevertheless, in al-Beruni's *Chronology of Ancient Nations* and Ibn Khaldun's *History of the World,* it achieved a "critical consciousness of function and procedure of the scholar" that "remained unparalleled for centuries." The latter's "sociological studies" antedate "modern European sociology by more than four centuries," but the same problems had already engaged another "Muslim author [Mas'udi] more than four centuries before his time."[28]

For several hundred years Western science rested largely on an Islamic foundation. The "Arabic writers," Sarton concludes, "led scientific thought for about three centuries [ninth to eleventh] and remained exceedingly influential for at least two more centuries [twelfth to thirteenth], but . . . after 1300 their influence declined, slowly at first, more rapidly later."[29] But even after 1300 they retained their prestige. Chaucer interlarded his poetry with allusions to Arabic writers—Avicenna, Rhazes, Alchabitius—and Greek authorities whom his contemporaries knew only via the "Islamic detour." As late as the seventeenth century Robert Burton still mentions them with respect. In themselves they are sufficient witnesses to refute the cliché of scientific Europe and spiritual Asia.

The scientific achievements of India and China are scarcely less worthy of respect. The three inventions which Francis Bacon extolled for changing "the appearance and state of the whole world"[30]—printing, gunpowder, and the compass—possibly origi-

nated in China. "Possibly," for the origin of gunpowder is still
obscure, and on this point scholars have challenged Chinese
priority. The fact remains, moreover, that whereas Europe recognized the revolutionary potentialities of all three of these discoveries, China apparently did not. They transformed the West,
but left the Far East virtually unchanged.[31]

By a very early date the Chinese had already revealed their
technological skill in engineering and irrigation. They had
learned to harness the forces of water and wind as sources of
industrial power. They had invented the crossbow and the
treadle, paper, the foot stirrup and the bellows[32]—and even
those exotic desert ships, the "cany waggons light" which Milton's "Chineses" steered before the wind. Their alchemy, phar-
macology, and divination may have been pseudosciences, but
so were the same arts in the "rationalistic" West.

To India the West is indebted for "positional reckoning,"[33] the
concept of zero, the so-called "Arabic" numerals, trigonometry,
and arithmetic. Both of the latter were, as Sarton observes, of
"Eurasian" parentage: "The mother was Hindu and the father
Greek." The notion of "sine" was discovered in India and developed by the Arabs.[34] The discovery of the differential calculus
has also been ascribed—with probability rather than certainty
—to India. The Ayurvedic medicine and astrology of the Hindus
may seem little more than pseudosciences today, but we recognize them as such only because modern science has outgrown
them.

In Indian logic we have encountered syllogistic reasoning
comparable to that of the West. The similarities extend even to
the distinction between syllogisms of three, four, or five members
respectively. In countering the "widely spread prejudice that
positive philosophy is to be found only in Europe," Dr. Stcherbatsky has thrown new light on "Buddhist logic . . . as the
culminating point of a long course of Indian philosophic history." In the nondualist (Advaita) philosophy of Shankaracharya
we have observed exegetical and controversial methods not dissimilar to those of rational theologians in Europe and Western

Asia—a fusion of logical procedure and textual interpretation and a dual reliance on the authority of reason and scriptural revelation that can be paralleled in the scholastic philosophy of medieval Christendom and Islam. In Oriental science, finally, we have met traditions that could until recently rival those of Europe and to which Western science has frequently been heavily indebted. For the greater part of our history the "secretions" of Maeterlinck's "subconscious" Eastern half of the global cranium have been, on the whole, just as scientific, just as rational, as those of the "Western lobe."

In the next two chapters we shall examine the reverse side of the problem. Just as the rational and scientific aspects of Eastern societies have been underestimated, so have the mystical and religious traditions of the West. In the following pages we shall consider the dual tendency to overstress the mystical aspect of the Orient at the expense of its rationalism and to exaggerate the rational aspects of the West at the expense of its mysticism.

V

EASTERN RELIGIONS
AND WESTERN CULTURE

"In the history of Western thought," declares the British philosopher E. W. F. Tomlin, in his (1950) introduction to Oriental philosophy, "there is a thing called philosophy and there is a thing called theology; and it has usually been possible, except in certain periods such as the Middle Ages, to distinguish between the two. In the history of Eastern thought there is only a thing called theology."[1] "For 3,000 years," asserts Dr. Edward Conze, a leading authority on Oriental thought and the author of several brilliant books on Buddhism, "Asia alone has been creative of spiritual ideas and methods . . . European thought has excelled in the elaboration of *social* law and organization, especially in Rome and England, and in the *scientific* understanding and control of sensory phenomena. . . . Philosophy, as we understand it in Europe, is a creation of the Greeks. It is unknown to Buddhist tradition, which would regard the enquiry into reality, for the mere purpose of knowing more about it, as a waste of valuable time."[2]

If pushed to its logical conclusion, this contrast would invalidate most of the comparative studies of European and Asian philosophy. If the West alone has produced true philosophers, then the histories of Indian and Chinese philosophy by Dasgupta, Radhakrishnan, Fung Yu-lan, and many others must be utterly beside the point. Indeed, the very title of Mr. Tomlin's book— *The Oriental Philosophers*—must be a misnomer. On the basis of his own distinctions he may legitimately compare European and Asian *theology*. Yet, if Dr. Conze is correct and all religions are Asiatic in origin, even this is impossible. One can only compare the primary and secondary spiritualities, indigenous and imported faiths—the different systems of "Asiatic" religion on Asian and European soil.

Even though both writers qualify their generalizations, the antithesis is not a happy one, and the qualifications themselves are not always accurate. To except the Middle Ages (with Mr. Tomlin) means ruling out a major part of the Western tradition. Nor is the exception altogether pertinent. Medieval schoolmen usually draw a sharp distinction between reason and revelation and the relative authority of philosophy and theology—a dichotomy that also underlay the frequently distorted doctrine of a double truth. In the Orient Shankara exhibits a similar awareness of the contrast. Like most of the scholastic theologians in the West, he throws his weight solidly behind the authority of revelation; but he, too, is fully cognizant of the difference between scripture and logic. In actuality, the distinction between theology and philosophy is fairly widespread in the East. As a modern Chinese philosopher, Dr. Fung Yu-lan, points out, the Chinese themselves differentiate clearly between Taoism, Buddhism, and Confucianism as philosophical systems and as religions.[3]

Oriental thought is too diverse to be comprehended in a single formula. Carvaka materialism is surely philosophy rather than theology. In the strictest sense, the Sankhya, Jain, and early Buddhist schools are atheistic; to describe them as theologies is at best an ingenious paradox.

Nor do Western philosophers consistently draw a distinction between philosophy and theology; both classical and modern thinkers often evolve a *natural* theology, a religious philosophy based ostensibly on reason rather than revealed truth. Aristotle's Unmoved Prime Mover, Plato's Demiurge and Idea of the Good, the Logos of the Neo-Platonists, Leibniz's Supreme Monad, and the Spirit and Absolute of the German transcendentalists are essentially theological concepts as well as philosophical abstractions. In none of these systems can one dissociate theology from philosophy without destroying its integrity and coherence.

2

Nor are Dr. Conze's qualifying phrases much more helpful. In fact, he loads his dice rather heavily, and his arguments are all too often a case of special pleading. In East and West alike, philosophy is usually an enquiry into reality and a search for the principles of what Dignaga calls "right knowledge." As to what this reality is, how far it can be known and by what means, philosophers in both regions show almost equal diversity. They are scarcely less varied in their conception of the grounds of right knowledge and in the motives underlying their thought. Critical philosophy, in the West as in the East, has usually concerned itself less with the nature of reality than with the limitations of the human mind; metaphysics has normally been contingent on epistemology. The majority of Western thinkers, whether classical or modern, would, like the Buddhists, regard "the mere purpose of knowing more" about reality as a waste of time—a pastime for the naïve realist. For many of them, the chief purpose of philosophy would, as for most Eastern schools, be predominantly ethical—the discovery and attainment of felicity and the highest good. Platonism culminates in the Idea of the Good, Spinoza's philosophy in the intellectual love of God. Kant exposes the limits of pure reason to leave greater scope for the practical reason, curbing the excesses of theory on behalf of ethics and faith.

Indeed, the very example Dr. Conze cites argues the exact opposite. The Buddhist tradition of skepticism toward the enquiry into reality was not, of course, directed against Western rationalism. It evolved in reaction against the metaphysical speculations of other Indian schools, against the theories of the Brahmins as to the nature of the ultimate reality—whether matter or God or soul. According to the Buddhist theory of right knowledge, none of these concepts could be validated by either perception or inference; and early Buddhism was, in fact, known as the "No-Soul and No-Substance doctrine."[4]

Dr. Conze exaggerates the nonphilosophical character of Buddhism and the contrast with Western thought. For other observers the differences are less striking. Stcherbatsky stresses the resemblances between Buddhist theory and the views of a host of Western philosophers—Leibniz, Bergson, Heraclitus, Sigwart; Aristotle and Kant and Herbart; Brentano, Bradley, and Bosanquet; Plato and Hegel; Bain and J. S. Mill.[5] Mr. Watts, in turn, finds "an almost uncanny affinity between some of the major trends of modern Western thought and Buddhist philosophy. Bergson, Whitehead, Wittgenstein, Schrödinger, Dewey, Korzybski, Heidegger, Whyte, Tillich—all in some quite significant respects think like Buddhists."[6] These convergences between thinkers widely separated in space and time are, on the whole, independent developments. They cannot be dismissed as borrowings.

Nor is political genius a unique characteristic of the West, as Dr. Conze apparently believes. For Xenophon, the perfect mirror of a prince was to be found in a Persian monarch, Cyrus. If an efficient civil service is a prerequisite for sound imperial government, China demonstrated her political aptitudes long before Europe. For such social enterprises as town planning, large-scale irrigation, and legal codes, the priority belongs to the Orient rather than the Occident.

The credit for many of the arts and sciences likewise belongs to the Orient. The Greeks themselves, for all their contempt for "barbarians," openly acknowledged their debt to the older civilizations of the Near and Middle East. Mycenaean culture took over the achievements of late Minoan society, but this Greek-speaking culture rested on an older, Asiatic foundation; the early Semitic civilization of Crete had its roots in the cultures of the Fertile Crescent. If Professor Lynn White, Jr. (author of *Medieval Technology and Social Change*) is correct, Western technology is ultimately indebted to the Orient for many of the inventions that revolutionized European society—to China for the foot stirrup, the mariner's compass, and the crossbow; to India for the spinning wheel, Arabic numerals, and the idea of perpetual motion; to Tibet for the vertical-axle windmill and the hot-air turbine. The "first crank is in a Han-dynasty model." Nor was China slow to adopt Western inventions; the horizontal water wheel—the first power machine—made an "almost simultaneous appearance" in Denmark, the Mediterranean region, and China. The Chinese were using cannon as early as 1356—very shortly after their appearance in Europe. Although "there is no evidence of Chinese stimulus to, or precedence over, the European developments" in the use of rockets, this invention was being exploited almost simultaneously—for spectacular or for military purposes—in both regions.[7]

Indeed, the migration of the arts—from Asia and Egypt to Greece and thence to Rome—was a commonplace of the ancient world. The myth of Cadmus was regarded as a historical allegory, a veiled account of the Oriental origin of the alphabet and the Asiatic source of most of the arts and sciences. Admittedly, many of these were pseudosciences, nor had the "true" sciences reached the level the Greeks subsequently gave them. The fact remains, however, that for classical antiquity the myth of Asia stressed the priority and excellence of Oriental art and science. It did not regard social and scientific achievement as distinctively characteristic of the West.

3

In pressing the claims of Eastern spirituality, Dr. Conze fails to avoid the usual pitfall of cultural diffusionists—the so-called genetic fallacy. Because most of the world's higher religions developed on Asian soil, he infers that true spirituality must be characteristically Asiatic: "All European spirituality has had to be periodically renewed by an influx from the East, from the time of Pythagoras and Parmenides onwards. Take away the Oriental elements in Greek philosophy, take away Jesus Christ, Saint Paul, Dionysius Areopagita, and Arabic thought—and

European spiritual thinking during the last 2,000 years becomes unthinkable."[8]

Parmenides and the Arabs, the pseudo Dionysius and Christ—this is such a curious medley of examples that it warrants more detailed examination. It would be unfair to take literally Dr. Conze's assertion that all religions are Asiatic in origin. A medieval schoolman could have plausibly argued such a thesis. (All pagan religions were, for him, either inventions of the devil or corruptions of the true religion revealed to Adam. And Adam, of course, was as impeccably "Asiatic" as the red clay of Damascus.) Dr. Conze is not speaking of *all* religions, but merely of the *higher* faiths.

The term smacks of provincialism, however; one may well ask with the Wife of Bath, "Who painted the leoun?" after all. The student of comparative religions measures the relative altitude of other faiths by his own. In practice he tends to restrict the term to religions that have a monotheist, monist, or dualist tendency, which have simplified the complex polytheism and animism of their ancestors and (in Platonic terms) reduced the Many to One. Yet this approach is not altogether satisfactory. Polytheism and animism still retain their popular attraction even within the framework of the "higher" faiths. Can we justly exclude the religion of Greece—the polytheism that underlies so much of the world's best sculpture, architecture, and drama; the philosophical monotheism that finds expression in Plato and Aristotle, the Eleatics and the Stoics?

Arabic thought hardly proves the point. In fact, it argues the contrary of Dr. Conze's thesis. What Europe borrowed from Islam was neither "religion" nor "spirituality," but philosophy and science. This was the principal channel through which medieval Europe recovered the learning of the ancient Greeks; it laid the theoretical foundations for the modern scientific West. Initially, it encountered sharp opposition from the Church; and the basis of this hostility was precisely that it was *not* spiritual, that it was secular and therefore profane. It was merely the wisdom of *this* world, not the wisdom of God; the product of human reason, not the voice of the Spirit.

The impact of Arabic thought seems, therefore, to invert Dr. Conze's thesis—to demonstrate the influence of the "scientific" and rationalistic Orient on the "spiritual" and mystical West. One remembers how bitterly one Western mystic—St. Bernard—fought against the new learning, and how savagely he attacked the logical methods of Abélard.

To cite Parmenides, Pythagoras, and pseudo Dionysius as instances of Asiatic spirituality may seem puzzling until one reads further and discovers how comprehensive are the claims the author advances on behalf of Oriental thought. Both Christianity and Greek philosophy are in large part, it appears, pale reflections of Brahmanism and Buddhism. Pyrrhonic skepticism derives from Madhyamika teachings, "probably" by way of the Jains. The Christian Gospels, in turn, show the influence of "Buddhist doctrines."[9]

In comparison with other writers on the subject, Dr. Conze is —as we shall see—highly conservative. Though he finds "a profusion of verbal coincidences" between Neo-Platonic literature and "the Prajnaparamita texts" of Mahayana Buddhism, he admits that these may represent parallel developments rather than direct borrowing.[10] Other scholars are far more audacious in stating such claims. Many of them categorically define the religions of Europe (and of Western Asia) as a derivative from India. Against this background Dr. Conze's claims for Oriental spirituality appear very modest indeed.

4

Since Nietzsche, cultural historians have recognized the tension between rational and irrational, Apollonian and Dionysian, elements in Greek civilization—the conflict between the bright Olympian deities and the dark gods of death and rebirth; the dualism of reason and emotion, logic and mysticism. Though most contemporaries would regard both aspects as equally Hellenic[11] like the complementary masks of comedy and tragedy, a minority regard the darker facet of Greek culture as an Asiatic intrusion, an importation from India by way of Persia. For Dr. Sarvepalli Radhakrishnan, author of *Eastern Religions and Western Thought,* "the Orphic, the Eleusinian, the Pythagorean brotherhoods, and Platonic schools" are essentially "alien in origin, alien to the spirit of Hellenism, predominantly Indian in character and content." Further affinities with Indian thought appear, he finds, in doctrines of the Eleatics, of Empedocles and Anaxagoras, and of Pyrrho and the Stoics.[12]

But India's influence on Western thought was not confined to the earlier phases of Greek philosophy. If Dr. Radhakrishnan is correct, it also left its imprint on Judaism and Christianity, Gnosticism and Neo-Platonism—and thus played a major role in the intellectual history of Europe. The Book of Enoch and the teachings of Jesus illustrate and continue an ancient Hindu tradition. The "striking resemblance" that the "Gospel story bears . . . to the life and teaching of Gautama the Buddha" is due neither to accident nor to natural evolution, but to Hindu and Buddhist influence. "The Therapeutae or the contemplative monks of Egypt . . . represent a blend of Alexandrian Judaism and Hindu beliefs and modes of life." Most of the elements in Philo's system "are those found in Hindu thought." Gnosticism fuses Platonic and Hindu elements, and Basilides "works Hindu and Buddhist thought into a Christian framework." Plotinus and pseudo Dionysius reveal an indebtedness to Brahmanism, and Clement of Alexandria is "deeply influenced" by Buddhist thought.[13]

These are not isolated views, and in advancing them Dr. Radhakrishnan cites a formidable array of scholars—Rawlinson, Winternitz, Garbe, Hopkins, Macdonell; Mayer, Lightfoot, Moffatt, Carpenter; Otto, Müller, Eliot, Pfleiderer; Petrie, Stutfield, and Inge. Though such authorities as these are not to be lightly dismissed, they are not always reliable. At times their opinions bear a striking resemblance to those of less conscientious scholars or the vagaries of Pacific Coast mystagogues.

Other writers have pointed to the analogies between idealistic monism in India and the West as evidence of a further debt to "Eastern spirituality." Though such analogies have been over-stressed, they do exist, and several European and American transcendentalists (or their successors) were undeniably aware of the parallel. In the first pages of *The World as Will and Idea* Arthur Schopenhauer stresses the affinities between his own philosophy and the Vedanta. Ralph Waldo Emerson, in verse and prose alike, frequently arrays his thought in the imagery and terminology of the Vedas and Upanishads. Yet in both cases the Orientalism is largely extrinsic—applied ornament rather than inherent structure. In both cases the allusions to Hindu thought reflect an awareness of similarity in viewpoint rather than fundamental doctrinal indebtedness. The thought of Schopenhauer and Emerson alike really springs not from Vedanta but from the German idealist tradition. Yet the similarities, as both men saw them, were so striking that they were able, without affectation, to emphasize the analogies between their own philosophies and those of the East.

Nor were they, by any means, the first "Western" thinkers to do so. Neo-Platonists and neo-Pythagoreans of late antiquity found similarities between their own doctrines and those of India's "gymnosophists." (The latter may have been members of the Jain Digambara sect; and just how much the Hellenistic and Roman worlds really knew of their doctrines remains a matter of doubt.) Patristic theologians cited them, along with the "Brachmanes" either as spokesmen of natural theology or as evidence for the diffusion and corruption of Hebrew truth. Renaissance Neo-Platonists and cabalists likewise claimed them as adherents to their own doctrines. Their own *philosophia perennis,* compounded of Hermetic and Pythagorean, Orphic and Judaic traditions, was (they maintained) the "secret doctrine" divinely revealed to Adam, Moses, and the patriarchs. Indeed, Abraham was really *"Abrahman"*(!),[14] and the monotheism he preached was merely the cabala which ancient India had received by oral tradition from Adam's posterity.

The Renaissance cabalists bring one perilously close to the esoteric precincts of modern theosophy. Yet even here one is still on European soil. For all their adulation of the "wisdom of the East," Mme. Blavatsky and Mrs. Annie Besant were not exotic fruits, but part of the indigenous flora of the Western landscape. They continued, possibly without realizing it, the traditions of Renaissance Hermeticism and, in a highly modified form, of German transcendentalism. What Heinrich Wölfflin observed of the classicizing artists of the Italian Renaissance is equally true of the Orientalizing philosophers and mystagogues of the modern West. "With unerring feeling," they "took from these admired models only those things which they themselves understood, that is, those things which they had already mastered for themselves. . . ."[15] With rare exceptions the Oriental element in modern Western thought is merely a veneer. For the most part, it points rather to a real or imaginary *sympathy* with Eastern philosophy rather than to real intellectual indebtedness. New England "Brahmanism," California Vedanta, Barbary Coast Zen —all are essentially Western developments. Instead of a wholesale borrowing from the East, they represent little more than a sentimental sympathy with Oriental thought, a vague hankering after the mysteries of the East. Such Orientalism is less essential than symptomatic.

This, then, is the background of Dr. Conze's insistence that all "European spirituality" is "Asiatic" in origin and must be periodically revived, like Antaeus, by fresh contacts with the soil from which it sprang. According to this interpretation, the entire mystical tradition in the West is exotic, derived from the Orient and—more specifically—from India. The Western mystics, from Plotinus to Evelyn Underhill, are citizens of a vast, invisible commonwealth stretching from Japan to Gibraltar and beyond to the New World—an Indian empire beside which the dominions of Ashoka and Akbar pale to insignificance.

Superficially, this conception confirms the proverbial contrast of spiritual East and rationalistic West by reducing European spirituality to a pale imitation or corruption of its Asian original. Yet, in actuality, it undermines the antithesis. If the principal schools of Greek philosophy really drew their inspiration from India, then the chief influences on Western rationalism are also Asiatic in origin.

But, in fact, there is very little evidence for this view. The alleged Indian influence on Hellenic and Judaic thought is largely a matter of guesswork. Most of the scholars Dr. Radhakrishnan cites wrote before the development of modern anthropological techniques and hence placed an exaggerated stress on parallels as evidence of borrowing. By the same line of reasoning, writers have "demonstrated" that Polynesians are Norsemen and that the pre-Columbian civilizations of the New World borrowed from the higher cultures of the Old.

Because the Mayas built pyramids and wrote in hieroglyphics, they must, it is assumed, have acquired their arts from Egypt. Because they were mathematicians and astronomers, they must have borrowed their science from the Chaldeans. Because they worked in jade, modeled pottery tripods, and imposed abstract linear designs on their stylized animal masks, they must, it is inferred, have been influenced by China. By this type of argument one might maintain—just as plausibly and just as erroneously—that Indian logicians derived their syllogisms from the Greeks. After all, was not Alexander the pupil of Aristotle? And was it not philosophy that he discussed with the naked sages of the Sind?

Despite commercial contact with India, Greek colonies on the Indian frontier, and the presence of Indian traders in Alexandria, there is little evidence that the Mediterranean world possessed extensive or accurate knowledge of Indian civilization—much less of the subtleties of Indian philosophy. The Upanishads were, on the whole, a secret doctrine,[16] and the penalties for revealing them to outsiders were as severe as the punishment for betraying the secrets of the Greek mystery cults. For overhearing them, a Sudra (a member of the fourth and lowest caste) might legally incur such tortures as having his tongue cut out and boiling oil poured in his ears. About the Greek mysteries we know very little indeed, and the accounts of them that are preserved in patristic writings are fragmentary and often misinformed—a distortion that cannot be attributed entirely to religious bias. If this was true of mysteries that flourished in the very heart of the Greek world, it must have been even more true of the complex and jealously guarded doctrines taught in a remote country and in a virtually unknown tongue thousands of miles to the east. Though Mediterranean traders and adventurers might have gained a superficial knowledge of Buddhist or Jain practices and beliefs, it is doubtful that they learned much about Hindu philosophy.

Whatever Indians made the arduous voyage to Alexandria would probably have been Jains and Buddhists or members of the Vaisya (merchant) caste. Caste laws tended to restrain Brahmins from foreign travel—though they may have been less rigidly observed than at a later date. There seems little likelihood that Alexandrian Greeks could have acquired much detailed information about the Upanishads and the philosophical traditions based on them.

Though there is no dearth of references to Indian beliefs—in Hellenistic geographers and historians and in patristic theologians and apologists—they are, for the most part, neither detailed, accurate, nor profound. What Clement of Alexandria reports of the Buddha is very superficial indeed. So are the allusions to Indian doctrines in Philostratus' *Life of Apollonius of Tyana.* For alleged Indian influence on Pythagoras, there is no real evidence other than the relatively late tradition that he had studied there. The belief in the transmigration of the soul is far too widespread to substantiate his debt to India. After all, Caesar ascribes the same opinion to the Druids. Finally, of the multitude of Greek and Roman philosophers whom Dr. Radhakrishnan regards as ultimately indebted to India, *none* explicitly acknowledges the debt. This cannot be dismissed as mere ingratitude.

In actuality, the clearest and fullest account of Indian society and its religious beliefs remains that of Megasthenes, ambassador of Seleucus I Nicator to the court of Chandragupta Maurya. As extensive quotations in Strabo and other writers indicate, the Hellenistic world depended heavily on his report for its knowledge of Indian civilization. Together with the reports of Alexander's generals, this apparently remained the most detailed and reliable authority on the subject.

Nor is Indian thought fundamental to Gnosticism. As Dr. Hans Jonas points out, the principal Oriental contributions to this

Hellenistic religion appear to have been "Jewish monotheism, Babylonian astrology, and Iranian dualism."[17] Despite certain striking resemblances—the antithesis of Knowledge and Ignorance as instruments respectively of liberation or bondage, the emphasis on the essential identity or affinity of the self with the transcendental Absolute—the fundamental differences are more impressive. Indian Vedantist philosophy is for the most part radically monist; Gnosticism, especially in its Iranian versions, is radically dualist. The Gnostic hostility toward the Creator-God and bias toward Satanism are altogether alien to Brahmanism; Brahma the creator and Vishnu the preserver are benevolent deities. The astral determinism, so characteristic of Gnostic thought, and the emphasis on fate (*heimarmene*) are primarily Syrian and Greek in origin; they differ from the basically *ethical* determinism of India as reflected in the concept of karma—the view that man's lot in this life is the reward or punishment for his merits or demerits in his prior existence. Furthermore, the existential status of the cosmos is radically different. As Jonas observes, "the removal of true divinity from the world does not deprive it of reality and make it a mere shadow or illusion (as in certain teachings of Indian mysticism)."[18]

Finally—and most significantly—neither the philosophical nor the mythological idioms of Gnosticism are Indian. The former is predominantly Platonic, the latter Iranian or Babylonian, Hebrew or Christian, Hellenic or Egyptian.

Zeus and Hermes and Helen make their appearance in Gnostic texts, along with Ptah and Jehovah, Christ and Adam, and the seven planets; the Indian deities, however, are conspicuously absent. Only in its later stages, with Mani and Bardesanes, does Gnosticism explicitly stress its affinities with India. In both cases, however, Buddhism is a minor strain in a syncretistic religion, side by side with Zoroastrian and Judaic elements. In both instances the dominant strain is Iranian dualism.

Of the alleged Indian influence on the Hellenistic West, all one can safely affirm is that several thinkers—Christian and pagan alike—recognized certain affinities between their own doctrines and the beliefs ascribed to certain Indian cults. When they mentioned the latter—as they occasionally did—they cited them not as ultimate authorities but as rhetorical examples, parallels that confirmed their own tenets. They were, on the whole, merely appealing to universal opinion and the common consent of mankind; they were *not* confessing a debt.

The argument from analogy is as dangerous in intellectual as in literary history. One can "prove" anything by it—even that the *Tibetan Book of the Dead* represents a positive debt to Egypt!

Such arguments as these are, we have suggested, special pleading. The scholar is really an advocate in disguise, and beneath the doctor's cap and gown one can detect the periwigged form of the barrister. The treatise on comparative philosophy or religion turns out, after all, to be a lawyer's brief. The case is now being fought out in the lecture hall instead of the battlefield, but the issue is still the same. It is still the familiar "Quarrel of Continents."

On the whole, the Asian case is a countersuit against the claims of the West to spiritual as well as intellectual pre-eminence, to superiority in the realms of religion as of science, to the lion's share in this world and the next. The Asian apologist counters such claims by affirming the superiority of his own religions or by arguing that the Western faiths are not really Western at all, but Oriental in origin. If his opponent finds the seeds of an indigenous philosophical mysticism in Plato and Pythagoras, he rebuts this argument by identifying them as disciples of the Brahmins. If his opponent is a classicist, he stresses the Oriental elements in classical civilization. By such arguments as these he pleads for "intellectual justice to Asia."

At other times, however, his primary aim is not theoretical but practical. His chief objective is not so much to rectify a historiographical injustice as to advertise a characteristic and eminently salable export of the East—to barter spirituality for machines and the technology of mysticism for that of the production line. At this point he discards the lawyer's brief for the merchant's brochure.

Like salesmen of less imperishable goods, he employs a two-

fold approach—extolling the merits of his own wares and emphasizing his client's urgent need for them. The West suffers from
spiritual malnutrition, the East from physical undernourishment.
Why not arrange a reciprocal trade agreement beneficial to both
parties? One can sympathize with this approach—perhaps the
need *does* exist, on both sides, and perhaps this is the answer.
Yet surely the tradesman protests too much. Such high-pressure
salesmanship is more likely to alarm his customer than persuade.

Like other merchandisers, in fact, he is sometimes careless
about his labels. He may be right in emphasizing the potential
value of Buddhism for the modern West. But cannot it stand on
its own merits? Must he try to sell it on the irrelevant and
actually meaningless grounds that it is Asian?

What bearing, after all, has St. Paul or Jesus Christ on the
matter? They belonged to an entirely different Asia—an altogether different society, civilization, and religious tradition—
from the Buddhist spirituality for which the modern apologist is
pleading. Surely they have little or no relevance to the question
of the latter's importance to the West—unless, of course, one
really regards them as crypto-Buddhists, as several Oriental
apologists come close to doing.

No, Asia is so ambiguous a word—and its meanings so diverse
—that unless one distinguishes sharply between its various
senses, one may easily trip over a common logical fallacy—the
Fallacy of Equivocation. When the religious historian argues
that since Europe found spiritual satisfaction in at least one
Asian religion, it must, necessarily, find similar inspiration in
another, he is talking about two very different Asian traditions.
There are many Asian religions, and each of them has its distinctive merits. But the historic links between them are often tenuous
indeed, and the fact that they are Asian is less significant than
their more localized origins—their derivation from India or China
or Japan.

Asian spirituality—that miraculous hormone which Maeterlinck's "Eastern lobe" of the brain "secretes"—is, in fact, as
elusive as the alchemist's elixir, which likewise claimed to be a
panacea for all ills. Like such concepts as "Asia" and "the Ori-

ental mind," it has only a verbal existence—not a real foundation in reality. To treat it as the common substratum of Oriental faiths—to present the Buddhist and Judeo-Christian traditions as two slightly different brands of the same wonder-working drug— is neither sound reasoning nor good semantics. It belongs rather to the linguistics of advertising. It is, in fact, a characteristic gimmick for selling a patent medicine.

vi

MYSTICISM

IN EUROPE AND ASIA

— · —
·

1

"Experience, next to thee I owe, Best guide." The speaker is Eve; and her better guide the Forbidden Tree. The fruit that opens her eyes confers a higher knowledge more closely akin to the intuitive intellect of the angels than to the rational discourse of man. This, it appears, is the taste of immortality, the savor of divine life and the fruition of divine essence. While her ecstasy lasts, she is deified, "a Goddess among Gods."

Eve's "experience" sounds perilously like mystical experience; and Milton's fiction should warn us against regarding the latter as consistently uniform. It is not invariably linked with religious devotion. Here, in fact, it is diabolical. There can be (as R. C. Zaehner, Spalding Professor of Eastern Religions and Ethics at the University of Oxford, points out) both a "sacred" mysticism and a "profane."

Experience, surely, is as dangerous a guide in comparative religion as in the Garden of Eden. Since mystical experience is common to most religions, it is not a reliable criterion for differentiating them. Yet this is a common fallacy in many comparative studies of the Western and Oriental faiths.

Dr. Radhakrishnan, for example, emphasizes the opposition between doctrine and experience. "The Hindu philosophy of religion starts from and returns to an experimental basis." "While [elsewhere] fixed intellectual beliefs mark off one religion from another, Hinduism sets itself no such limits. Intellect is subordinated to intuition, dogma to experience, outer expression to inward realization. Religion is not the acceptance of academic abstractions or the celebration of ceremonies, but a kind of life or experience. It is insight into the nature of reality (*darśana*), or experience of reality (*anubhava*)."[1] "The chief mark of Indian philosophy in general is its concentration upon the spiritual." Reason is "insufficient," and intuition is "the only method through which the ultimate can be known."[2]

"The religions of the world," in Radhakrishnan's opinion, "can be distinguished into those which emphasize the object and those which insist on experience. For the first class, religion is an attitude of faith and conduct directed to a power without. For the second it is an experience to which the individual attaches supreme value. The Hindu and the Buddhist religions are of this class. For them religion is salvation. It is more a transforming experience than a notion of God."[3]

Is this really a valid distinction? an appropriate classification for *all* the higher religions? Does it actually differentiate Hinduism and Buddhism from the non-Indian faiths—from Christianity and Islam? Do not the latter also stress "the spiritual"? Do not most of them likewise involve salvation (though sometimes with different meanings and connotations)? Do not most of these also preach an inner transformation?

On the other hand, is this classification strictly true of Hinduism and Buddhism? Most of the popular devotional cults in both religions *do* emphasize the object—a divine "power" that is (even if only in appearance) "without." Surely the *Bhagavad-Gita* places a very heavy emphasis on an attitude of faith and conduct directed to Vishnu. "He is the highest," the god proclaims through his avatar, "who worships Me with [unflinching] faith." The "best knowers of Yoga" are not the worshipers of the "Unmanifested," but the devotees of the personal "Lord"—those "who, fixing their minds on Me, worship Me with perpetual de-

votion, endowed with supreme faith. . . ."[4] Arjuna's God is not
only "Father of the moving and unmoving world" but also—significantly—"its *object* of worship."

And what of the myriad personal deities who are objects of
popular faith throughout East and South Asia—such Hindu
deities as Shiva and Kali, Rama and Krishna and such Buddhist
divinities as Amitabha and Avalokiteshvara (Kuan-Yin)? The
cults devoted to the latter are among the largest in China and
Japan; and legend and iconography alike emphasize the miraculous efficacy of an "attitude of faith."[5]

Radhakrishnan rightly deplores the "tendency . . . to distinguish Eastern mysticism from that of the West, or, to be more
precise, Hindu mysticism from the Christian, by contrasting the
immense ethical seriousness of the latter with the ethical indifference of the former. Christian thought, it is said, is dynamic
and creative. It affirms the reality of the world and the meaning-
fulness of life. Hindu thought, on the other hand, is said to deny
the reality of the world, despair of human life, poison the very
springs of thought and activity, and exalt death and immobility.
It does not create power and purpose directed to high ends."[6]

This is another conventional stereotype of the East, and of
India in particular. Even so objective a scholar as Dr. Rudolf
Otto, author of *Mysticism East and West*, does not escape it. "It
is because the background of Sankara's teaching is not Palestine
but India," he asserts, "that his mysticism has no ethic. It is not
immoral, it is a-moral."[7]

For Dr. Albert Schweitzer, in turn, the fundamental attitudes
of the Christian and Hindu religions are diametrically opposed.
The essence of one is "world and life affirmation"; of the other
it is "world and life negation."[8]

Both of these overstatements spring from the fallacies we have
outlined earlier. Both authors overemphasize the distinctions
between East and West. And both overgeneralize from inadequate evidence, ignoring significant exceptions. The "reverence
for life" that Schweitzer finds so prominent in the Indian tradition cannot, surely, be "life negation." If "nirvana" is really

"samsara" (as in certain Mahayana sects), then the opposition between "world negation" and "world affirmation" tends to disappear. The elements of nature mysticism one finds in Japan and China—in Shinto, in Taoism, and in Zen—surely involve some sort of "world and life affirmation." So do the practical and worldly doctrines of Confucius.

Conversely, Schweitzer underplays the elements of "world and life negation" in the West—Christianity's antithesis of world and spirit, its sharp distinction between the sacred and the secular, its emphasis on "mortifying the flesh," its ideals of the contemplative life and renunciation of the world.

Otto's belief that the soil of India is morally sterile—that the pervasive salt of other-worldliness somehow inhibits the growth of a true "ethic" there—likewise rests on insufficient evidence. Ignoring the rigid personal and social morality of the caste system, he also overlooks the ethical content of Karma-Yoga (salvation through works). The *Bhagavad-Gita* is, in fact, a moral treatise as well as a devotional exhortation. The argument centers, in large part, on duty, and on the relative value of knowledge and works as avenues of approach to God. Krishna exhorts Arjuna to "work" without desire for the fruits of work; to "perform right and obligatory actions, for action is superior to inaction." "The place which is attained by the Jnanis (wise men) is also reached by the Karma Yogins (men of action). He who looks upon wisdom and the performance of action as one, is a true Seer."

Nor does Raja-Yoga—the physical and mental discipline that has become, for many Westerners, the classic prototype of Indian mysticism—lack an ethical foundation. If it ends in samadhi (superconsciousness) it begins, all the same, in morality. Of the traditional eight stages of Yoga the first two (the Five Vows and Five Observances) are largely ethical in character.

Differences between Eastern and Western spirituality cannot, however, be so rigidly defined or so sharply contrasted. Hinduism and Christianity alike resist the attempt to treat them as a set of logical contraries. In several respects they display impressive resemblances. Otto devotes an entire book to the similarities and differences between two of their representatives—Shankara and Meister Eckhart:

> Brahman, high above the personal God; the personal God submerged and disappearing in the suprapersonal Brahman; the identity of the soul and Brahman; salvation as identity with Brahman; Brahman determined as the unqualified, pure Being and Spirit, without attributes, without distinctions within itself; the world lacking real being, floating in the indefiniteness of Maya and Avidya—all these have, point for point, their parallels in Eckhart, extending even to a surprising identity of phrase.[9]

Both theologians show scant sympathy for "nature mysticism" and prefer to combine the mysticisms of "God" and "soul" (Brahman and atman).

"The distinction of superpersonal and personal, *nirguna* and *saguna,*" Radhakrishnan points out, "is found in all mysticism, Eastern or Western." The three stages of the Hindu's path to perfection—"purification, concentration, and identification"—correspond to the Purgative Way, the Contemplative Way, and the Unitive Way conventional in Western mysticism. For the nature of this "identification" or "superconsciousness" (samadhi) the author turns, in fact, not to an Indian contemplative but to a Greek; he quotes Plotinus.[10]

Nevertheless, after effectively discrediting the dichotomy of Eastern and Western mysticism, Radhakrishnan and Otto promptly resurrect it in a different shape. For the former, the real contrast between East and West is not so much the distinction "between Hinduism and Christianity" as the difference "between religion and a self-sufficient humanism": "While religion is taken more seriously in the East, humanism is," he maintains, "the predominant feature of Western life. Hindu religion, like all true religion, is essentially 'otherworldly.' "[11]

One need not quarrel with this distinction; nevertheless, like most that we have examined, it needs to be qualified. Though it may be a fairly just summary of the *current* orientation and emphasis of contemporary Indian and Western cultures, it is not accurate historically. In the course of the centuries both traditions have undergone numerous modifications in response to internal and external pressures. They resist so simple a formula.

Otto's detailed comparison between "the two principal classic types of Eastern and Western mystical experience"[12]—the thought of Meister Eckhart and Shankara—likewise dispels many of the false dichotomies his predecessors have evolved about Europe and Asia. But, as he himself acknowledges, neither man is entirely typical of "Eastern" or "Western" mysticism. Nor are the differences between them typically Eastern or Western. Some of the contrasts he emphasizes seem doubtful. Others have a limited validity when applied specifically to Shankara and Eckhart, but are not true of Indian and Christian mysticism as a whole.

"Is this Brahman a *living* God?" he demands—and proceeds forthwith to contrast the "vitality" and "movement" of Eckhart's deity with the inert immobility of Shankara's. The former's mysticism, he declares, is "dynamic," the latter's static. "The eternal 'repose' of the Godhead, which Eckhart mâintains, has a different meaning from that of the resting Sat in India. It is both the principle and the conclusion of a mighty inward *movement,* of an eternal process of ever-flowing life."

This antithesis may seem convincing if one limits one's inquiry to Shankara's impersonal Brahman. It disappears, however, as soon as one applies it to the personal Isvara. The Lord of Ramanuja and the *Bhagavad-Gita,* the personal divinity of Bhakti-Yoga (the "way of devotion"), is very much a "living God." In fact, all the dynamic qualities—the movement, the vitality, the power—that Otto finds conspicuously absent in Shankara's unmanifested Brahman are prominent attributes of the manifested Isvara.

The dramatic epiphany scene in the *Gita,* where Krishna reveals to Arjuna his "Universal Form" ("with infinite power, with numberless arms, the sun and moon [his] eyes, [his] mouth as the blazing fire, heating this universe with [his] own radiance" and "swallowing all the worlds with [his] blazing flames"), is

nothing if not dynamic. Like the God of the Old Testament and
of St. Paul, he too is a "consuming fire."

The antithesis between dynamic and static mysticism is not,
therefore, a valid basis for differentiating Christian and Indian
mysticism—much less for contrasting the spirituality of the entire West with that of the whole East. Nor is this distinction
altogether accurate in Shankara's case. For—as Otto himself
points out—the latter's commentary on the *Gita* contains a positive theistic element, and Shankara "proclaims and defends
Iśvara, the Lord, the personal God. . . ." For the "apara vidya"
(the "lower knowledge"), he is a "passionate theist." Indeed,
"the whole Bhakti-marga, the way of salvation, as . . . personal
reverence or worship, prayer, praise, and the private devotion of
love and trust in a personal redeeming God, are also to be found
in Śankara. . . . God under this aspect [Iśvara] pours Himself
into and unfolds Himself in his creation. . . ."

"Pours," "unfolds"—such metaphors would seem to imply both
movement and vitality. In actuality, Shankara's system is broad
enough to include more than one variety of mysticism. It leaves
room for Bhakti-Yoga as well as Jnana-Yoga, for devotion as well
as knowledge. The values that Otto misses in one facet of Shankara's mysticism are present elsewhere in his system in a different form.

There is, to be sure, a difference in tone and imagery—and
Professor Otto makes much of this. "A wheel rolling out of
itself," "a stream flowing into itself"—these metaphors of Eckhart's "would be quite impossible for the One of Śankara." Similarly, Eckhart's image of the "soul that seeks God with rage" is
essentially Gothic rather than Indian.

Imagery, however, has only limited value as a tool of comparative criticism. It may tell us something about the style of
certain works and occasionally something about the authors.
But, like any sharp instrument, it must be handled with care. For
it cuts both ways; one can prove almost anything by it. To take
the differences between Eckhart's metaphors and Shankara's not
only as representative of the men themselves but as typical of

Eastern and Western mysticism means pushing inference very far indeed—and on the basis of very slim evidence. Moreover, one must be sure that one is really comparing "commensurables" —works that are sufficiently similar to permit significant comparison or contrast. In actuality, Shankara and Eckhart are not writing the same kind of work at all. Their approach to imagery is distinctly different. Nor is the function of their metaphors truly comparable.

Otto consistently overlooks these differences due to genre and intent. Shankara is emphatically *not* preaching a sermon, as Eckhart is. On the contrary, he is writing extended textual commentaries—on the *Gita,* on Badarayana's Sutras, or on the Upanishads. His primary purpose is exegetical—to elucidate the meaning of the text, to explain away its apparent contradictions, and to refute contrary interpretations. The literary genre in which he is writing is so different from Eckhart's that it is irrelevant to attach much weight to divergences in imagery or tone.

As for his images, he usually derives them from the particular Vedic texts he is discussing, and even here his primary intent is exegetical rather than rhetorical. He is chiefly concerned with what the scriptural images really *signify.* He is not, primarily, trying to exhort his hearers by tropes and schemes, not endeavoring to stimulate devotion by rhetorical colors and poetic images. Instead he is attempting to set forth—clearly, logically, unambiguously—what the Vedas, with their ambiguous terminology and their curious mixture of philosophical and figurative language, really *mean.* The purpose of Eckhart's sermons, with their freer and more imaginative use of imagery, is quite different. They are, for the most part, meditations on the divine nature or exhortations to spiritual contemplation, and their images are admirably adapted to these ends. Though they may begin with a Biblical text, they are not textual commentaries like Shankara's works. In these very different contexts images have rather different functions and values. In a sermon or meditation they are aids to devotion—means of stimulating an audience's imagination; their effectiveness consists in the fact that they are sensuous and intelligible symbols for an ineffable reality that transcends thought. In a textual commentary they are, in most instances, ambiguous figures whose real meaning needs to be defined and analyzed—pinned down definitively once and for all. In this respect their poetic or rhetorical character can be a disadvantage rather than an asset, since it may stand in the way of clearer definition.

Shankara and Eckhart naturally bear the stamp of their different cultural and religious backgrounds. One does not challenge Otto's assertion that the latter's mysticism springs from "the soil of Palestine," the former's from "the soil of India." Nor does one deny his contention that mysticism is not "the same" in East and West, that "Christian mysticism is not Indian mysticism, but maintains its distinctive character, clearly explicable by the ground from which it rises."[13]

One does, however, regret his tendency to overgeneralize. On the basis of the alleged differences he finds between two individuals, he draws conclusions about Indian and Christian mysticism as a whole and—more dangerous still—about the "inner spirit" of Europe and Asia. He attempts "to show within the framework of formal agreement the peculiar spirit, the genius et numen loci, which, in spite of structural resemblances, colors very differently the inward experiences of mysticism in the two regions of East and West."[14]

Why "East and West"? The contrast can be significant only if one still thinks in terms of the dichotomy of Orient and Occident. The author has not entirely emancipated himself from the myth of Asia.

Oriental mysticism is as complex, as multiform, and—in some manifestations—as bizarre as an Indian divinity, with her manifold arms and tenfold heads, her benign and terrible aspects, her popular and esoteric modes, her oscillation between the extremes of bloodlust or erotic orgy and passionless spirituality. The same dark goddess who could inspire the hymns of Sister Nivedita and Tagore could also evoke the excesses of thuggee (which so shocked the British) or the animal sacrifices at Kali-Ghat (which so dismayed the American tourist, Miss Mayo). The same paradoxes, the same extremes of passion and tranquillity, vulgarity and refinement, erotic and ascetic zeal, also characterize the labyrinthine windings of the *via mystica*.

The Oriental religions and their various types of mysticism are, as we shall see, even more diverse than those of the West. Many of them disagree—in their destinations, their starting points, and their avenues of approach. Not all of them aim at enlightenment. Not all of them seek an undifferentiated Absolute. And even to these there are numerous ways and means. Like the walls of Paradise, the roads to samadhi and nirvana are built of contraries.

2

For many of our contemporaries, the difference between East and West symbolizes the antithesis between intuition and discursive reasoning. The Western philosopher, like the fisherman in Josetsu's well-known painting, is forever endeavoring to catch a catfish with a gourd—vainly attempting to grasp reality by methods that are manifestly irrelevant. Since ultimate truth is inconceivable, it eludes logical definition. Since it is inexpressible, it defies verbal statement. Neither affirmation nor negation strictly applies to it, and all descriptions are merely relative.

Undifferentiated and unconditioned, transcending the contradictions of the phenomenal world (samsara), it is too elusive to be seized on by reason and too ineffable to be comprehended in words. Instead of approaching it mediately and indirectly through logic, one must realize it immediately, directly, as personal experience. Instead of theorizing about it, one must apprehend it by pure intuition—through systematic meditation (dhyana), through ecstatic devotion (bhakti), or by sudden insight (samadhi or satori). For these observers, true knowledge belongs primarily to mysticism and—more particularly—to the mystic East.

In one form or another, these doctrines can be found in several Oriental faiths. But they undergo many a metamorphosis, and in elaborating them different sects sometimes contradict one another. There are numerous varieties of mysticism—numerous types of mystical experience and as many approaches to it or interpretations of its significance. What is true of one variety is not necessarily true of all. The doctrine that nirvana and samsara are "one and the same" is "necessary and vital to the mood of the Mahayana"; yet, as Rudolf Otto points out, it would be "sheer madness" for Shankara.[15] The latter also rejects the doctrine of the Void, so significant for Mahayana thought.

Similarly, Shankara and the yogis disagree on several crucial points. The old Yoga school "believed in a personal, almighty, omniscient and commiserative God,"[16] quite different from Shankara's impersonal Absolute. In fact, the latter's type of mysticism "stands in sharpest contrast to the pure atman-mysticism of the Yoga."[17] Indeed, Otto argues, Shankara is not a typical mystic at all. On the contrary, he "represents a mysticism of a very special type which stands in . . . sharp antithesis to other types of mystical experience." Its peculiarities stand in still stronger relief when contrasted with other non-Indian forms of Oriental mysticism, such as "the Taoist and Zen schools of China."[18] These involve a nature-mysticism distinctly different from Shankara's fusion of two traditional Indian strains—the mysticism of Brahman and atman, God and Soul.

The popular Western conception of the Oriental mystic has, in fact, little historical basis. It is merely a highly questionable synthesis of diverse and sometimes incompatible doctrines. Its philosophical foundations would appear to be Vedanta and Mahayana idealism; and its classical representatives the yogi, the lama, and the Zen adept.

In reality, these are very different; and their disagreements are fully as significant as their similarities. Like a portrait by the mannerist painter Arcimboldo, the archetypal Eastern mystic is a composite figure; the appearance of unity is an illusion. Shankara does not really conform to the popular Western stereotype of the Oriental contemplative; nor, for that matter, does a Zen master like Hui-neng. They differ widely from one another in method and emphasis, and they are just as far removed from the yogi and sannyasi. Zen Buddhism (as Suzuki informs us) attaches far less importance to meditation and trance as techniques for achieving satori than its original name (dhyana) would suggest. In fact, this was the issue that divided its northern and southern schools in China—the former stressing "gradual" and the latter "abrupt" enlightenment.

Shankara's biographers often stress his personal experience of samadhi (superconsciousness). Nevertheless, his writings place relatively little emphasis on mystical techniques as means of salvation. Instead, they attach primary importance to the correct interpretation of scripture as essential to true knowledge and deliverance.

Despite superficial resemblance, the Oriental religions usually display striking variations in method and emphasis, theory and practice. Not infrequently they aim at diverse goals. Taoism, for instance, resembles the Indian faiths in stressing nonviolence and in regarding ultimate reality as ineffable and inexpressible. ("The Tao that can be uttered is not the true Tao.") In this respect it approximates Brahman and nirvana, the Hindu and Buddhist conceptions of the Absolute. In other respects, however—and particularly in its relationship to the world process (to nature, society, and history)—it differs radically from them.

For Taoism, neither nature nor time is unreal; they are the effects and accidents of the unpredictable and sometimes quixotic power which underlies the cosmos. They are rather like the surface of a torrent; they move and are moved in an unseen current. The Tao flows through them—as apparently arbitrary, purposeless, and directionless as a constantly shifting stream. It is a moving force—"a motion and a spirit that impels"—and it "rolls through all things."

Unlike Brahman, the Tao demands rather an attitude of the will than absolute knowledge. One seeks conformity rather than identity with it; the important thing is not so much to contemplate it as to resign oneself to it. And it is equally different from nirvana; only with the Mahayana doctrine "nirvana is samsara" do the two concepts tend to converge. In spite of its formative influence on Zen Buddhism, there remains a fundamental difference of emphasis. The keynote of Taoist mysticism is less enlightenment (samadhi or satori) as in the Indian religions, than harmony with nature.

There are, to be sure, affinities between many of these religions in their emphasis on nonattachment and disciplined contemplation. Yet surely a similar—if not equal—emphasis appears in Western monasticism. The objects of meditation vary—even among the Oriental faiths—and the colorless ideal of nonattachment often takes on the shading and coloring of particular creeds; its implications vary with its context. Buddhism, for instance, eschews the extreme asceticism and "mortification" of the yogi and sannyasi. The Middle Way lies between—or rather beyond —attachment and detachment.

The popular image of the yogi as the classic type of the Oriental mystic has, of course, a limited validity inasmuch as elements of yogic discipline can be found in most of the Indian religions. One of the oldest seals unearthed in the Indus Valley depicts a bearded god sitting cross-legged in meditation— possibly, as several scholars suggest, a prototype of Shiva Mahayogi (the "Great Yogin"). In Indian epic the warrior may practice Yoga on the battlefield itself or go into trance in the very thick of combat. Though these techniques achieved their definitive expression in Raja-Yoga and Patanjali's *Aphorisms,* they are not restricted to Hinduism. Both Buddhists and Jains likewise practice a method of concentrated meditation. A few Sinologists detect yogic elements even in the *Tao-Te-Ching*— but these must remain purely conjectural, since the text is notoriously ambiguous.

All the same, Yoga is scarcely representative of Oriental mysticism as a whole. Other schools and sects assailed its doctrines, and at best there existed an uneasy truce between them. Though the *Bhagavad-Gita* seems heavily indebted to it for certain elements—the emphasis on concentration, nonattachment, and devotion to Isvara—the poem transmutes its borrowings into something quite different. The principal emphasis falls not on

Raja-Yoga but on Bhakti- and Karma-Yoga—the way of devotion
and works. To the Bhakti cults, moreover, the traditional Yoga
ideal of kaivalya (a "complete isolation or independence" attended with supernatural glory and magical powers) was
anathema. Indeed, as Otto observes, the later bhaktas condemned
the yogis with their kaivalya, and "denied them the final capacity
for redemption. . . ."[19]

The Oriental faiths show equal diversity in their views of the
relative value of experience, devotion, and scriptural authority.
Zen paintings portray eminent masters in the act of tearing up
the sutras or chopping up an image of the Buddha. Buddha himself rejected the authority of the Vedas, as did the Jain leader
Mahavira. Where Shankara maintained that salvation could be
achieved only through the doctrine revealed in the Vedas, the
Bhagavad-Gita declared that to "the knower of Truth, all the
Vedas are of as little use as a small water-tank during the time
of a flood, when water is everywhere." Where Shankara emphasized knowledge of the unmanifested Brahman, the *Gita*
stressed devotion to the personal Isvara. After manifesting his
"supreme godly form" to Arjuna, Vishnu declares that "neither
by the Vedas, nor by austerities, nor by charitable gifts, nor by
sacrifice, can I be seen as thou hast seen Me, but by singlehearted
devotion alone I can be known in this manner . . . and perceived
in reality and also entered into. . . ."[20]

The doctrines we have outlined are not, furthermore, at all
peculiar to the Orient. Western religious traditions exhibit the
same tendencies and emphases. Western theologians have likewise exalted mystical over dogmatic theology, and intuition above
discursive reason. The "neti neti" (not this, not this) of the
Upanishads and Nagarjuna's "Eight No's" can be paralleled in
the negative theology of the pseudo Dionysius, St. John of the
Cross, and Walter Hilton. The Flemish and German pietists—
Ruysbroeck and Meister Eckhart among them—also stress the unconditioned character of ultimate reality. For Nicolas of Cusa,
Godhead lies beyond the realm of reason and logical contradictions
—in a "coincidence of opposites"; the "wall of Paradise" is built
of "contraries."

The manifold varieties of mysticism refuse to be pressed into such artificial categories as Oriental and Occidental. "Those differences," as Rudolf Otto reminds us, "are revealed in both the East and West, and are not divided into East *and* West."[21]

Let us return to Josetsu's painting of the fisherman who attempts to capture the catfish with a gourd. This is, of course, a Zen allegory, and it is directed specifically against certain trends in Buddhist philosophy—the tendency to overemphasize theory and to stress doctrine rather than experience. His criticism reflects the traditional Zen viewpoint, and its basis is largely epistemological rather than metaphysical. He directs his attack less against the *doctrines* of other Mahayana sects than against their *methods*. He is objecting not so much to what they say as to the fact that they try to say it at all. He does not quarrel with their beliefs; these, for the most part, he accepts. His criticism is precisely that the *substance* of their doctrines has eluded them through their very attempt to reduce it to dogmatic statement. Reality—"Suchness"—can no more be comprehended in words than a catfish can be caught with a gourd.

Though Zen methodology is obviously poles apart from Kantian logic, Josetsu's painting is really a *Critique of Pure Reason*. He too—we may observe—affirms the impossibility of knowing the thing-in-itself through discursive reasoning. As with Kant's strictures against the metaphysics of Leibniz and Wolff, the Zen objection to Mahayana philosophy centers on method.

The fact that Josetsu's criticism is directed against other Mahayana schools ought to make us skeptical of the antithesis of intuitive East and discursive West. It should also put us on guard against the stereotypes of a single Oriental mysticism and the archetypal Eastern mystic. But such clichés die hard. Like most mythical creatures, they are extraordinarily long-lived, and an isolated example is hardly enough to defeat them. To realize their hybrid and composite character—to recognize the Chimaera as indeed a chimera—one must examine their parts. And these are in most cases quite disproportionate and incompatible—as absurd, in fact, as the legendary synthesis of lion, serpent, and goat.

That these clichés have seemed plausible is readily understandable. In the first place, the "myth of Asia" has given them persuasive force; it is, after all, a comparatively easy step from the notion of the "unity of Asia" to that of the "unity of Asian mysticism." Secondly, the elusiveness, the ambiguity, and—as some Oriental philosophers would insist—the inadequacy of their philosophical vocabulary is partly responsible. Taoists, Buddhists, and Vedantists alike frequently stress the inadequacy of words or concepts to comprehend absolute reality. Hence they sometimes describe it either in purely negative terms or else as something beyond both affirmation and negation. Many of them regard it as devoid of all qualities—unmanifested, unqualified, undifferentiated. Many of them insist that it can best be apprehended through immediate experience. And, in varying degrees, they stress the method of concentrated meditation as a preparation for direct insight or intuition. It is tempting, therefore, to infer that they are all talking about the same undifferentiated reality and the same experience or intuition, but it is by no means certain that these terms have the same meaning in all cases. The fact that Brahman and Suchness and Tao are all described as "unutterable" does not permit us to conclude that they are also "identical."

Thirdly, in recent discussions of Oriental conceptions of reality there is a marked tendency to overemphasize their mystical, empirical elements and to understress the rational, philosophical traditions behind them. The notion of reality as *nirguna,* "without qualities," is actually both a theological and a philosophical concept, and in both respects it has close parallels in the West. It may, as several contemporary critics suggest, reflect actual mystical experience. But it also results from philosophical speculation about the relationships between substance and accidents, between the first cause and its effects, between transcendental unity and the multiplicity of phenomena, or between ideas and the realities they refer to (the thing-in-itself). "Suchness" is indescribable because the human mind cannot grasp the thing-in-itself. The ultimate Tao is unqualified because it is the cause of both positive and negative qualities. Brahman is undifferentiated because it is pure substance dissociated from all attributes, or because it is the simple reality behind and beyond the appearance of multiplicity—the One behind the Many. In most of these religious systems the concept of an unconditioned Absolute results from a complex blend of religious experience and metaphysical or epistemological speculation. If reason ultimately recognizes its limitations and yields to mystical immediacy, it makes this surrender partly—perhaps largely—on rational grounds. To neglect either the empirical or the rational element in Indian or Chinese mysticism obscures its composite character—its dual debt to reason and experience.

The negative approach that sometimes characterizes these religions is equally complex. Essentially, it reflects the impossibility of defining the indefinable or describing the indescribable. Yet it also results from the logical necessity of dissociating substance from its attributes and the unconditioned first cause from its (conditioned) effects. To some extent it may also reflect the method of progressive concentration and abstraction characteristic of certain Oriental methods of meditation.

Nevertheless, one can easily exaggerate its importance. Actually, it is only one of several methods for approaching the problem of reality. Nor is it altogether so "negative" as it seems. Neither Shankara's arguments concerning the *nirguna* Brahman nor Mahayana interpretations of nirvana and the Void are entirely negative. On the contrary, they seem to bear a rather close resemblance to the concept of zero, which (as Leonard Bloomfield observes)[22] appears not only in Indian mathematics but also in Panini's Sanskrit Grammar. Linguistically, this usually refers to the uninflected form of a noun. As it does not mean " 'nothing,' but rather the 'significant absence of something,' " it can be a highly appropriate term for an "unmodified" reality, a pure substance without accidents or qualities.

This approach is not, however, essentially Asiatic. At least one commentator explains Eckhart's *nihte* (the "nothingness" of the creature and the "ultimate condition of the blessed") in terms of the "mathematical notion of zero."[23]

3

The tendency to reduce Oriental mysticism to a single stereotype—emphasizing an impersonal Absolute rather than a personal deity, stressing the "unqualified" rather than the "qualified" Brahman—is responsible for many of our current misconceptions about the Eastern religions. Ignoring the devotional and ethical aspects of Hindu and Buddhist piety, commentators sometimes transform both of these religions into a sort of Neo-Hermetic theosophy, a combination of the mystical techniques of Raja-Yoga and the absolute idealism of Advaita philosophy. Yet in actuality there is a strong admixture of both Bhakti- and Karma-Yoga (to use the Hindu terms) in both faiths.

The same observers often assume—quite wrongly—that the mystical experience and its content are uniformly the same. Oriental mysticism, they insist, is consistently preoccupied with samadhi; and this, in turn, has no other object or content than the nondifferentiated Absolute.

If this view were strictly accurate, then one would be justified in accepting Professor Northrop's views and equating Eastern spirituality with "the undifferentiated aesthetic continuum." But is this really the case? For an answer, let us examine several of the more important texts and doctrinal statements. These can speak for themselves.

1. Of the traditional "Eight Stages" of Yoga according to Patanjali, the first five need not concern us here; they deal primarily with the moral, religious, or physiological preparations for meditation. The last three stages (or samyana) are more important. Dharana (concentration) consists in "holding the mind on to some particular object." An "unbroken flow of knowledge in that object" is dhyana (meditation); and "when that, giving up all forms, reflects only the meaning," it is samadhi (superconsciousness).[24]

But the matter is not so simple as it appears. Actually, there are several distinct varieties of samadhi ("with-question," "without-question," and "seedless"). The last of these results from restraining *all* mental "impressions"; and this also can properly be called undifferentiated.

Moreover, the object of meditation is not, as a rule, the undifferentiated Brahman. Actually the yogi worshiped the personal Isvara and acknowledged the real existence of individual souls. Both in theory and in practice, there could be innumerable objects of meditation; and most of those listed in the *Yoga Aphorisms of Patanjali* are not religious at all. The overwhelming majority are purely physical—the sun, the moon, the polestar, the navel circle, the hollow of the throat; and the purpose of concentrating on them is to acquire supernatural powers. Thus, "by making *samyana* on the strength of the elephant" and other animals, "their respective strength comes to the *Yogi*." This is far removed indeed from transic absorption in an "undifferentiated aesthetic continuum."

2. Though Patanjali declares that the yogi can achieve samadhi by devotion to Isvara, the personal "Lord," the *Aphorisms* do not emphasize this point. For the higher aims of Yoga one must turn to the *Bhagavad-Gita*. By meditating on "Me," Krishna (i.e., Vishnu) declares, a "Yogi of subdued mind, practising union with the Self" can achieve "Self-knowledge" and experience the "infinite bliss which is perceived by the purified understanding":

He whose heart is steadfastly engaged in Yoga looks everywhere with the eyes of equality, seeing the Self in all beings and all beings in the Self. He who sees Me in all and all in Me, from him I vanish not, nor does he vanish from Me.[25]

The primary emphasis of the poem falls, however, not on yogic exercises or on wisdom, but on the Yoga of disinterested action and devotion to a personal God. For the "Lord" of the *Gita* is not Shankara's undifferentiated Brahman but the "lower Brahman"—the personal Isvara.

3. Despite his criticism of certain doctrines of the Yoga schools —especially their belief in "individual souls" and in "an all-knowing, all-powerful Lord" in addition to them—Shankara

agrees with Badarayana in recognizing the value of their meditative discipline. "At the time of perfect conciliation the Yogins
see the unevolved Self (the highest Brahman) free from all
plurality." This "presentation" of the Highest Self "before the
mind" is, he declares, "effected through meditation and devotion."[26]

Nevertheless, there are several varieties of meditation, and
not all of them have equal merit. Though the highest is directed
to the undifferentiated *nirguna* Brahman, the Vedas also enjoin
meditation on the "qualified" *saguna* Brahman under his several
aspects. This type of meditation, however, merits only an inferior
reward; its "fruit" is "lordship over the worlds," and this falls
"within the sphere of the Samsara," as "Nescience" has not "yet
been discarded." Meditation through symbols ranks still lower;
for "the symbol" itself is "the chief element in the meditation,"
and "the meditation is not fixed on Brahman." Unlike the two
superior modes, this does not lead to final "release" or to the
"world of Brahman."[27]

Shankara's system also contains room for intuition. This is the
"final result of the enquiry into Brahman," and it complements
scripture and inference as "means of knowledge." By means of
"rishi-like intuition," saints have perceived their identity with
"the supreme Self."[28]

Shankara's chief concern, however, is not meditation but knowledge; and he draws a sharp distinction between them. Though
"meditation and reflection are indeed mental," they depend on
the meditating person and may, accordingly, "either be performed
or not be performed." Knowledge, on the other hand, "depends
entirely on existing things," and can be neither "made or not
made."[29]

This contrast between knowledge and meditation resolves
many of the apparent contradictions in the Vedas. Noting that
"the scriptural texts concerning Brahman disagree in so far as
representing Brahman as qualified by form and again as devoid
of form," Shankara suggests that in chapters devoted to the
"highest knowledge" the "elements of plurality" are "mentioned
merely to be abstracted from." On the other hand, in "chapters

treating of devout meditation," they are actual injunctions to meditation and cannot be set aside.[30]

For Shankara, knowledge does not depend "on Vedic statements or on the mind of man," but on existence. And since Brahman alone truly exists, knowledge of the higher Brahman is the only true knowledge. Nevertheless, it is through the correct (i.e., the Advaita) interpretation of the Vedas that man discovers his identity with absolute reality, and thus achieves release from birth and death:

> . . . for the fact of everything having its Self in Brahman cannot be grasped without the aid of the scriptural passage "That art thou." . . . It . . . is the task of the Vedanta-texts to set forth Brahman's nature. . . . From the devout meditation on this Brahman there results as its fruit, final release, which, although not to be discerned in the ordinary way, is discerned by means of the sastra. . . . Release is nothing but being Brahman.[31]

Preaching a radical monism, Shankara argues that plurality and duality are illusions. Only the highest Brahman—the Absolute—truly exists. Neither the world nor the individual has substantial existence. The illusion of separate identity springs from "nescience" (avidya); through knowledge (vidya) of his identity with the Higher Self, the individual is released from the illusions (maya) of the phenomenal world, freed from the cycle of transmigration (samsara), and reunited with transcendental reality:

That same highest Brahman constitutes—as we know from passages such as "that art thou"—the real nature of the individual soul, while its second nature, i.e., that aspect of it which depends on the fictitious limiting conditions, is not its real nature. For as long as the individual soul does not free itself from Nescience in the form of duality—which Nescience may be compared to the mistake of him who in the twilight mistakes a post for a man—and does not rise to the knowledge of the Self, whose nature is unchangeable, eternal

Cognition—which expresses itself in the form "I am Brahman"—so long it remains the individual soul. But when, discarding the aggregate of body, sense-organs, and mind, it arrives, *by means of Scripture,* at the *knowledge* that it is not that aggregate, that it does not form part of transmigratory existence, but is the True, the Real, the Self, whose nature is pure intelligence; then knowing itself to be of the nature of unchangeable, eternal Cognition, it lifts itself above the vain conceit of being one with this body, and itself becomes the Self, whose nature is unchanging, eternal Cognition.

For,

> . . . bondage is due to the absence of knowledge of the Lord's true nature; release is due to the presence of such knowledge . . . the only thing needed is that the knowledge of Brahman should be conveyed by Vedic passages sublating the apparent plurality superimposed upon Brahman by Nescience, such as "Brahman is one, without a second." . . . As soon as Brahman is indicated in this way, knowledge arising of itself discards Nescience, and this whole world of names and forms, which had been hiding Brahman from us, melts away like the imagery of a dream. . . . Just as pure water poured into pure water remains the same, thus . . . is the Self of a thinker who knows.[32]

Undeniably, these doctrines offer a limited support to Northrop's views concerning the "undifferentiated aesthetic continuum." Shankara would probably have preferred the term "cognitive" to "aesthetic," and it might be more accurate to speak of "pure subjective intelligence." Nevertheless, the "undifferentiated" clearly occupies a central position in this system. "Non-differenced intelligence," the Vedantist declares, "belongs to the soul and the Lord alike, as heat belongs to the sparks as well as the fire." There is an unqualified (*nirguna*) knowledge whereby the unqualified Brahman is known and the distinction between subject and object is lost; "for as soon as there supervenes the comprehension of the non-dual Self . . . all objects and knowing agents vanish. . . ." "Brahman as the eternal subject (. . . the inward Self) is never an object," and this insight removes "the distinction of objects known, knowers, acts of knowledge, &c., which is fictitiously created by Nescience."[33]

This is, however, only one aspect of Brahman as revealed in the scripture and interpreted by Vedanta philosophy. Shankara unequivocally stresses the positive value of meditation on particular attributes and qualities emphasized in the Vedas; these aspects of Brahman are unmistakably "differentiated." The "qualified" (*saguna*) knowledge of the qualified Brahman is valid so far as it goes, for this too has Vedic authority behind it. (Indeed, the distinction between "lower" and "higher" knowledge and *saguna* and *nirguna* Brahman really represents an attempt to resolve the inherent contradictions in the scriptures themselves. The obvious inconsistencies in the Vedas must somehow be accounted for, without challenging their infallibility.)

Though the apex of Shankara's system is mystical union, his method of approach is predominantly rational. The "unqualified" knowledge of the "unqualified" Self really depends on a recognition of the soul's essential identity with Brahman. This insight, in turn, is necessarily contingent upon a correct interpretation of the Vedic texts; and this Shankara sets himself to demonstrate. To establish it, he employs every available means of logical proof. Though his end is essentially mystical, his method belongs rather to dogmatic than to mystical theology.

4. Between Shankara's philosophy and that of several Mahayana schools there are certain obvious affinities. Both teach an idealistic and nondualistic (Advaita) doctrine of reality. Like the highest Brahman, *Bhutatathata* ("Suchness" or "transcendental truth") is indefinable and indescribable. Like Brahman, it is neither Being nor Nonbeing (*sat* nor *asat*). Since it is above "name" and "form" (*namarupa*), no qualities can be predicated of it. As with the higher and lower Brahman, "Suchness" has two aspects, "conditional and nonconditional, or the phenomenal world of causality and the transcendental realm of absolute freedom."

Moreover, like Shankara, the Mahayana distinguishes two kinds of knowledge, "conditional" and "transcendental" truth.[34] As in Vedantist philosophy, this higher truth can be apprehended intuitively through "perfect wisdom"—prajna or *sambodhi.*

"A similar distinction between manifested and unmanifested reality underlies the Mahayana doctrine of the *trikaya* (the three 'bodies' or 'aspects' of the Buddha)—as unmanifested Absolute, as the 'Body of Bliss' manifested to the Bodhisattvas, and as the 'apparitional body' manifested to man."[35] The last of these belongs to the so-called "historical" Buddhas, who appeared on earth as human beings. Suzuki compares this body to a "God incarnate" or avatar; and Conze regards it as "a fictitious magical creation which goes through the motions of descending from heaven, leaving home, practising austerities, winning enlightenment, gathering and teaching disciples, and dying on earth, in order to aid and mature beings of little insight."[36] (Late Hellenistic civilization offers obvious—though surely independent—parallels, in the Monophysite belief in a phantom Christ and the Gnostic distinction between the Absolute and an incarnate Saviour-god.)

Unlike Shankara's Absolute, however, the "unmanifested" Buddha (Dharmakaya) is not—in the strictest sense—entirely without qualities. As Suzuki points out, it differs from Brahman "in that it is not absolutely impersonal, nor is it a mere being." On the contrary, it is "capable of willing and reflecting"; it is *"Karuna* (love) and *Bodhi* (intelligence), and not the mere state of being."[37]

5. Finally, let us turn to Dharmakirti's conception of mystical experience—the "intelligible intuition of the Saint" (*yogi-pratyaksa*). According to his *Short Treatise on Logic,* this is "produced" from a "state of deep meditation on transcendental reality." Dharmottara amplifies the point in his commentary:

The saint or yogi experiences *directly* and *immediately* a transcendental reality that the philosopher can "elicit" only after "logical criticism." This is "direct knowledge, just as (sensation) and other varieties of direct cognition are. Yoga is ecstatic (direct) contemplation. The man who possesses this faculty is a

Saint." His "direct knowledge" has the "vividness (of direct perception), and just for this reason it ceases to be [a synthetic, logical] construction."[38]

On the surface, this theory seems to have much in common with the Zen doctrine of "abrupt enlightenment."[39] *Beneath* the surface, however, there is a profound difference in emphasis. The experience of satori or samadhi is of cardinal importance to Zen and to most Mahayana sects. For Dharmakirti, on the other hand, the theory of "intelligible intuition" has relatively little importance; he devotes exactly one sentence to it. In Stcherbatsky's view, it is merely a "loophole" which Buddhist logicians felt compelled to leave in order "to support the religious theory of a Saint and of a Buddha." In Dharmakirti's treatise it serves merely as an "illuminating contrast" to emphasize the limitations of our "two sources of knowledge"—perception and inference, the senses and the understanding:

> The agnostic attitude of Dharmakirti is expressed with great decision and all logical sharpness. His Omniscient Being is the unapproachable limit of human cognition.[40]

Elsewhere, in fact, Dharmakirti argues that only the Buddha himself—the supreme Yogin—can possibly intuit "the undifferentiated Absolute"; the "ordinary Yogins can intuit only its subject-object aspect."[41] By this view, "non-differenced intelligence" would appear to be almost as inaccessible in the "mystic East" as in the "scientific West." Dharmakirti shows little faith in the possibility of directly experiencing the "undifferentiated aesthetic continuum."

In their conceptions of the mystical experience, the role of meditation and its object, and the nature of the Absolute, Oriental discussions of mysticism show significant divergences. Their accounts of the catfish vary, and so do their piscatory techniques. Some of them are not altogether contemptuous of the gourd. It cannot "catch" the catfish, to be sure, but it can at least maneuver it into a strategic position, to be grasped by other means. Or, perhaps they are not after the same catfish at all.

PART THREE

Art and Aesthetics

vii

THE WESTERN IMAGE
OF ASIAN ART

●　●
●

1

Thus far our analysis has centered on modes of knowledge. But
the conventional stereotypes are not confined to philosophy and
religion. They apply to the entire complex of European and Asian
civilizations—to their literature and art, their music, their total
culture. The sensibility of the Orient, critics inform us, differs
radically from that of the West; and this contrast affects patterns
of feeling as well as of thought. Asian art is an organic expression
of the "Oriental temperament," just as Asian philosophy is a
characteristic revelation of the "Oriental mind." Aesthetics and
metaphysics have a common origin in the regional "genius," the
"inner spirit" of the East—or, as Lafcadio Hearn believed, the
"Race Ghost."

In accepting this dichotomy as our frame of reference, we
impose an artificial scheme of classification on European and
Asian cultures alike. The art and literature of both regions become little more than a set of logical contraries. We distort their
true character by overstressing their differences and minimizing
their similarities.

Similarly, we exaggerate the unity of Oriental art by ignoring
its diversities and seeking instead a single comprehensive formula.
This bias toward oversimplification frequently leads us to take
one facet of a particular tradition as characteristic of Eastern

culture as a whole. In actuality, there is neither a common Asian tradition nor a common Oriental aesthetics: There are numerous artistic traditions, and they vary widely with nationality and religion, period and school. Notwithstanding India's vital contribution to Buddhist iconography, Chinese and Japanese art have always displayed marked differences from that of Hindustan. Despite important cross-influences between Persia and China, their artistic traditions have remained, on the whole, separate and distinct. Their interaction differs from that between European and Iranian art largely in degree. The latter's affinities with Europe in classical antiquity and the Middle Ages are almost as significant as its links with China.

The argument for the unity of Oriental art usually depends on similarities of style (which are sometimes fortuitous, if not imaginary) or on direct and indirect influences (which are even more debatable and difficult to trace). Scholars are still uncertain how far Persian ceramics were indebted to China, and vice versa. Though they recognize impressive resemblances between Chinese and nomadic bronzes, they are still undecided as to which culture was the borrower. Moreover, even where the pattern of influence is relatively clear, it often represents a *convergence* of different traditions rather than a common tradition. Both Persia and China readily altered what they borrowed, assimilating it to their native heritage, accommodating it to their indigenous styles. In this respect also, the pattern of cross-influences is not dissimilar to that of Europe and the Near East.

Differences of nationality, period, and school are not, however, the only factors that make for diversity. Style and technique— and whatever cultural values they manage to convey—are strongly conditioned by subject, genre, and medium. If it is irresponsible to generalize about Eastern and Western sensibility on the basis of one art form—painting or sculpture or music— it is just as unscrupulous to draw sweeping conclusions about the Oriental or Occidental mind from a single genre—religious architecture, landscape painting, or bird-and-flower prints. Equally ingenuous is the tendency to theorize about Eastern and Western aesthetics on the basis of a single medium—ceramics, scroll paintings, or bronzes. For aesthetic value is usually closely identified with the nature, function, and material of the particular work of art; these condition its shape and ornament, its iconography and choice of motifs, its relative degree of realism or stylization. It would be ridiculous to pontificate about Eastern and Western art by contrasting a Hellenistic Poseidon with a Han dynasty belt-buckle, merely because both are of bronze. But it is scarcely less absurd to base one's conclusions on the differences between an oil painting of a Venetian courtesan and a *sumi-e* (monochrome) of Bodhidharma, simply because both are portraits.

Furthermore, the excellence of a particular art form and its historical importance rarely guarantee its immortality. As certain media are manifestly more vulnerable than others, the art most characteristic of earlier periods does not always survive. Music is as volatile as the air on which it depends; to know what ancient Greek or Chinese or Indian music *really* sounded like one would have to ascend, like Chaucer, eagle-borne to the House of Fame. Painting—the most important of the visual arts—is also the most fragile. The pictures that survive are not always the best or the most representative. A few frescoes in cave temples, a few scraps of silk miraculously preserved in buried cities of the desert, and several incomplete scrolls (undoubtedly of great age, but also of dubious authenticity) that have somehow escaped the fate of most imperial collections—these are our only real evidence for ancient Indian and Chinese painting. In the West our knowledge of classical Greek painting is restricted largely to vase decoration, Alexandrian funeral portraits in encaustic, and a few Roman, Etruscan and South Italian murals. These provide little evidence for theorizing about the early painting of any of these cultures—much less for drawing sharp distinctions between Eastern and Western aesthetics in their earlier stages.

The critic of Oriental art has not altogether emancipated himself from the fallacies of the cultural historian. In his hands the myth of Asia becomes the unity of Asian art. The dichotomy of East and West becomes the opposition between Oriental and Occidental aesthetics. As a result, he applies to art and literature the same antitheses that other scholars have detected in religion and philosophy—the opposition between experience and theory, mysticism and logic, contemplation and practicality, understanding and exploitation of nature. The art of the Orient, he insists, is intuitive and symbolic; that of the Occident scientific and realistic. The Eastern artist projects himself into the objects he is painting and portrays them from within; the Western craftsman sees them merely as external objects and paints them from without. The former realizes his essential identity with all other beings; rocks and streams, trees and mountains, insects and birds, men and beasts—they are all instinct with the same universal life. The same Tao flows 'hrough all; they all possess the same "Buddha-nature." Realizing that their nature is also his own, the Oriental expresses their "inner spirit."

The Western artist, on the other hand, is a dualist; he fails to perceive his essential identity with nature and regards himself as separate from and superior to the objects he paints. He is, therefore, merely an observer, not a participant. Nature remains an aggregate of objects, nothing more; a yellow primrose is merely a yellow primrose. The Westerner "imitates" nature, giving meticulous attention to accidental details and external aspects. The Oriental "expresses" nature and grasps the essentials. The one aims at mere verisimilitude, the other at true reality.

These views were widely current earlier in the century, and they are still echoed today. They represent, however, a comparatively recent development in the stereotype of Oriental art —a development based largely on Chinese and Japanese aesthetic theory and the paintings of a few influential (but not altogether representative) Far Eastern artists. Unfortunately, few Western critics had access to the masterpieces of Far Eastern painting or to Sino-Japanese manuals on the subject; only within the last hundred years have these exerted any appreciable influence on the European image of Asia. Only gradually, moreover, were they able to displace (or force reappraisal of) an earlier stereotype, the conception of the "gorgeous East"—a myth whose fortunes we shall retrace in a later chapter.

Firsthand acquaintance with Sino-Japanese painting enabled Western critics to perceive some of the fallacies of the older stereotypes of Asian art. But it did not emancipate them from the myth of Asia. On the contrary, they brought to their studies a preconceived notion of the unity of Asian sensibility, and they attempted to fit Far Eastern painting into this frame of reference. In three representative examples, ranging in date from the early 1860's to the first decade of this century, we find the Western critic approaching Chinese or Japanese art directly, occasionally achieving fresh insights—yet nevertheless seeking therein a formula valid for Asian aesthetics *as a whole.*

Let us begin with one of the earliest European appraisals of Japanese painting, a lecture "On Japanese Art" by John Leighton, a Fellow of the Royal Academy, published in book form in 1863. His address is important in at least three respects. In the first place, its early date makes it invaluable as a statement of the impression that Japanese art produced on European connoisseurs. (The discourse was delivered at the Royal Institution of Great Britain on May 1, 1863, in connection with an exhibition of Japanese art.) Secondly, it emphasizes several qualities that have subsequently become clichés in Western criticism of Oriental art. Finally, it illustrates the Westerner's characteristic tendency to generalize about the "Oriental mind" on the basis of his limited acquaintance with one or two Eastern cultures. Even the distinctions Leighton draws between Chinese and Japanese painting are arbitrary and, by modern standards, invalid.

"In contrasting the arts of China and Japan," he declares, "what strikes one forcibly is the marked difference of labour, the Japanese aiming to produce the greatest possible effect at the least expenditure of trouble, whilst the Chinese make pains a principal virtue; they toil and spin, but lack inventive power, *working from instinct rather than from the dictates of reason— a fault with all Asiatics,* in greater or lesser degree. . . ." This notion of the intuitive, irrational character of Oriental painting will become a commonplace of Western criticism.

Like many later critics, Leighton is impressed by the absence of chiaroscuro: "The arts of Japan may be said, in an eminent degree, to depend upon the picturesque, though rarely to reach the pictorial, that is to say, they never produce a picture, because the principal element of pictorial art is wanting; light and shade . . . they know not of." This is a half truth, but it is still an article of faith in European criticism.

Lamenting their lack of perspective, he grants, nevertheless, that Japanese artists are "very judicious" in their use of color. But this he explains—grotesquely—on racial grounds. Sensitivity to color, he insists, varies with the degree of pigmentation in the artist himself. The darker the race, the greater its feeling for color. Western Europe, of course, prefers somber and sober hues. "But to the East, where colour reaches its climax, *as it tans the skin and renders man fit to support primitive hues,* the love of which is perhaps to be found most highly in the Negro, though in the Hindoo must be sought the subtle appreciation of it. Leslie has somewhere said, the only perfect specimen of colour he had seen was in a Chinese picture. What he would have said to those of Japan we can only conjecture,—colour with perspective, and shade nowhere."[1]

Leighton's opinions became the dogmas of later critics. Some of them took color as the keynote of Oriental art in contrast to the Western sense of form. Others attributed the absence of chiaroscuro and the alleged lack of perspective in Far Eastern painting to a fundamental difference between the European and the Asian mind. These too contrasted Oriental "instinct" with Occidental "reason," though they generally expressed the opposition differently—as the contrast between intuition and theory, spontaneity and science.

2

Unlike Leighton, the Anglo-American essayist Lafcadio Hearn could boast of a firsthand acquaintance not only with Oriental art but with the Orient itself. Settling in Japan after a career as journalist, novelist, and short-story writer in the United States, he married a Japanese woman, adopted Japanese dress and the Japanese way of life, and dedicated his remaining years to interpreting Japanese culture to the West. Nevertheless, in his writings we observe the same bias we have encountered in Leighton's essay—a tendency to treat Japanese art as representative of the Orient as a whole and to exaggerate its differences from that of the West.

"What a contrast," he exclaims, "between the emotional and intellectual worlds of West and East! . . . When one compares the utterances which West and East have given to their dreams, their aspirations, their sensations—a Gothic cathedral with a Shinto temple, an opera by Verdi or a trilogy by Wagner with a performance of *geisha,* a European epic with a Japanese poem —how incalculable the difference in emotional volume, in imaginative power, in artistic synthesis!"[2]

In this passage Hearn is contrasting the Orient (rather unfavorably, and certainly unfairly) with the Occident. His remarks occur in his essay on "The Genius of Japanese Civilization" (published in *Glimpses of Unfamiliar Japan* in 1894), and their purpose is to emphasize the former's ingrained incompatibility with Western culture—to argue that the "national genius" can assimilate Western science and technology, but not "Western music, Western art, Western literature. These things make appeal extraordinary to emotional life with us; they make no such appeal to Japanese emotional life." Today this view has become so patently anachronistic that it needs no refutation; in all three areas—art, literature, and music—the Japanese have mastered Western styles without losing their own. Hearn was an observer, not a prophet, and it would be uncharitable to blame him for a false prognostication. His observations concern us here not because they are poor soothsaying, but because they illustrate several characteristic weaknesses in comparative criticism of European and Asian art.

In the first place, Hearn leaps unashamedly from one level of abstraction to another. Though he is really discussing Japan, he does not hesitate to apply his conclusions to the entire Orient.

He magnifies the apparent contrasts between Japanese and European culture into a global distinction—the "emotional and intellectual" opposition of "East" and "West."

Secondly, like many other writers, he bases his generalities on insufficient evidence. The examples he draws from Western culture are cosmopolitan; they include Germany and Italy, Greece and Rome. His instances from Eastern civilization, on the other hand, are provincial; they are limited strictly to Japan.

Thirdly, they represent a "comparison of incommensurables" (as a British scholar once observed of Milton and Dante). If one were seriously comparing European and Asian civilizations, one would compare an epic with an epic—the *Iliad* or *Odyssey* with the *Ramayana* or *Mahabharata,* not with a *haiku* or a *tanka*— lyric forms that approach the conciseness of epigram. One would compare European opera with Cantonese opera or with the dance drama of southern India (*kathakali*)—not with a geisha performance!

For his architectural analogies Hearn naïvely (or perhaps disingenuously) juxtaposes the most complex of European religious buildings and the simplest of Asian temples. Besides, there is a notable difference in medium—stone and wood. The analogy would have been fairer had he contrasted his "Gothic cathedral" with Oriental religious architecture of comparable magnitude —Borobudur or Angkor Wat, the Hindu temples at Trichinopoly, Madura, and Rameswaram, or the Friday Mosque at Lahore. This would have provided a juster basis for comparing "East and West."

But that would, perhaps, have been beside his purpose. His real topic is not "the East," but Japan. He is anxious to prove that the latter is too "dainty" and "delicate" to master the "emotional volume" of Western art. "Japanese life" and culture, he insists, are "small"—and to emphasize this point he compares the largest and most pretentious of European art forms with the slightest— the "daintiest"—of the Japanese. The contrasts would have been more significant had he compared "commensurables"—the geisha performance with the cabaret, music hall or ballet; the "Japanese poem" with the lyric, ode, or epigram; the Shinto temple with the simplest of Greek and Roman shrines. The parallel between No play and European religious drama could have been significant, or the analogy between the theme of revenge in Jacobean and Kabuki drama, or even the point of honor in French and Japanese tragedy.

Finally, the contrast in magnitude—the emphasis on European "volume" and Japanese "daintiness"—is equally adventitious. What of the Momoyama castles? The Toshogu shrine? The burial mounds of the early emperors? The more grandiose Buddhist temples? The colossal Buddhist bronzes at Nara and Kamakura? Even in comparison with the architecture of the West, these are neither "small" nor "dainty." Actually Hearn has slanted his evidence to prove a preconceived opinion—a cherished personal conviction that has proved to be wrong.

Hearn's view is typical of the Western attitude toward Japan —and Asia in general—around the turn of the century. For years European and American aesthetes had been refashioning Japanese culture in their own image—or at least to their own tastes. They had identified the nation with its art; in the fullest sense of the word, the society was "picturesque." Hearn's Orient, in fact, was really Japan—and almost exclusively the Japan of the aesthete. Like many other writers of his generation, he brought his own aesthetic principles with him and projected these on what he felt and saw. His account of his "First Day in the Orient" does not, of course, represent his mature views, but it is characteristic of the subjective, "impressionistic" approach he shared with other representatives of the "art for art's sake" movement. He did not, like an eighteenth-century tourist, view a landscape through a Lorraine glass and rave about the "sublime" emotions it evoked. He did, however, see it within the frame of reference of a Japanese print—and analyze the "sensations" it aroused. The Japan he encountered was strongly colored by *fin de siècle* romanticism, and his record of his experiences is actually romantic art—"sentimental" rather than "naïve" poetry (in Schiller's phrase).

"First impressions," "lost sensations of those first experiences," "delicious surprise," "fancy," "illusion," "fantastic prettiness," "aesthetic sentiment," "forgotten memories of picture-books"— these are the characteristic idioms of romanticism, the mirror of the poet's own mind. "Elfish everything seems." There is a "romance" in the very "consciousness" of being in the East— "the real sensation of being in the Orient, in this Far East so much read of, so long dreamed of. . . ." Like Dante's *Commedia* or the Renaissance conception of the *Odyssey*, this precious travelogue is actually a pilgrimage of contemplation, an interior journey through the author's own soul. It ends appropriately—though not (as in Dante's instance) with the Beatific Vision. For at a Shinto shrine:

> . . . I look for the image of the Deity or presiding Spirit between the altar-groups of convoluted candelabra. And I see—only a mirror, a round, pale disk of polished metal, and my own face therein, and behind this mockery of me a phantom of the far sea.
>
> Only a mirror! Symbolizing what? Illusion? or that the Universe exists for us solely as the reflection of our own souls? Or the old Chinese teaching that we must seek the Buddha only in our hearts?[3]

This gifted writer journeys to the Far East only to discover the mirror of his own sensibility.

For Hearn the centuries of Japanese isolation had merely created "aesthetic distance" by exaggerating that country's detachment from the "real" world—the "utilitarian" West. The relics of feudal and aristocratic ceremonial enhanced its value as a work of art; it was "archaic," "traditional," and "stylized," as a work of art ought to be. Indeed, here was a society wholly founded on the principle of "art for art's sake." A veritable Utopia of the *beaux-arts,* it lived for no other purpose than painting china, carving ivory, printing exotic landscapes, and embroidering flowered kimonos. Here were the very cliffs and waterfalls of Hiroshige and the genre scenes of Hokusai—"Hokusai's own figures [as Hearn exclaimed] walking about in straw rain-coats, and immense mushroom-shaped hats of straw, and straw-sandals"!

In the eyes of the West, social realities were indistinguishable from aesthetic conventions. The Japanese mind seemed defined once and forever in the idiom of its art. Its "floating world" was firmly anchored now; the sportive samurai, the geishas, the men about town, and the courtesans of the Yoshiwara safely confined within the lacquered or bamboo frames of its superlative wood-cuts. Its political history seemed as remote and colorful as a Tosa scroll; its inner tensions and external conflicts merely lent vitality to its paintings. Japanese civilization, in short, was a *tableau vivant,* like the scenes on a Kabuki stage or in a puppet theater.

This was a valid, though exaggerated, aspect of the "real" Japan, just as Yeats's Byzantium was a valid, but highly personal, view of the real Constantinople. But it was, of course, tragically incomplete. This was the Japan of the connoisseur—not of the statesman, the soldier, or the businessman. And the connoisseur, like the artist, is eclectic. He selects fastidiously, and sees what he chooses to see.

What Lafcadio Hearn saw was an artifact. (Yeats, sailing in imagination to Byzantium, saw an "artifice.") And, like Yeats, he converted what he saw to a personal symbol.

When events seemed to contradict this picture—when Japanese forces defeated the Russian Navy, occupied Manchuria, and invaded China, the West formed another stereotype, contradictory and almost as exaggerated: an image of a nation of fanatic militarists. Since the samurai and the artist seemed incompatible, Westerners sought for an explanation to the contradiction. They did not have to look hard to find it. Since the stereotypes could not be false, the obvious answer was that the nation itself was inconsistent—self-contradictory, if not perfidious. A host of books sprang up, like dragon's teeth, to explain the paradox—ranging from *Cannons and Cherry Blossoms* (*Kirschenblüten und Kanonen*) to Ruth Benedict's scholarly treatise, *The Chrysanthemum and the Sword.*

Yet, in actuality, neither cliché really embodied the *essence* of Japan; each merely emphasized a different facet of a highly complex society. Nor is the seeming paradox significant; it exists in most societies—and not least in those of the West.

3

Whereas Leighton and Hearn had founded their notions of Asian art almost exclusively on Japan, Laurence Binyon based his ideas on China as well. Moreover, he explicitly rejected the earlier stereotype of Eastern art, derived chiefly from the ornate styles of the Near and Middle East. An earlier critic, writing anonymously on "Byzantine Architecture" in the *Edinburgh Review* (October 1904), had contrasted "the Eastern sense for colour" with "the Western sense for form"—and explained this opposition in terms of the antithetical temperaments of Europe and Asia. "Form," he had argued, "is chiefly a matter of the intellect," whereas color "is emotional and appeals to the senses." Thus it was only natural "that the Western temperament, intellectual rather than sensuous, should excel in form rather than colour; while the Eastern, sensuous rather than intellectual, should excel in colour rather than form." He had also raked up the old chestnut of Oriental decadence: "The impotence that saps the emotional temperament has waited on the East."[4]

Binyon correctly diagnosed the limitations of his predecessor's conception. It was based, he observed, on the myth of the "gorgeous East"—the "vague associations of luxury and sensuous magnificence" conveyed by "carpets and embroideries, lustrous wares and richly ornamented metal-work, familiar to our eyes in our shops, as Aladdin's trays of rubies and the glowing furniture and background of the 'Arabian Nights' . . . are familiarly impressed on our imagination, with the same vague and sumptuous effect." But it also depended on inadequate evidence: "We say 'the East,' with how huge a generalization!"[5]

This habit of thinking in terms of the categories of East and West has become so deep-rooted that critics have difficulty in emancipating themselves from it. Even when they succeed in refuting one erroneous version of this antithesis, they often substitute another. Thus the very first chapter of Binyon's influential book on *Painting in the Far East,* originally published in 1908, defines the frame of reference for the entire volume—"The Art of the East and the Art of the West." After observing that this dichotomy had long been "traditional," he poses the question of its significance: "In what precisely does this antithesis exist [*sic*]?"

Binyon's answer foreshadows a more recent stereotype—the image of the intuitive and spiritual Orient. For the notion of the "gorgeous East" (derived primarily from West and South Asia) he substitutes a stereotype founded largely on a narrow, one-sided view of Chinese and Japanese painting. Like other critics, he clings tenaciously to the opposition of East and West, even though he rejects his precursor's version: "If we are to compare the art of the East and the art of the West, in their essential character and differences, we must take as our type of the former the pictorial art of China." There is, he maintains, a "central tradition of Asian painting," and its origin is to be sought in China. It is in this art that "the genius of Asia" has found its "highest and most complete expression."[6]

In looking for the "essence" of Oriental art, in taking Chinese painting as its principal "type," and in treating the latter's differences from modern European painting as "typical" of European and Asian aesthetics as a whole, Binyon commits the same fallacy as his predecessor. He too overgeneralizes from inadequate evidence.

For all its merits and despite its undeniable impact on Central Asia and the Far East, Chinese art is hardly typical of the entire Orient. The Japanese often showed great originality in assimilating and transforming what they borrowed from the mainland; in painting as in architecture they developed distinctive styles of their own. Though the early Buddhist art of Central Asia often reflects Chinese influence, it is heavily indebted to India for its iconography, and not infrequently to Iran. The Chinese contribution to Islamic art, in turn, seems to have occurred fairly late—

much later than Binyon was willing to admit. Whereas Binyon reduced Islamic painting to a mere offshoot of Chinese art, later scholars have emphasized the former's links with the West. Thus, in Sir Thomas Arnold's opinion, "the chief sources from which Muhammadan painting derived its origin were the schools of Christian, Sasanian, and Manichaean painters that had been working long before the rise of Islam; and Chinese influences were superadded at a later period."[7]

Binyon's belief that medieval Persia recognized the "traditional antithesis" between Eastern and Western art and preferred the former also lacks sufficient foundation. In a trial of skill between Greek and Chinese artists, he asserts, the latter were judged superior in painting and the former in polishing. But this is not the usual version of the story. In Nizami's *Sikandar-namah* (*c.* A.D. 1200) it is the *Westerner* (the Rumi) who excels in "painting forms" and the *Easterner* (the Chini) who is "supreme in polishing." Moreover, as Arnold points out, this narrative "leaves us unfortunately in the dark as to the real artistic characteristics of these rival schools of painting." Even the national identity of the painters is "indeterminate." The Rumi may be a native of Asia Minor—and hence a subject of the Seljuk Turks—rather than a Roman or a Byzantine. The Chini, on the other hand, may belong to Chinese Turkestan or merely to "the country to the east of Northern Persia" rather than to "China proper."[8] Even though the terms may mean little more than "Westerner" and "Easterner" (as Arnold suggests), this is not the "traditional" antithesis between East and West; for the "Westerner" may not be a European at all, but an Asian artist who follows the styles of the Near or Middle East.

The biases of this earlier generation of Orientalists seem quaint today; for we approach the Orient with a different set of prejudices. In Hearn's account of his first day in Japan we have observed an extreme example. Admittedly, this was written long after, from notes; and it does not, of course, reflect his mature views. But the highly subjective approach is characteristic not merely of Hearn but also of observers and commentators today. We look for the "essence" of a culture—and distort it by imposing an artificial unity upon its actual diversity. We bring our own preconceptions to what we observe. And we are—not infrequently —more concerned with our own experiences than with the true nature and meaning of *what* is experienced.

All three of the critics whose views we have examined helped to stimulate Western interest in the art of the Far East, but none of them was able to resist the temptation to treat this tradition as typical of the Orient as a whole. Having inherited a notion of the unity of Oriental art, they proceeded to superimpose this notion on the relatively fresh materials they were examining. In this way they distorted art history. One doubts that Binyon, for instance, would have exaggerated quite so boldly the influence of Chinese on Islamic art if he had not already come to believe in a characteristically Oriental aesthetics antithetical to that of the West and if he had not already committed himself to the thesis that the essence or ideal of Asian art was really to be found not in the Near and Middle East but in China and Japan.

The Sino-Japanese stereotype in Western art criticism developed late, only after intensive scholarly study of the languages and iconography of China and Japan. Until comparatively recently, Western notions of Asian art were based chiefly on the Near and Middle East. The myth of the "gorgeous East," which had developed primarily through luxury trade with Western Asia, provided the frame of reference in terms of which Europeans first approached the cultures of India and Southeast Asia, China and Japan. In the following chapter we shall consider some of the factors responsible for the evolution of this conception and its decline.

viii

THE

GORGEOUS EAST

. .

1

To Western eyes Asia's aesthetic decadence was inseparable from moral corruption and from political and religious excesses. The great Asian empires were despotisms; they represented the characteristic vice of monarchy, as Aristotle defined it. Their kings were tyrants, and their peoples slaves. Worse still, they worshiped their tyrants as gods—a theological blunder but a political outrage.

Though Xenophon might extol a Persian as the ideal ruler—though Macedonian and Roman emperors alike would soon emulate their Asian predecessors and assume divine honors with the crown—the early Greeks and Romans regarded the Eastern despotisms with mixed admiration and loathing, envy and dread. These were richer, more powerful, and in many respects more "civilized." But they constituted a political menace. Athens and Rome had had a hard enough time ridding themselves of their own tyrants; the Eastern societies represented, literally, the apotheosis of tyranny. Political liberty was a rare exception in the Mediterranean world, and the Athenians and Romans were painfully aware of the fact. "Despotism is all right for Asians [Aristotle is, in effect, admonishing his royal pupil, the incipient conqueror and god of Asia], for they are naturally slaves. But we Greeks are naturally *free. Para kalo,* respect our liberty—and leave us alone."

The Greek myth of the luxury and decadence of Asia was really a political *exemplum,* an implicit warning against the dangers of tyrannical government. The vices of style, like moral vices, seemed closely associated with political vices, the "defect" or "excess" of the monarchical form of government. When Greek or Roman critics condemned the "Asiatic" style in rhetoric as "meretricious," they were making a moral, as well as an aesthetic, judgment. When Greek or Roman authors deplored the concubines and eunuchs of the royal households of Asia, they were phrasing not merely an ethical but a political indictment.

The myth of the sensual and luxurious Orient was, in part at least, an argument for the preservation of Athenian and Roman liberties.

The voice of the Stoic moralist sounds at times remarkably like that of the Hebrew prophet denouncing the fleshpots of Egypt, the fleshly delights and worldly splendors of Babylon. To the Greeks, Busiris was as much a byword for tyranny as was another Egyptian Pharaoh to the Israelites. The fate of Sardanapalus entailed much the same warning as Belshazzar's feast. Before very many centuries had passed, Western writers would, in fact, stress these very parallels.

Like democratic Greece and republican Rome, ancient Israel also had ample reasons—moral, political, and religious—to fear the powerful empires of the Near and Middle East. Their military organization and "power politics" menaced the security of smaller states; their state religions, centering around a semidivine king as the representative of the national gods, jeopardized the worship of Jehovah; their luxury and sensuality threatened to undermine the moral law. Threatened on several fronts by hostile empires—Egypt, Babylonia, Assyria—the prophets denounced their enemies in terms that would subsequently mold Western opinion of the Orient—magnificence and tyranny, voluptuousness and paganism, extravagant display of wealth and the "vain ostentation" of military power. These charges profoundly affected the medieval conception of the East, and they survived well into the Renaissance.

Echoes of these charges recur in the poetry of John Milton—

usually with sinister overtones. In *Paradise Regained* the splendid vision of the imperial capitals of the East—Babylon and Nineveh, Persepolis and Ecbatana, Bactra and Hecatompylos and Ctesiphon—is, after all, a Satanic lure. For all the allusive splendor of their names, they belong to the kingdoms of the world; their power and glory are diabolical. In *Paradise Lost* the allusions to Oriental magnificence are, if anything, still more pejorative. Satan's throne outshines "the wealth of Ormus and of Ind,

> *Or where the gorgeous East with richest hand*
> *Show'rs on her kings barbaric pearl and gold. . . ."*

The splendid building where he sits in conclave like a "Sultan" with his "Divan" surpasses the "magnificence" of Babylon and Cairo. Such passages as these combine medieval and Renaissance conceptions of the Orient with Biblical attitudes toward the wealthy, despotic empires of the East.

For, like the Old Testament, the New Testament had also strengthened the image of Asian magnificence. Aside from their symbolic significance, the precious gifts that the Eastern wise men brought to Bethlehem reinforced the stereotype of the Orient as the home of gold and spices and exotic wealth. Medieval and Renaissance artists exaggerated this emphasis. Since they identified the Magi with Oriental monarchs cited in the Psalms, they frequently took the opportunity to invest them with the robes and retinues appropriate to their princely rank —and thus intensified common belief in Asian magnificence.

Commercial factors also contributed to this opinion. Since Europe continued to import luxuries from Asia until well into modern times, by land or sea, it continued to associate the Orient with sensuality and wealth. Travelers' tales of the imperial courts and royal harems heightened belief in Asian pomp and decadence. If the stereotype of the "gorgeous" and voluptuous East showed signs of growing dim, Oriental romances—either composed by Western writers or translated from Eastern originals—gave it fresh coloring. It endured well into the Victorian era, and in fact it seriously distorted Fitzgerald's translation of Omar Khayyám; in Fitzgerald's hands, the Persian mystic became a "typical" Asian voluptuary, and his verses a sort of refined *Carmina Burana*. Dedicated to the pursuit of wine, women, and song, he differed from the goliards only in his finer taste, his subtler palate.

The myth of the "gorgeous East" remained for centuries the most common stereotype of Asia until it was finally displaced by the myth of the "spiritual East." In our own century the image of "royal" Asia has yielded to that of "mystical" Asia. The Orient of the emperor and the spice merchant has become the Orient of the bonze and the sadhu.

Both clichés have strongly influenced our views of Asian art. Though in actuality they have little in common, both claim to be representative of Asia as a whole. They involve, as a rule, very different strata of society and entirely different Asian cultures. The Western stereotype of the "gorgeous" East originated through contact with the Near and Middle East. The image of the "mystical" East resulted from contact with Indian philosophy or with Japanese and Chinese Buddhist thought. They involved entirely different civilizations. Nevertheless, they were regarded as typical of Asia as a whole. Once they had entrenched themselves firmly in Western opinion, observers applied them to the rest of the continent. The sensuality and corruption of the Chinese imperial court, with its concubines and eunuchs, the wealth and pomp of the Indian princes, with their jeweled garments and ornate palaces, seemed just as characteristic of the luxurious Orient as did the Turkish and Persian monarchs, or the Arab and Moorish rulers.

This image lent credence to the Western conception of Oriental art as essentially "ornamental," "decorative," ostentatiously "gorgeous" in its colors and materials and overelaborate in its design. This was the Orient of Chinese embroideries, Persian carpets, gleaming and overdecorated brass, gilded Buddhas, and carvings in chalcedony and amethyst, lapis lazuli, and jade. Oriental art was literally "precious" both in its materials and in its style. The inventory of almost any collection of Chinese snuff bottles reads like an apocalyptic description of the walls of the New Jerusalem.

2

The clichés of Oriental luxury, opulence, and decadence have not been confined, however, entirely to Asian societies. In antiquity, and again in the Renaissance, they were applied to styles that a modern critic would not hesitate to regard as European or Western. Rhetoricians of both periods regarded the ornate "Asiatic" style in Greek and Roman oratory as antithetical to the restrained "Attic" style with its distaste for affectation and its emphasis on simplicity and natural grace. The former style— believed to have originated among the Greek-speaking population of Asia Minor—was allegedly characterized by excessive use of the "Gorgian" figures of speech (rhetorical schemes or "colors" named after the influential sophist whom Plato has satirized in a dialogue on rhetoric).[1]

Both Cicero and Quintilian attributed the popularity of this style to the bad taste of the "Asiatic" orators and their audiences, in comparison with the refined tastes of the Athenians. "What reception would a Mysian or Phrygian have had at Athens," demands Cicero, "when even Demosthenes was censured as affected? If he had ever begun to sing in the Asiatic manner, in a whining voice with violent modulations, who would have put up with him?" The peoples of "Caria, Phrygia and Mysia, where there is least refinement and taste, have adopted a rich and unctuous diction which appeals to their ears." Quintilian, in turn, describes the orators of the Asiatic schools as "corrupt" or "decadent" and compares their rhetorical style to the "effeminate use of . . . cosmetics." The distinction between the two schools— Attic and Asiatic—belongs, he insists, to antiquity. "The former were regarded as concise and healthy, the latter as empty and inflated; the former were remarkable for the absence of all superfluity, while the latter were deficient alike in taste and restraint." Like Cicero, he attributes the difference between these two styles to the character of the orators and their audiences: "The Athenians, with their polish and refinement, refused to tolerate emptiness and redundance, while the Asiatics, being naturally given to bombast and ostentation, were puffed up with a passion for a more vainglorious style of eloquence."[2]

Such charges as these were double-edged. They could be—and were—turned against Athenian and Roman orators themselves. Not a few Renaissance authors accused Isocrates and even Cicero of "Asiaticism." For some of these critics, moreover, the "Asiatic style" was associated specifically with the rhetoric of display, as contrasted with the language of philosophy. It served the specious eloquence of the sophist instead of the naked truth enunciated by the wise man. It was sensual rather than rational; its jingling rhythms beguiled the ear instead of instructing the mind. It was an art of applied decoration and meretricious ornament—a verbal cosmetic that John Milton would denounce as the "varnish" on a harlot's cheek.

This rhetorical controversy over the "Asiatic" and "Attic" styles helped to establish a frame of reference for criticism of the other arts. Subsequent writers would contrast Eastern and Western painting in similar terms. The analogy would extend even to the alleged "Asiatic" sensuality and delight in color—whether it be the hues of the dyer, the tints of the painter, or the "colors" of the rhetorician. The so-called "Asiatic" style was, however, widely employed by writers we should normally call European or Western—patristic authors like St. Augustine and Renaissance "Ciceronians" like Cardinal Bembo. Here again one observes the ambiguity of the myth of Asia, and the futility of attempting to define cultural frontiers. These have never, of course, coincided with the Urals or the Hellespont. The Mediterranean was less significant as a geographical barrier than the Alps; it was an aid rather than an obstacle to commerce, and to the communication of styles and motifs, values and ideas.

With merchants, colonists, and conquering armies, styles and motifs passed as readily between Europe and the Near and Middle East as migratory birds. As they gradually adapted themselves to their new environments, they tended to lose their distinctive character—as Greek or Syrian or Persian or Egyptian. Their significance consisted less in their alien origin than in their function and meaning in their new context. They became part of the "cultural ecology" just as the English sparrow and the starling have adapted themselves to the American scene. In the "European" civilizations that dominated the Mediterranean and the Near East in classical antiquity and the Middle Ages—the Hellenistic, the Roman, and the Byzantine—the distinction between Europe and Asia became increasingly meaningless. As the Oriental divinities advanced on Rome, they acquired Roman citizenship, like St. Paul. If the leading Roman tragedian was Spanish, the principal comic writer was an African. The Greek and Latin fathers of the Church included Africans like Augustine and Asians like Basil and Gregory. Like all creative cultures, these societies combined different and often conflicting traditions— and transformed them into something new. Hellenistic and Oriental influences converged in Christianity, as in Gnosticism and Neo-Platonism. But in all three instances they united—like chemical elements—to form a new and fairly stable compound, with characteristic properties of its own. In the early centuries of our era it would have been meaningless to attach geographical labels to them. For, in origin as well as in character, they were neither distinctively European nor Asian. Eclectic, cosmopolitan, they represented a confluence of several streams. Hellenistic and Asian civilizations met and mingled, like the Ganges and the Jumna.

The same cosmopolitanism is evident in art and literature. Asian legend became Greek myth. The monsters of the "Oriental imagination"—the griffon, the dragon, and the sphinx—became incarnate in European sculpture. Architectural devices that can be traced to Sumer became the Roman arch and the Roman dome; Asia received them back, transformed, from her conquerors—just as at a later date Europe learned Greek science from the Arabs. It was an Asian—Theodore of Tarsus—who brought classical learning to England and indirectly, through Alcuin, laid the foundations for the Carolingian renaissance. At a still later date, stories from India—the legend of the *Seven*

Sages, and tales from the *Panchatantra* and the *Jatakas*—made their way to Western Europe; they were no longer distinctively Indian or even Arab, but an integral part of the European heritage. In such cases the distinction between "European" and "Asian" is a hindrance rather than an aid to understanding.

Conversely, classical art left its impact on India and China, through the Greek colonies in Bactria and Sogdiana or more indirectly through Persia. Yet this was not altogether an "alien" influence. It represented—practically from the beginning—a fusion of Eastern and Western styles and motifs. It was never exclusively or distinctively "European." If Gandhara sculpture influenced Mathura, the latter reciprocated; the later Gandhara styles, recent scholars have argued, show the influence of the more characteristically "Indian" styles developed in Mathura.[3] Greek or Roman influences on T'ang ceramics and metalwork were soon assimilated into the native tradition; they enriched the vocabulary of forms and ornamental motifs, but they neither reshaped nor displaced the indigenous styles.

3

That the Western image of Asian art was largely based on the Near and Middle East was only natural; classical and medieval Europe knew them better. Though the ancients had traded both directly and indirectly with India, they knew little about China except that it was the source of silk; the mysterious people who produced it were, accordingly, "Seres"—a name that survives well into the seventeenth century with Milton's allusion to the "plains of Sericana." Direct contacts with China in the later Middle Ages—such as the prolonged visit of the Polos—were sporadic, and indirect trade hardly gave a fair impression of Chinese art. Marco Polo's account of his travels tended, in fact, to reinforce the notion of the gorgeous, wealthy, and despotic East. A few celadons did make their way westward, and were highly valued by princes—less for their aesthetic qualities than for the belief that they changed color in contact with poisoned food.

Renaissance voyages of exploration opened up a new era. With the establishment of mercantile colonies and missions in China and Japan, Europeans had the chance to observe the range and variety of Far Eastern art even though they rarely saw or appreciated it at its best; a thriving export trade soon extended this opportunity to their cousins at home. Japanese lacquer, Chinese porcelains and Coromandel screens soon became domesticated, enhancing the decor of Western drawing rooms. A crucial scene in Wycherley's *Country Wife* hinges on the fashionable rage for chinaware. Europe developed a taste for Oriental decorative art.

Nevertheless, its knowledge of other art forms—painting, sculpture, and poetry—remained severely limited. An Italian iconographer, Lorenzo Pignoria, included Hindu and Buddhist figures in his *Discourse on the Gods of the East and West Indies* on the basis of information supplied by a Jesuit missionary to Goa (1553) and Japan (1565).[4] Included in late editions of Cartari's *Images of the Gods*, this work circulated widely during the seventeenth century. But the pictures themselves bear little resemblance to Oriental iconography, and Pignoria's treatise is often highly inaccurate. This source of information, moreover, would soon be severely curtailed, with the suppression of the European missions in Japan and the exclusion of all Westerners except for the Dutch trading post at Nagasaki.

Though Western art influenced Japanese painting and a few European artists introduced Occidental techniques into China, East Asian styles in painting had little impact on Europe until the nineteenth century. The Persian miniatures and Mogul paintings that found their way into Western collections belonged to a different Asia. The early European conception of Far Eastern painting was derived largely from porcelains and lacquered screens. As early as the seventeenth century Western Europe was decorating lacquered cabinets in the Japanese manner. In the following century it imitated or adapted Chinese porcelains and furniture and introduced Chinese designs into silverware; many of the finest eighteenth-century teapots are modeled after the severely simplified patterns of Yi-hsing pottery. This was the century that saw the vogue of *chinoiserie* and *japonaiserie*—with

Oriental motifs in garden pagodas, painted figurines, and wallpaper. But this was little more than an exotic variant of rococo aesthetics; it is not surprising that the West continued to think of Oriental art as essentially an art of decoration: light, amusing, "picturesque"—and trivial.

Not until French artists (impressionists and postimpressionists)[5] "discovered" the Japanese prints—and assumed that these coincided with their own aesthetic ideals—did Europe even approach a serious understanding of Far Eastern pictorial art. By the early 1860's Parisian connoisseurs had developed a keen interest in Japanese woodcuts and bric-a-brac; and—partly through the exertions of James McNeill Whistler and Dante Gabriel Rossetti—the taste for Japanese motifs and mannerisms had begun to spread in Britain. Its influence has been traced in Édouard Manet's celebrated *Olympia* (painted in 1863 and exhibited two years later) and in paintings exhibited by Whistler in 1865. Before the end of the century other painters—Gauguin, Degas, Toulouse-Lautrec, Matisse, and numerous others—also derived inspiration from the Japanese print. The qualities that they found in it were precisely those that seemed most at variance with the established "academic" style in Britain and France —and most useful to them, accordingly, in their attempt to "shock the bourgeoisie" and challenge the artistic Establishment. These qualities subsequently became familiar clichés in the comparative criticism of Oriental and Occidental painting.

What did these artists see in the Japanese print? In the first place, two-dimensionality, the frank recognition that the picture plane is a flat surface and not an arena for tricks of perspective— not a peep show. This was not altogether true, since most Oriental art *does* attempt to convey the idea of relative distance, and several ukiyoe (or woodblock print, literally "floating-world-picture") artists consciously emulated the Western techniques for achieving perspective. But the difference between these pictures and those of the Western beaux-arts tradition was clear enough for the French revolutionaries to make their point.

In the second place, color—and color conceived primarily as a plane, in terms of a flat surface. This was, in part at least, an accident—a result of the artist's medium. It was more or less inevitable in a block print, but a painting usually displayed subtler variations of color, and even some degree of shading. Nor is it true of the earliest—and, by our standards, the best—works in the ukiyoe tradition; these were often in black and white, with pale washes in tan or yellow (and later red or blue or green) often added by hand. But again that did not matter to the European artist. He was primarily concerned less with ascertaining the real nature of Japanese art than with registering a protest against the academic Establishment. The substance of his protest was that the latter overlooked the true nature of painting and usurped the functions of sculpture and architecture (a charge Binyon echoes)—that its emphasis on scientific perspective and the illusion of solid form violated the real nature of pictorial art.

Thirdly, line. For this they would praise Oriental art just as they lauded Botticelli. This too suited their conception of painting as essentially two- (rather than three-) dimensional. This too served to emphasize the "picture plane" in contrast with the academic stress on three-dimensional or "solid" form.

Fourthly, subject matter. Though this was sometimes romantic, it often dealt with the type of world—in fact the "half-world," the *demi*monde—which some of these artists knew (or professed to know) best. It portrayed the Edo version of the *vie Bohème*, the life of courtesans and prostitutes, dilettantes and men about town. By academic standards such subjects were "low" and therefore inappropriate for serious art. For the young revolutionaries they were reality, the world as it actually is and life as it is actually lived.

This relatively late contact with Japanese pictorial art helped to qualify the older stereotype of the "gorgeous East." Nevertheless, in some respects it was unfortunate that Europe acquired its first serious awareness of the real value of Far Eastern pictorial art through the block print instead of the fresco or the picture scroll. It is, perhaps, even more regrettable that the discovery was made by artists in revolt against the "established" Western tradition. Both of these accidents had profound results. In the first place, critics formed their judgment of Oriental painting from a form that was by no means typical of Oriental art as a whole—a form, moreover, that had laws and techniques of its own, due to its peculiar medium; a form, finally, that was often despised (unjustly perhaps) by serious artists in the land of its birth. Hokusai was proverbially "mad" about "painting," not about woodcuts. This was a popular rather than an aristocratic art, and in Japan it suffered much the same disrepute that the drama suffered in Elizabethan England, where even Shakespeare could not sweeten the "dyer's hand" of the common playactor. Despite the stigma attached to them, both were great arts. But one cannot understand Elizabethan poetry from the drama alone; nor do the ukiyoe prints alone provide an adequate basis for understanding Oriental painting as a whole.

These late nineteenth-century artists—French, British, American—consciously put into practice the principles they *thought* they found embodied in the Japanese prints. They too emphasized the flat surface, the planes of color or monochrome, the significant line. But with the possible exception of Whistler's *Nocturnes* and some of Matisse's drawings, their works remained far removed indeed from the spirit and technique of Oriental painting. The notion of art for art's sake would have seemed frivolous to many—if not most—Oriental painters.

Less than a decade after Manet and Whistler had begun to exploit the aesthetic principles they had discovered—or thought they had discovered—in the ukiyoe print, the Meiji Restoration in Japan inaugurated a new stage in Western contacts with the Far East—a stage equally significant for European appreciation of Oriental art. For Westerners were now able to examine a few of the real masterpieces of Japanese painting—not merely export ware or (at best) prints executed by competent artisans rather than by the original artist. Some of them would study directly under Japanese masters, devoting years to learning the different brushstrokes and the capabilities of the Japanese brush (or *fude*). Others would examine the manuals of painting—such practical or theoretical works as the *Mustard-Seed Garden* and Hsieh Ho's six canons. They were now able, at long last, to appreciate the range and diversity of Far Eastern tradition.

Yet this broader acquaintance with Chinese and Japanese painting entailed fresh difficulties. Confronted with this wider horizon, the Western critic was apt to lose himself or to blur his vision by gazing too fixedly on the rising sun. Not only did he find it difficult to discard his own preconceptions, the product of his Western training; he was now vulnerable to those of the Orient as well. Many of these Occidental students never outgrew the bias of the particular Oriental masters under whom they studied. Others adopted viewpoints fashionable in the art circles of Tokyo or Kyoto. Henry P. Bowie, an American traveler who visited Japan in 1893, studied painting under Japanese masters for nine years, and subsequently wrote a book on the subject (*On the Laws of Japanese Painting*, published in 1911), for instance, consistently undervalued the merits of the Japanese print. Others interpreted Japanese—or Chinese—art primarily in terms of Buddhist values. We have encountered this bias already in Hearn and Binyon, and we shall meet it later in Ernest F. Fenollosa. In recent years Western critics have tended to approach the painting of the Far East in terms of Zen intuitionism or Taoist spontaneity—concepts that we shall examine in the following chapter.

In our own time Japanese art has come to stand for qualities our ancestors would probably have called "Attic"—radical simplicity, economy to the point of severity, extreme understatement —and, along with these, a technique of studied nuance, a conscious manipulation of overtones, and a skillful exploitation of symbolic or allusive "resonances." Such a view has little in common with the "gorgeous East" that many of these very ancestors believed in—yet our attitude is perhaps almost as narrow, and as exaggerated, as theirs. Both views spring from too one-sided an approach to a varied and often contradictory aesthetic tradition. Ours is based, perhaps, on an overemphasis on Zen monochromes, theirs on fascination with the embroidered robes of courtesans, the gold and silver ornament of lacquered trays, the floral decorations on Momoyama screens.

The geisha's flowered kimono in an ukiyoe painting and the Zen patriarch in an ink drawing involve aesthetic principles almost as incompatible as the mores for which, in a sense, they stand. Yet both are perhaps equally representative of Japanese art. (Historically, in fact, the painting of the geisha is the more truly Japanese; for the Zen monochrome, like its subject, derives from Chinese rather than Japanese tradition.) Neither, however, represents *the* "Japanese tradition." Our own emphasis on the severity of Japanese art is almost as inadequate as our ancestors' admiration for its richness, its sensuousness, and its "decorative" aspects.

For, in fact, both views—however extreme—contain an element of truth. Radical simplicity may indeed be characteristic of the *best* in Far Eastern art, but it is scarcely typical of the tradition as a whole, which can range from austerity and elegant understatement to baroque luxuriance. As the art historian Hugo Munsterberg observes, "the love for extreme simplicity and restraint, the emphasis upon subdued colors, *the dislike of gorgeousness and ostentation* are not at all typical of the *characteristically Japanese* phases of Japanese culture such as the Heian, the Momoyama, and the Edo periods, but are Chinese importations which were introduced by the Zen monks of the fifteenth century."[6] Though the Toshogu shrine at Nikko and the Katsura detached palace at Kyoto were built during the same years, they are "exact opposite[s] in spirit as well as in structural detail"— the former "all garish display," the latter the "very essence of simplicity." Together they indicate "the dual nature of the Japanese soul."

Thus far we have considered some of the aesthetic implications of the notion of the gorgeous East and its significance for art criticism. In a later chapter, "The Eastern Despot" (on the myth of Asian despotism), we shall explore a few of its political implications and its significance for economic and social theory. In the next three chapters we shall examine other conventional stereotypes of Oriental art and their relationship to Western conceptions of Eastern modes of knowledge and expression, attitudes toward nature, and conceptions of ultimate reality.

REALISM

AND PERSPECTIVE

. .

1

Realism, imitation, scientific perspective—for many critics these are qualities that radically differentiate Western art from that of Asia; and their roots are to be sought in the Western mind itself. For the Occidental, reality is objective—a group of geometrically defined objects in mathematical space. Man and the world about him are separate and distinct—like mind and matter, thought and extension, in Cartesian dualism—and there can be no real communication between them. He remains a detached observer and nothing more. But for the Oriental they are ultimately the same. The same Tao, the same Buddha-nature, the same "Suchness," belongs to both; the appearance of duality is merely an illusion. Hence Oriental and Occidental aesthetics are diametrically opposed. The one "realizes"—and gives expression to— man's unity with nature. The other contemplates or "imitates" nature as an external thing. The one is instinct with the "breath of life" (*ch'i*); it renders the spirit. The other, for all its meticulous realism, is "dead," inasmuch as it reduces living nature to formal geometry, solid bodies arranged in space; it captures the form.

Let us re-examine these "distinguishing characteristics" of Western art (as critics usually regard them) and their proverbial neglect by Eastern culture. Are they strictly applicable to European aesthetics as a whole? And are they altogether alien to that of Asia? Is the antithesis really so absolute as popular opinion asserts? Does not Oriental art, in fact, often pursue comparable ends or values by somewhat different means?

"Realism"—the word is so often coupled with "naïve" that it seems deceptively simple. Actually, like "idealism" and "naturalism," it sometimes has different meanings in philosophy, literature, or art. Moreover, it becomes still more ambiguous, varies still more widely in meaning, once one raises the question "What *is* real?" Finding a plausible answer may be the responsibility of the philosopher, but it has unmistakable significance for the artist and the poet; insofar as these may consciously attempt to imitate or express "reality" (as some do), they are naturally concerned as to precisely what it is that they are imitating or expressing.

Few artists, either in the West or in the Orient, would pretend to be imitating "ultimate reality." Most would regard it as inconceivable and hence inexpressible, since literature and art are inextricably immersed in "name" and "form" (*namarupa,* as the Indians put it). If literature reduces reality to words or "names," art reduces it to "forms." In the strictest sense, therefore, neither can be truly realistic.

For the Platonists and medieval philosophical realists, *ideas* were real; they had substantial existence, they were not mere figments of man's reason. Though Aristotle and the nominalists dissented from this opinion, though Plato himself condemned art as an illusion (the imitation of an imitation), this view nevertheless provided a basis for European aesthetics. Aristotle asserted the superiority of poetry to history on the grounds that the former imitated the universal—the general idea— whereas the latter dealt largely with particulars. In this sense, a realistic art would be essentially "idealistic," and this term has often been applied to phases of both Oriental and Occidental art. Asian art, critics insist, portrays the "type," the species, rather than the individual. But this quality does not actually differentiate it from Western art; an analogous emphasis on the type occurs in ancient Greece and in Renaissance Italy. That the poet

imitates the universal in and through the particular was a commonplace of Renaissance literary theory, and painters and
sculptors likewise paid more than lip service to Aristotle's principle of "ideal" imitation.

But perhaps these "types"—these "names" and "universals"—
are *not* real; perhaps they are no more than names and the only
reality inheres in the particular. This is the nominalist point of
view. In this case, artistic verity might require a faithful rendition of particulars, a meticulous reproduction of detail. This is
the conventional meaning of realism in art and usually in literature. In the Western rhetorical tradition it underlies the emphasis
on *enargia*—the quality of vividness, lifelikeness, or actuality
that results from mentally placing the scene before one's very
eyes, visualizing it as immediately present.

In contrasting the "realistic" art of the West with the "idealistic" tradition of the East, critics usually emphasize the former's
resort to "scientific perspective" in organizing space and its use
of "tactile" or "sculptural" values in modeling figures. Yet is this
not really a confusion of terms? Both techniques belong, as a
matter of fact, to the "idealistic" art of the Renaissance. The
Renaissance, in turn, was attempting—in part at least—to realize
the aesthetic principles of classical antiquity; this too was, for
the most part, an "idealistic" art. Just how far the Renaissance
actually succeeded in "imitating" the ancients remains, however,
a matter of dispute; though it claimed to be realizing their
aesthetic principles, it had only a partial and subjective conception of classical art. For its major innovations it was not, apparently, indebted directly to the classics. The "scientific perspective"
invented by Brunelleschi developed in large part out of medieval
optics. As for modeling through light and shade, there were
indeed notable precedents in antiquity (as in the Villa of the
Mysteries at Pompeii); but there is little indication that the
Renaissance was influenced by them. Its concern with plastic or
"tactile" values in painting was, apparently, an independent development—and in achieving them it derived greater inspiration
from antique sculpture than from antique painting.

Moreover, in prating of Western realism, few, if any, of these commentators draw the necessary distinction between the "realism" of the Dutch and Flemish schools and the "idealism" or "naturalism" of the Italian. For the sake of preserving their cherished "East-West antithesis" they oversimplify both the Oriental and Occidental traditions. Like the artists of China and Japan, those of classical Greece usually depicted the universal rather than the particular, the type rather than the individual. With the notable exception of portraiture, the artists of the Italian Renaissance usually did likewise; they too were concerned with proportion, symmetry, and "ideal form." They too imitated the idea. For all its plasticity, theirs was not essentially a "realistic" art.

Western art is no more consistently realistic than Far Eastern art is consistently symbolic. The most that one can say is that the latter has, on the whole, carried the principle of economy of means to a higher degree of refinement and with greater consistency than one normally finds in Western (or for that matter Indian or Persian or African) art. The West has at times been very much preoccupied with symbolism; this has, in fact, been one of the principal criticisms often levied against the Middle Ages, with its "types" and "antitypes," its "allegorical senses" and "transumptive" modes—and against the Renaissance, with its mania for hieroglyphics and emblems, its manuals of allegorized mythology, and its complex fusion of symbols and images from a wide variety of heterogeneous sources—classical and Biblical, Egyptian and cabalistic, medieval and modern.

Conversely, the Orient has often professed to be aiming at realism. Indeed, it was the realism of Chinese painting that impressed medieval Persians. It could, in their opinion, "represent a man with such fidelity to nature as to make him seem to be breathing" or "laughing, and even all possible varieties of laughing, each in its own peculiar way." Its pictures of "trees, animals, birds, flowers, fruits, and human beings . . . lacked nothing except soul and speech."[1]

The degree of realistic detail usually varies not only with school and period but with genre. The horses of Kung K'ai and Jên Jên-fa[2] are "realistic," even though they may be "typical" horses rather than individual animals and though Fenollosa would probably dismiss them as "Tartar realism." Ch'ien Hsüan's pictures of small animals and insects—rats feeding on a melon, frogs and dragonflies in a lotus pond—show meticulous attention to detail; such subjects challenged the painter to demonstrate his skill.

Chinese ancestor portraits are equally scrupulous in depicting details of physiognomy; here the artist is concerned as a rule with the individual rather than the type. Though this is an official portraiture—magisterial, formal, stylized—it is not impersonal. The office is merged with the man, the type with the individual. As in Roman portrait busts, the costume and posture may be thoroughly conventional, but the features are personalized. The Confucian principles binding the family to its head are not only abstract laws but living human ties expressed in flesh-and-blood relationships. In these ancestor portraits—in Confucian art as in Confucian morality—abstract ethical values are realized concretely in particular individuals.

The sculpture of the Kamakura period often seeks to enhance realism by such devices as inlaying the eyes with crystal. But other realistic effects are usually contingent on the subject—undercutting in rendering the drapery of a standing Buddha or Bodhisattva, details of armor or musculature in a tutelary guardian, the wrinkles of an old man or woman, the skeletal structure of an emaciated ascetic. These too reflected the realistic tastes of the age, but they also represented a challenge to the sculptor's mastery of his craft, his skill both as artisan and artist.

Moreover, realism has long been a well-established term in the critical vocabulary of Oriental art. William Cohn emphasizes the "realistic Han tradition" and the Yüan dynasty's "tendency towards realism" and "predilection for verisimilitude."[3] William Willetts points out the "new note of pictorial realism" in the animals and plants of Ch'ien Hsüan.[4] Hugo Munsterberg distinguishes several varieties of realism in Japanese art. Though the "realism of the Nara age" appears in its sculpture, "it never loses itself in naturalistic detail, but is tempered with a strong feeling for abstract design. Like the art of classical Greece or

Renaissance Italy, the result is a work which might be called ideal naturalism, for the elements of physical beauty are combined with the spiritual ideals of Buddhism." The picture scrolls of the Kamakura period reveal "a greater emphasis upon realistic detail" than those of the Heian period, while its sculpture expresses "the same vigorous, realistic spirit as the paintings." "The most original development, and one which perfectly expressed the realistic tendencies of the age, was the growth of portrait-sculpture." Okyo Maruyama, in turn, "developed a realistic manner which gave expression to the materialism of the bourgeoisie." Though this was partly due to his study of "Western illustrations," it also reflected the influence of "the more realistic Chinese painting of the Ming and Ch'ing dynasties." His "faithful copying of nature" is "best seen" in his "sketches of flowers and plants and animals."[5]

Far from being alien to the East, the principle of "likeness or imitation" occupies a central position in Asian aesthetic theory; nor is it altogether different from the Western concept. In the opinion of Ananda Coomaraswamy, former curator of Indian art at the Boston Museum of Fine Arts, it shows affinities with scholastic views—principally those of St. Thomas Aquinas and Meister Eckhart—but differs from the Renaissance viewpoint. According to one Indian writer, "representation" or "likeness" (*sadrsya*) is "essential to the very substance of painting." Others apply the term "imitation" (*anukara*) to the drama. The Chinese principle of "shape resemblance" seems "to define art as an imitation of Nature," and a Japanese critic regards music and dancing as pure "imitation."

Nevertheless, *sadrsya* does not, Coomaraswamy insists, "imply naturalism, verisimilitude, illustration, or illusion in any superficial sense. . . . What the representation imitates is the idea or species of the thing, by which it is known intellectually, rather than the substance of the thing as it is perceived by the senses." *Sadrsya* is essentially "visual correspondence" or the "correspondence of formal and representative elements in art."

Similarly, Chinese writers insist that "it is not the outward appearance as such, but rather the idea in the mind of the artist, or the immanent divine spirit, or the breath of life, that is to be revealed by a right use of natural forms." One praises an artist for expressing the "idea" in "few brushstrokes." Another observes that "the painters of old painted the idea and not merely the shape." Asian art is essentially "ideal [Coomaraswamy concludes] in the mathematical sense: . . . not in appearance, but in operation."⁶

Even with Coomaraswamy's qualifications, this conception of "likeness" and "imitation" does not provide a valid basis for a sharp dichotomy between Eastern and Western art. Chinese practice did not always conform to theory. Several of the writers Coomaraswamy quotes are really registering a protest against the practice of their own age; they are deploring the current emphasis on mere "resemblance." "Those painters who neglect natural shape and secure formative idea," one laments, "are few." "What the age means by pictures is resemblance."⁷ Even if these aesthetic jeremiads are exaggerated, as perhaps they were, they would seem to indicate that "Asiatic art" was *not* always "ideal in the mathematical sense"—that, on the contrary, it was at times predominantly naturalistic or realistic.

2

Western art, critics often point out, is preoccupied with space; it stresses solid forms in organized distance. In its concern for scientific perspective it betrays its desire for infinity; though parallel lines seem to converge toward a remote vanishing point, they are themselves infinite in extension and they will never meet. For Oswald Spengler, this was symbolic of the aspirations of the modern West; in his philosophy of comparative civilization, the handling of space became the touchstone for distinguishing the major cultures and their essential characteristics—a criterion that sharply differentiates the European mind from the Arabic or the Chinese. For other critics, the Renaissance delight in perspective exhibits the same obsession with infinity that impelled Western voyagers to circumnavigate the globe, astronomers to reject the

Ptolemaic for the Copernican universe, philosophers to posit a plurality of worlds, and dramatists like Marlowe to portray the world conqueror, the magician, and the financier-magnates dedicated to the pursuit of infinite power, "knowledge infinite," or "infinite riches."

Eastern art, on the other hand, critics insist, remains satisfied with the limitations of the picture plane. It is essentially an art of line—sometimes merely of outline. Though it realizes the aesthetic and symbolic value of empty space, it does not attempt to organize the picture through scientific perspective or to convey the idea of infinity. It confines itself to line entirely, or to color and line. Though certain schools preferred the "boneless" manner, eschewing linear outlines for washes in ink or color, they did not employ these plastically. They remained committed to an essentially two-dimensional art. The differences between Oriental and Occidental aesthetics reduced themselves, in short, to the distinction between plane and solid geometry!

This tendency to read too much into the aesthetics of space— to interpret the artist's attitude toward plane or depth as the symbolic expression of his world view—is not uncommon even in recent comparisons between Eastern and Western art. Its most extreme statement, however, appears in Spengler's *Decline of the West*. Taking the *"kind of extension as the prime symbol of a Culture,"* the author draws a sharp contrast between classical Greece and the medieval and modern West, between the "Apollonian" and the "Faustian" man. The "prime-symbol of the Classical soul is the material and individual body, that of the Western pure infinite space." Chinese culture, in turn, stressed the "intensely directional principle of the Tao" and developed landscape gardening into a "grand religious art." The "Chinaman *wanders* through his world, . . . conducted to his god or his ancestral tomb . . . by friendly Nature herself." Similarly, his "paintings take the beholder from detail to detail"; it is "direction in depth that maintains the *becoming* of space as a continuously-present experience."[8] For Spengler, the Renaissance was a "revolt" against the "Faustian spirit" of the Gothic. Nevertheless, its attempt to revive the forms of classical antiquity was

actually an egregious failure; the Faustian craving for the infinite
finally triumphed in the discovery of perspective. With the sixteenth century, "painting becomes polyphonic, 'picturesque,' in-
finity-seeking. . . . The technique of oils becomes the basis of an
art that means to conquer *space* and to dissolve things in that
space. . . . The background as symbol of the infinite conquers the
sense-perceptible foreground, and at last . . . the depth-experience
of the Faustian soul is captured in the kinesis of a picture. The
space-relief of Mantegna's plane layers dissolves in Tintoretto
into directional energy, and there emerges in the picture the
great symbol of an unlimited space-universe which comprises the
individual things within itself as incidentals—the *horizon*."[9]

Spengler's art criticism differs in several significant respects
from that of the other writers we have examined. For one thing,
he is not concerned with the antithesis between East and West.
(As a matter of fact, he frequently stresses the affinities between
Chinese and Western culture.) The primary antithesis that engages him is the contrast between classical civilization and that
of the modern West. The Greek temple and the Gothic cathedral
"differ precisely as the Euclidean geometry of bodily bounding-
surfaces differs from the analytical geometry of the position of
points in space referred to spatial axes." Classical sculpture, "the
art of the naked body standing free upon its footing and appreciable from all sides alike," represents a decisive refusal "to
transcend sense-limits in favour of space." It is "rigorously *non-
spatial*" and springs "from a plane art, first obeying and then
overcoming the fresco." Whereas classical art stresses the "plastic"
values, the art of the modern West emphasizes "depth-experience."[10]

At this point we encounter another marked difference between
Spengler and the comparative critics of East and West. Where he
exaggerates the distinction between Greek and later Western art,
they tend to underemphasize it. Where he opposes linear perspective to "plastic" form as contrasting symbols of radically different world views, they generally link both concepts together as
signs of the same Western attitude toward reality—the same
preoccupation with three-dimensional realism, the same mathe-

matical conception of nature. Where he identifies Greek sculpture as a "plane art" and stresses the "visible brush-strokes" and "atmospheric" effects of Venetian painting, they associate both of these primarily with the art of China or Japan.

Yet in one respect they agree—the symbolic import of carved or painted space. For them, as for Spengler, "the arts of form" (*die bildenden Künste*) have an almost sacrosanct significance as "the clearest type of symbolic expression that the world-feeling of higher mankind has found for itself."[11] For them also, the aesthetic representation of "extension" is the keynote to a culture —though they usually express this idea in other words. The Western emphasis on "plastic" form and scientific perspective, the Eastern art of line—these reflect strikingly different concepts of nature, cultural attitudes as far apart as the rising and the setting sun.

These views, however, are decidedly one-sided. Interpreting the mind of the East almost exclusively in terms of its art, they ignore the extent to which comparable values find expression in other forms. Is Indian sculpture deficient in plastic values? Does Hindu architecture lack mass or solidity? Are Hindu and Buddhist cosmology indifferent to the notion of infinity?

In fact, the Orient was no less obsessed than the West with the idea of infinite space and a plurality of worlds. In contrast to the finite cosmos which Europe reluctantly discarded under the impact of modern astronomy (a cosmos equally limited in *time* and space), India had traditionally conceived the universe in terms of billions of leagues and cosmic cycles lasting milliards of centuries.

Even for us, who are accustomed to think in terms of light-years, the numerical imagery of the Lotus Sutra appears staggering. When the Buddha delivers a sermon on Vulture Peak, his audience includes "eighty thousand Bodhisattvas [enlightened spirits dedicated to the salvation of man] . . . who had propitiated many hundred thousands of Buddhas," achieved renown in "many hundred thousands of worlds," and "saved many hundred thousand myriads of kotis [ten millions] of beings." A ray from the Buddha's forehead extends over "eighteen hundred thousand

Buddha-fields in the eastern quarter" so that "all those Buddha-fields" appear "wholly illuminated by its radiance." Visible are "thousands of kotis of Stupas, numerous as the sands of the Ganges" and measuring in height "no less than 5000 yoganas and 2000 in circumference." The speaker has pursued his career "in presence of kotis of Buddhas . . . during an inconceivable number of kotis of Aeons." To each of his chief disciples he promises an epoch in which his lifetime will last twelve hundred intermediate kalpas, his true law twenty and its counterfeit as many. The lifetime of an earlier arhat (enlightened sage) had endured for fifty-four hundred thousand myriads of kotis of aeons, yet it is still too remote to calculate:

> . . . suppose some man was to reduce to powder the whole mass of the earth element as much as is to be found in this whole universe; that after taking one atom of dust from this world he is to walk a thousand worlds farther in [an] easterly direction to deposit that single atom; that after taking a second atom of dust and walking a thousand worlds farther he deposits that second atom, and proceeding in this way at last gets the whole of the earth element deposited in [the] eastern direction. Now . . . is it possible by calculation to find the end or limit of these worlds?[12]

The question is not purely rhetorical. It demands an answer, and this is inevitable under the circumstances: "Certainly not!"

But the numerical imagery itself *is* largely rhetorical. Its purpose is to extol the "knowledge and sight" of the speaker, who can remember so remote a day.

Moreover, it also served a "soteriological function," as Mircea Eliade points out. "Simply contemplating the panorama" of "incalculables" and aeons "terrifies man and forces him to realize that he must begin this same transitory existence and endure the same endless sufferings over again, millions upon millions of times; this results in intensifying his will to escape" into nirvana.[13]

Hindu cosmology posits an incalculable number of universes, each subject to periodic dissolution (Pralaya). A complete cycle

(Maha Yuga) lasts 12,000 "divine years" (360 years each) or a total of 4,320,000 years. A thousand such Mahayuga constitute a Kalpa; fourteen Kalpa make a Manvantara. A Kalpa is equivalent to a day in the life of Brahma; another Kalpa to a night. A hundred "years" of Brahma constitute his life—311,000 "milliards of human years"! Buddhism in turn divides the Kalpa into a number of "incalculables," and these are "connected with the career of the Bodhisattva in the various cosmoses."[14] Estimates of the duration of a Kalpa vary, however, ranging (as Conze observes) between 1,344,000 and 1,280,000,000 years.[15]

Equally innumerable are the number of universes existing simultaneously in infinite space. A tale in one of the Puranas relates how the god Indra was cured of his ambition by a lecture on cosmogony:

> Who will number the passing ages of the world, as they follow each other endlessly? And who will search through the wide infinities of a space to count the universes side by side, each containing its Brahma, its Vishnu, and its Shiva? Who will count the Indras in them all—those Indras side by side who reign at once in all the innumerable worlds; those others who passed away before them. . . ?[16]

Here again the function of this emphasis on mutability and infinity is ethical and soteriological. Both by precept and by parable, Indra learns the future rewards and penalties of good and evil actions and the way of "redemption" through non-attachment.

A preoccupation with infinity—either of space or of time—can hardly be regarded as peculiar to the West. Oriental art may not express this concept through linear perspective, but Oriental literature emphasizes it in other ways—and on a scale that would have seemed preposterous to the man of the Renaissance. It is not, however, altogether alien to what Kant termed the "mathematical sublime."

The Indian sense of space seems, perhaps, very different in quality from that of the man of the Renaissance or Spengler's

"Faustian man." It dwarfs ambition instead of stimulating it. Instead of an object of delight, it becomes a source of pity and fear. Yet the concept of infinite space could produce the same reactions in the West. Pascal could experience terror in contemplating the empty spaces beyond the stars. In Chirico and Dali the linear perspective that so delighted the Renaissance becomes a *horror vacui,* a sense of fear.

The Oriental attitude to infinite space also has a double aspect, benign as well as fearful. Space is filled with island-universes, "pure" and "impure" Buddha-fields. The latter (as Dr. Edward Conze observes) may be "identical with the natural and *impure* world systems . . . inhabited by creatures in all the six states of existence." But the former are jeweled paradises inhabited by the blessed.[17]

To express the notion of infinity in his art, the Oriental painter or sculptor had several obvious means at his disposal. He could use actual symbols or signs—though this would amount to little more than writing the word "infinity" or "innumerable" across an image. He could suggest an infinite attribute by multiple arms or heads—or by multiple images, like the statues of Kannon at Sanjusangendo. This, however, would merely denote an infinite quality—wisdom or compassion—rather than infinite space. The latter task fell to the landscape painter. When China developed "a pure landscape art," Dr. William Cohn declares, "spatial effects gradually became one of the determining factors. Not the reproduction of an isolated, in some way restricted and . . . tangible space was here sought for . . . , but the insertion of a scene in a floating, boundless and immeasurable universe. The conception of this mysterious infinity is not transmitted through the adherence to a fixed viewpoint and a perspective in the Western manner. It is brought about by changing the viewpoint, by gradations of brush-tone and by including the more or less untouched picture surface to add to the impression of the painting."[18]

Moreover, though the Orient did not utilize linear perspective to suggest depth, it did (apparently) on occasion make use of converging lines to organize a picture. In some of the Buddhist frescoes in the Tunhuang caves, the lines of various architectural features in the foreground would, if extended, intersect at the figure of the central Buddha. This triangular arrangement, with a lake or platform in the foreground forming the base and sides of a triangle and the central Buddha the apex, occurs frequently in the paradises of Amitabha and other Buddhist divinities. In one of these, as Basil Gray comments, "the perspective is skilfully organized to converge on a spot not far behind the principal figure. This is done by acute diminishing of the buildings right and left."[19] Additional and slightly larger triangles (likewise converging at or behind the central figure) are formed by the lines of architectural features or rows of figures in the right and left foreground. In other paintings at Tunhuang Mr. Gray finds "masterly composition in depth" or "an exaggerated perspective converging always not far behind the picture plane but with a shifting viewpoint."[20]

The plastic values critics find notably absent in Far Eastern painting are demonstrably present in many of the Buddhist cave paintings in India and Central Asia. In Indian painting, as Coomaraswamy observes, "generally there is relievo, that is to say modelling in abstract light, painting being thought of as a constricted *mode* of sculpture."[21] Nevertheless, for obvious reasons, one must look for them primarily in sculpture. In China this art never achieved the high status of painting, and (as William Willetts points out) it usually conforms to the "native" tradition of "linear conventionalization."[22] Yet it would be hard to deny the "plasticity" of T'ang mortuary figurines—courtiers, horses and camels, and stable grooms from Central Asia; of the life-size arhats modeled in glazed pottery during the Liao dynasty; or of the Sung statues of Bodhisattvas. Japanese sculptors of the Kamakura period achieved a high degree of excellence; they were hardly deficient in plastic values. Nor were the sculptors of India; indeed, Willetts notes the effort of Indian Buddhist sculpture "to recapture the full plasticity and rhythm of bodily movement so convincingly rendered by its oldest schools."[23]

Early Buddhist paintings in Japan and China likewise made

use of shading for modeling figures and thus invested them with plastic or "tactile" values. The paintings at Nara are a case in point. This feature derives, of course, primarily from India, where it appears in a higher degree in the cave paintings at Ajanta. Though it is not typical of Far Eastern painting as a whole, it nevertheless demonstrates that Buddhist art is not characteristically indifferent to the illusion of solidity. It also underlines the fallacy of taking Far Eastern painting as characteristic of Asia as a whole.

That Far Eastern painting ignores plastic values and makes no attempt to convey the idea of three-dimensional form is, then, at the very most a half-truth. Even less true is the belief that it lacks perspective. For centuries, its landscape artists have preached and practiced the "law of the three distances"—a principle also observed by certain schools in the West. Oriental art too differentiates between fore-, middle-, and back-ground. It too aims at the illusions of space and distance.

It is true, of course, that they often flatten the background. But this is not unusual in Western landscapes, and the purpose is fairly obvious—to increase the illusion of space and distance. Only rarely do they flatten the foreground and middle ground. Though they often separate and differentiate the two, it is not strictly true that they reduce these to two-dimensional planes. The position of rocks and trees in the foreground suggests relative distance. In the middle ground a fishing boat or two on a lake conveys the idea of its relative expanse; or a series of superimposed planes suggests the mass and shape of a mountain. Contrary to common opinion, stylization is not incompatible with the illusion of solidity; in the more "stylized" landscapes, the series of roughly parallel lines employed to suggest the receding planes of a rugged mountain reminds one of a contour map. These lines involve the same principle but with a different application— to suggest horizontal rather than vertical extension, horizontal depth rather than height.

Moreover, both Japanese and Chinese painters stress the importance of diminishing size and intensity to suggest distance. One must omit the details of distant peaks and trees, or they will appear nearer than they are. Remote objects must be smaller than those close at hand, or they will not appear remote. Though these precepts seem obvious, they are nonetheless significant; for they demonstrate the artist's concern with three-dimensionality, his desire to achieve the illusion of extension.

It is true that, until recently, the Orient never carried these tendencies to the extremes one finds in the modern West. Scientific perspective and a fixed point of view, chiaroscuro, and the exaggerated use of shading in modeling figures—these are not, on the whole, characteristic of medieval European painting. They are largely the legacy of the Renaissance (though partly anticipated by classical antiquity), and neither Renaissance nor post-Renaissance artists have been altogether consistent in observing them.

In painting architectural space—porches, courtyards, the interiors of palaces and cottages—Far Eastern and Western traditions are less divergent than critics often suppose. The preference for oblique rather than frontal views, the approach to a scene from the side or a tilted angle, the composition of interior scenes through diagonals—these are not peculiar to Far Eastern painting; on the contrary, they frequently occur in medieval European art, and one encounters them much later in such painters as Tintoretto.

3

Critics have likewise overemphasized the "scientific" element in Western art, largely through concentrating too narrowly on a small group of Renaissance artists who united the skills of painter and scientist. "The Renaissance," as Erwin Panofsky correctly observes, "was a period of *decompartmentalization*," and one of the barriers it broke down was the separation of the "liberal" and "mechanical" arts. With the proverbial versatility of the Renaissance man, the practicing artist could also be a both theoretical and experimental scientist. "Much of that which was later to be isolated as 'natural science' came into being in

artists' studios. And, perhaps the most important point, the rise
of those particular branches of natural science which may be
called observational or descriptive—zoology, botany, palaeon-
tology, several aspects of physics and, first and foremost, anatomy
—was . . . directly predicated upon the rise of the representational techniques. . . ." In placing "perspective on a truly scientific
basis"—conceiving the painting "as a plane cross section through
the pencil or rays connecting the eye of the painter . . . with the
object or objects seen"—the artist laid the foundation of "both
projective and analytical geometry." The fifteenth century produced a "continuous series of 'painter-anatomists,' running from
Pollaiuolo to Michelangelo" and Alessandro Allori, who "placed
anatomy in the service of art." Leonardo da Vinci, on the other
hand, "placed art in the service of anatomy and thereby became
the founder of anatomy as a science."[24]

Dagobert Frey (according to Earl Rosenthal) likewise stresses
"the affinity of art and the natural sciences in the fifteenth century." In his opinion, "the Renaissance idea of the world was in
the main determined by the study of optics, perspective, geometry, cartography, and astronomy," and "the visual concept of
space which resulted from these studies was reflected in its art
forms, most clearly in painting."[25]

As this union of artist and scientist has, apparently, no parallel
in Oriental art, critics are justified in emphasizing its implications
for Western painting—particularly in the representation of space
and the treatment of the human form. But it is, on the whole,
peculiar to the Renaissance. Though later artists built on the
Renaissance achievement, they were rarely so "scientific" in their
attitude toward anatomy and perspective.

"From the whole of Asia," Coomaraswamy asserts, there "cannot be adduced . . . such a thing as a treatise on anatomy designed for use by artists."[26] This is probably true; but is it not
due in part to the linear techniques of Far Eastern painting? to
the symbolic nature of much of Hindu and Buddhist iconography?
and (more significantly) to the Oriental medical traditions themselves? The ivory figurines on which the ladies of China or Japan
used to indicate their ailments show so little anatomical detail

that they could at best designate the general location of the symptoms.

Again, Coomaraswamy's observations on Western perspective are partly justified. "In Western art the picture is generally conceived as seen in a frame or through a window, and so brought toward the spectator; but the Oriental image really exists only in our own mind and heart and is thence projected or reflected onto space."[27] This is actually an echo of Alberti's comparison between the picture plane and a *"pariete di vetro"*—"an imaginary windowpane *through* which we look out into a section of space." But it is not true of the entire Western tradition—even since the Renaissance; and it scarcely applies to the Middle Ages. In both periods a picture was regarded "as a material, impenetrable surface on which figures and things are depicted"—in contrast to Alberti's view.[28] The "whole Middle Ages," declares Heinrich Wölfflin, believed it "impossible to reproduce spatial reality in depth on a flat surface." Hence they were "content with a system of representation which merely contained references to objects and their spatial relation, but made no attempt to compete with Nature." It was left to the Renaissance (as Vasari remarked of Masaccio) to conceive of painting as "the imitation of things as they are."[29]

By judging European and Asiatic aesthetics largely in terms of the contrast between Renaissance or post-Renaissance oil painting and Zen monochrome, critics are—once again—comparing "incommensurables." The Western line drawing, sketch, or water color would—as several scholars point out—be a sounder basis of comparison. Moreover, unlike Western painting, that of China and Japan has traditionally been intimately associated with calligraphy—a fact that has decisively affected its style and technique.

This narrowness of focus has had unfortunate results for comparative criticism. Not only has it made the differences between Eastern and Western traditions seem greater and more fundamental than they are; it has also exaggerated the contrasts between European and Asian sensibility or temperament. Worse still, it has tended to obscure the actual diversity of Oriental art and to foster a highly illusory picture of its essential unity. Far Eastern painting becomes little more than a visual expression of Zen and Taoism. Chinese pictorial art becomes the criterion by which Oriental aesthetics—and virtually all Asian art forms—are judged.

This summary is, of course, merely a description of a trend. Few critics *consciously* follow the pattern of reasoning I have outlined. But it is, nonetheless, often implicit in their arguments. And it is largely responsible for the common opinion of Oriental art as indifferent to plastic values, as hostile to realism, and as spontaneous and intuitive rather than studied. It has also led them to exaggerate other aspects of Eastern painting—its asymmetry, its radical simplicity, its reliance on suggestiveness and nuance. In varying degrees, these qualities may be characteristic of Zen monochrome paintings (*sumiye* or *suiboku*), but they are not true of the whole complex of Asian art.

Buddhist iconography is not, on the whole, asymmetrical; often, on the contrary, its organization is highly formal and its figures are carefully balanced—as in medieval Christian iconography. Nor is it spontaneous or individualistic. With the notable exception of Zen portraiture, it is, like most religious art, conservative and bound by strict conventions—sometimes to the point of rigidity. The composition and iconography of recent Tibetan paintings are still very close to those of the early Buddhist art of China, Japan, and Central Asia. On many of these, a careful observer can detect the original lines traced from a master design and later painted over. Though highly symbolic, this tradition is scarcely characterized by either radical simplicity or suggestive understatement. Indeed, in portraying the "terrifying" aspects of its divinities, it goes to the opposite extreme.

The popular conception of the "spontaneous" painter who dashes off an entire landscape in a moment of inspiration is scarcely typical. This was not the practice of Kuo Hsi, who appears to have been the classic type of the Taoist individualist. According to his son, he had "studied under a Taoist master, *in consequence of which he was ever inclined to throw away what is old, and take in what is new.*" He disliked the laborious revision practiced by certain other painters: "To sketch out the picture once, and then try to reconstruct it . . . to do twice what could have been once, to do thrice what could have been twice, to trace again every curve, and thus be always trying to improve, . . . such is what he meant by painting with a proud heart." Like other "intuitive" painters, he attempted to identify himself with his subject and then paint "unconsciously": "A true artist" should "be capable of understanding and reconstructing in his own mind the emotions and conditions of other human beings, both in pointedness and obliqueness. . . . Having accomplished this understanding of others, he should let them out unconsciously through the tip of his brush."

Nevertheless, Kuo Hsi did not always complete a picture at one sitting. Sometimes he left them "unfinished for ten or twenty days at a time, probably because he was not disposed toward them. That is what he called the idle mind of a painter."[30] "Having drawn a picture," his son continues, "he would retouch here and add there; augment and adorn it. If once would have been sufficient, he would go back to it for the second time. If twice would have been enough, he would go back to it the third time."[31]

Similarly, the belief that the Oriental painter (unlike his Western counterpart) invariably paints from memory contradicts the facts. Chinese painters themselves assert that they went directly to nature for their models, especially in sketching.[32] As Willetts observes, "not all European artists . . . have worked directly from a model; landscapists especially have often relied on memory and working notes combined. . . ." Conversely, certain Chinese painters, "especially landscapists, did make working sketches of their subjects *sur le motif*."[33]

Most of the critics whose views we have discussed in this chapter have contrasted the aesthetics of Oriental and Occidental cultures primarily in terms of different modes of knowledge. Europe and Asia, they suggest, have evolved different artistic forms because they possess different conceptions of truth. Their characteristic modes of expression reflect contrasting modes of cognition—different ways of perceiving or *conceiving* things. From these basic psychological or epistemological differences have arisen most of the antitheses noted in the preceding pages— realism versus idealism; imitation of reality versus intuition of reality; scientific elaboration of external detail versus spontaneous rendition of essential insight; conceptions of forms as solid or merely linear; conceptions of space as three-dimensional or as confined exclusively to the two-dimensional plane.

For these critics, the fundamental differences between the aesthetics of Europe and Asia amount to a difference in orientation. The former tends to approach the work of art primarily in terms of its relationship to some external object; the latter, on the other hand, usually conceives the work of art chiefly in terms of its relationship to the mind of the artist. The former accordingly stresses the objective element—the latter the subjective element—in aesthetics. For the West, art is first of all representation; for the East it is, essentially and primarily, expression.

In challenging this dichotomy, we have seen that neither extreme can be entirely, or even predominantly, characteristic of either European or Asian art. Indeed most of these antitheses can be found, albeit in varying degrees, in Oriental and Occidental art alike.

In the following chapter we shall consider some of the contrasts that Western art historians have drawn between Oriental and Occidental conceptions of nature. From the problem of *how* the artist perceives and expresses "reality" we shall turn to the allied problem of *what* he believes this "reality" to be.

NATURE IN
FAR EASTERN ART

———

. .
.

1

If the stereotype of Asian religion is essentially Indian, that of Eastern art is predominantly Chinese. Where the former interprets the Oriental mind largely in terms of Vedantist or Buddhist monism, the latter explains Oriental aesthetics primarily in terms of Sino-Japanese art. In this field it narrows its scope still further: to painting and poetry, and—more specifically—to the styles and motifs most closely associated with Zen or Taoist concepts.

For many critics, these philosophies are the cornerstones of Far Eastern aesthetics. They molded its salient features, established its artistic standards, and determined its criteria of taste and style. More than any other factor, they have allegedly shaped the Oriental "sensibility" and the forms of Oriental art.

Despite its narrowness, this view is more than a half-truth. Chinese and Japanese cultures are undeniably deeply indebted to Taoist and Zen attitudes. Paradoxically, through their very emphasis on inaction (*wu-wei*), both exerted a significant influence not merely on literature but also on political and private morality. Like Western romanticists—Rousseau, Shelley, the Godwins—Taoism stressed the "natural" man, unwarped by the artificial conventions of society. In ethics, it emphasized spontaneity and individuality; in politics—inactivity, passive resistance and *laissez faire*.

Zen likewise aimed at realizing the original nature (*Tathata*) inherent in man, as in all other beings. In its ethics it too stressed spontaneity and the expression of individuality. Nor was it devoid of political implications. The feudal lords of Japan respected it as an effective discipline for their soldiers and an ideal psychological preparation for warfare. Its techniques of concentrated meditation induced calm. Its belief in nonattachment removed anxiety about the fruits of action—and could, therefore, be as efficacious for the Japanese samurai as for the Indian hero Arjuna. These features, however, were not peculiar to Zen; they belonged to most Buddhist sects as well as to Hinduism. What *was* characteristic of Zen was an emphasis it shared in part with Taoism. By stressing effortless and unpremeditated action, it enabled the warrior to strike his blow without hesitation or forethought. In this respect Zen training would become closely associated with such arts of combat as jujitsu, fencing and archery.

The impact of Taoist and Zen attitudes on the fine arts was still more significant. Painting and poetry, ceramics, architecture and landscape gardening—all of these owed much to the characteristic emphasis on nature and spontaneity. So did the gentle art of tea drinking—an institution that, directly or indirectly, influenced the arts of expression and design.

In Japan all of these art forms reflect the "spirit" of Zen, but it is easy to exaggerate their indebtedness. They are not—as Langdon Warner, formerly Field Fellow of the Fogg Museum, Harvard University, points out—the "results of Zen," as critics often assert, but they have been modified by it. They have, as it were, acquired its qualities by intincture or infusion—as boiling water assumes the taste of tea dust. For many Westerners the cult of Zen has become a form of connoisseurship; a discriminating palate can detect the subtlest variations in flavor—and announce (like the wine-tasting ecclesiastic at Montefiascone) *"Est! est! est!"* Some Zen tasters have so sensitive a palate that like R. H. Blyth, author of *Zen in English Literature and Oriental Classics,* they can identify the distinctive savor of Zen in one line out of a thousand English verses.

"It is this flavor and taste of Zen," Warner continues, "in the mouths of the Japanese which for five hundred years has fostered an art of simple things without glitter and embellishment, a decorous attitude toward other persons and a keen appreciation of all that is suggested rather than stated. Zen habits of mind ran through the warp of Japan to subdue and harmonize the whole fabric."[1]

The Taoist's preoccupation with nature was to have profound implications for his art. Not only did it affect his choice of subject, but it also influenced his style and his attitude toward his medium. In seeking to express and reveal nature, the craftsman preferred to stress the intrinsic beauty of natural materials rather than to overlay them with extraneous ornament. Form was, accordingly, rather the natural and inevitable expression of the material than an arbitrary pattern imposed from without. It was organic rather than artificial; the function of art was to conceal art.

The sculptor must, ideally, reveal the nature of the Uncarved Block. The painter must respect the character of the Undyed Silk. The mirror maker must produce a polished surface capable of assuming the shapes and hues of all sorts of objects, while remaining unaffected and unmodified by them.

All three of these examples are, in fact, conventional Taoist or Zen symbols for essential reality—the original, unqualified nature of man and the universe. As such, they may serve to underline the affinities of these Far Eastern philosophies with Hindu thought. For the Mahayana concept of "Suchness" or "Buddha-nature" (*Bhutatathata*), so significant in the Zen vocabulary, has much in common with the "unqualified Brahman" (*tat*) of Vedantist philosophy. The Vedic equation *tat tvam asi* ("thou art That") is really as fundamental to Zen monism as to Shankara's. Aside from their different religious contexts—the divergent traditions of Hinduism and Mahayana Buddhism—the chief difference lies in their approach and methodology. In their attempts to realize "That"—the ultimate reality—Shankara and the Zen patriarchs stress different means.

With this respect for the natural, as opposed to the sophisticated and artificial, went a love of nature in a broader sense—the cult of natural scenery and natural life, delight in insects and flowers, birds and animals, mountains and streams. These were infused with the same universal spirit—the Tao—or shared alike in the universal "Buddha-nature."

The Taoist's emphasis on spontaneity (*tzu-jan*) and purposelessness (*wu-hsin:* literally, "no mind") was inseparable from his devotion to nature and his concern with the natural. For spontaneity meant self-expression—a free outpouring of the inner spirit; and purposelessness meant a surrender of conscious volition to the same spirit. A spontaneous, "unpremeditated" art is also a pure art, an essential art; for it is a direct expression of the innermost nature of things. Insofar as the artist cultivates the quality of *muga* (effortlessness—the Japanese reading of Chinese *wu-wo*, "without ego") and does not intervene consciously in the "creative process," he allows nature—or the Tao in and beyond nature—to express itself through him. In this way art becomes a manifestation of reality; it catches the spirit or essence of the things it depicts. And precisely because it is a "selfless" art, it can be simultaneously a manifestation of the Tao and an expression of the artist's Self.

Perhaps this is why so many Taoist and Zen painters usually rank as "individualists." The very fact that they *are* so classified ought, however, to put one on guard against taking them as paradigms or "types" of Oriental art. At times this can become as inspirationless, as mechanical, as convention-ridden, and as devoid of "spirit" and spontaneity as much of the academic art of the West. Henry Bowie acknowledges seventy-two "important" *laws* of Japanese painting. As in the West, the student learns his craft by imitation—by copying the masters. Though at times this can be very free (witness the very different results by artists who profess to paint in the "style of Ni Tsan"), it can sometimes prove very mechanical indeed. "In copying," Bowie informs us, "the teacher usually first paints the particular subject, and the student reproduces it under his supervision. . . . In tracing, thin paper is placed over the picture and the outlines . . . are traced according to the *exact order* in which the original subject was executed, an order which is established by rule. . . ."[2]

This is, admittedly, a technique of instruction. As such, it does not differ appreciably from the method whereby—in Western Europe—Renaissance schoolboys learned the principles of Latin style and neoclassical art students the principles bequeathed by Renaissance painters and sculptors. These too had their "laws"— their rules of grammar and rhetoric and logic, or their rules of proportion and perspective. These too had their classical models to imitate.

One can—and many critics often do—exaggerate the spontaneity of Oriental painting, and also its feeling for nature. Undoubtedly the great masters achieved both, but they are rare.

Chinese art critics seldom find all six of Hsieh Ho's principles exemplified in one man; the common burden of their complaint is the almost universal failure of their contemporaries to live up to the Six Canons, and in particular the criterion of "Spirit-Rhythm, Life-Movement."

Like most great traditions—those of Sumeria and Egypt, classical Greece and Renaissance Italy—those of China and Japan carried within themselves the germs of their own decay. The sensibilities that helped to create the tradition also helped to destroy it. They became the symptoms of old age—for there is an aesthetic as well as a physical senility; and art, like man, can suffer a hardening of the arteries. Styles and values that once appeared new and vital become conventional; conventions become norms; and these in turn become "rules" and "laws." Far Eastern art is no exception to this pattern; it owes its continued vitality largely to the importation of alien traditions—Indian, Central Asian, European—and to the friction between these and native traditions—Confucian and Buddhist, Taoist and Persian, and (in Japan itself) between Chinese, Western, and Yamato (Japanese) styles.

Indeed, the Taoist and Zen contributions to Far Eastern culture are fully intelligible only in the larger context of Chinese or Japanese society as a whole. With their emphasis on spontaneity, individualism, and informality, they complemented—but did not undermine—the rigid moral and political codes of two ancient and convention-ridden societies. For Ruth Benedict, Zen was, in part, a reaction against the feudal character of Japanese culture, with its emphasis on moral and social, personal and political obligation; its preoccupation with *on*, "obligations passively incurred," and *giri*, duties to "liegelord," "official family," and oneself. Taoism, in turn, was, to some extent, an antidote to Confucian ethics in private life and an overemphasis on ceremonialism and bureaucracy in the state. (As a matter of fact, however, the Taoist celestial hierarchy far outdid the empire in its formal chain of command and its complex Tables of Organization!) There was no rigid line of demarcation between these ideologies; it was rather a matter of propriety and decorum. A man adapted his creed and mores to his situation. At the barbecue pit in his California garden, the American general doffs his uniform, gold braid, and stars for Bermuda shorts and a sport shirt. On the Costa Brava the British Minister discards his bowler hat, school tie and Oxford-gray flannel for bathing trunks. Retiring to the country, an impeccably Confucian bureaucrat might similarly embrace Taoism. Resigning his official duties, a Japanese court noble or feudal lord might shave his head and become a Zen monk. There was no inconsistency in this; the change of customs, like the change of costume, accompanied a transition from public to private life, official to personal values.

Far Eastern painting is not, in fact, the spontaneous rapture of a child of nature. On the contrary, it is in many respects the reaction of a sophisticated, self-conscious, and overcivilized society to the inevitable inconvenience of being civilized. Here again the analogy with eighteenth- and nineteenth-century romanticism in Europe is inescapable. Before the guillotine cut short her charades, the Queen of France enjoyed disguising herself as a dairymaid or a shepherdess. Fashionable poets masqueraded in verse behind the *personae* of shepherds or fishermen. Fashionable ladies temporarily closed their salons to seek the Sublime by mountains and waterfalls and to retrieve natural innocence in the bosom of Nature herself—in rural retreats that

were still within easy reach of society. The cult of nature in
Oriental art is not altogether different—though artists adored
Fuji and T'ai Shan instead of Mont Blanc; sailed along the Hsiao,
the Yangtze and Lake Biwa instead of the Rhine, the Stour, or
Lake Léman; and did their painting in Peking and Hangchow,
Tokyo or Kyoto instead of Paris and London and Rome. They
were, for the most part, metropolitan sophisticates who longed
for rusticity. We have their counterparts today in the Angeleños
who crowd the national parks each summer, or the New Yorkers
who flock to Maine or New Hampshire, and return with water
colors (the record of their own, or another's, experience), sketches,
and relief.

"Wherein," demands Kuo Hsi, "do the reasons lie of virtuous
men so loving sansui [landscape—from Chinese *shan-shui,* 'mountains and water']? It is for these facts: that a landscape is a
place where vegetation is nourished on high and low ground,
where springs and rocks play about like children, a place which
woodsmen and retiring scholars usually frequent, where monkeys
have their tribe, and storks fly crying aloud their joy in the scene.
The noisiness of the dusty world, and the locked-in-ness of
human habitations are what human nature, at its highest, per-
petually hates; while, on the contrary, haze, mist and the Sennin
sages . . . are what human nature seeks, and yet can but rarely
see. . . . What a delightful thing [then] it is for lovers of forests
and fountains and the friends of mist and haze, to have, at hand,
a landscape painted by a skillful artist! To have therein the opportunity of seeing water and peaks, of hearing the cry of monkeys, and the song of birds, *without going from the room!*"[3]

Art is thus a surrogate for the direct experience of nature. It
offers a means of escape from town life, a vicarious retreat from
the real metropolis into a painted wilderness. Is this so very
different from the services that the landscape painters of
Western Europe provided for their patrons? That Ruysdael and
Hobbema provided for the burghers of Amsterdam, Gains-
borough and Constable provided for the merchants of London,
or the Barbizon school provided for the *bourgeois gentilhommes*
of Paris?

2

For many critics, the differences between Eastern and Western art spring from fundamentally divergent attitudes toward nature. Since the same writers usually regard Taoism and Zen as largely responsible for the treatment of nature in Far Eastern painting, the key to the differences between Eastern and Western painting would appear, therefore, to lie in the contrasts between Taoism and Zen on the one hand and Western conceptions of nature on the other. This seems to be the real crux of the matter.

For Professor Northrop, Western painting (like other facets of European culture) is preoccupied with "the theoretic component." This characteristic emphasis radically affects style and technique and reduces art to science: The West is "so fascinated with this theoretic component" that it has turned the "aesthetic component into a . . . mere handmaid, whose sole value is the conveying of the theoretic component." By "the use of theoretically controlled and defined techniques such as perspective," it "uses the aesthetic materials and the aesthetic continuum not merely in and for themselves for their own sake, but also analogically and symbolically to convey the theoretic component of the nature of things of which they are the mere correlate or sign."[4]

Chiang Yee, author of several books on Chinese painting and calligraphy, draws a sharp contrast between Chinese and Western approaches to nature—and explains the former primarily in terms of Taoism. In his essay on "The Philosophical Basis of Chinese Painting," he acknowledges the Buddhist and Confucian contribution to Chinese art, but awards the palm to Taoism. For the Confucians, painting was primarily a "means of promoting culture and strengthening the principles of right conduct"; their emphasis on suppressing the emotions tended to stifle poetry and painting alike. It was Taoism, with its feeling for nature, that stimulated the growth of a great pictorial tradition. Of the three great religious and philosophical systems in China, "only Taoism is without preconceptions and strives to see life as it is," recognizing that the "Eternal Law" is responsible for "the rhythm of life in nature." "Tao models itself after nature," and to "identify oneself with Tao is to identify oneself with nature."

The Chinese love of nature differs from the Western attitude "in that its aim is identification with her, not imitation or 'conquest' of her." (Of course we should note that identification is an ambiguous word. The Chinese idea of identity with the Tao is not the same as the Indian goal of identity with Brahman; it involves realization of the common spiritual force underlying nature rather than the recognition that nature is an illusion—a unity of life and spirit rather than a unity of mind. Spiritual harmony with nature and internal, as opposed to external, conformity would be less equivocal terms.) "Taoistic insight is the source of the intense delight which Chinese poets and artists" take in the details of nature—a single bird or flower, a fish or insect. It exhibits a "sympathetic insight" into inanimate objects, for it regards them as alive, as possessing "selves or souls."

Such a view has profound implications for painting, for "it is the soul which must emerge from the picture, and the technique which achieves this is permissible—the simpler the better. . . ."[5]

Okakura Kakuzo, Japanese critic and author of *The Book of Tea*, points out the aesthetic implications of the Taoist emphasis on relativity and emptiness. "The Tao is in the Passage rather than the Path. It is the spirit of Cosmic Change." The Tao is the Infinite; but "Infinity is the Fleeting, the Fleeting is the Vanishing, the Vanishing is the Reverting." Hence Taoism "accepts the mundane as it is and, unlike the Confucians and the Buddhists, tries to find beauty" in the world about it.

Moreover, the Taoist doctrine that "only in vacuum lay the truly essential" underlies the tendency of Far Eastern art to stress "the value of suggestion":

In leaving something unsaid the beholder is given a chance to complete the idea and thus a . . . masterpiece irresistibly rivets your attention until you seem to become actually a part of it. A vacuum is there for you to enter and fill up to the full measure of your aesthetic emotion.

The same emphases recur in Zen Buddhism. This too stresses individualism and relativity. This too aims at "direct communion with the inner nature of things." This too recognizes "the mundane as of equal importance with the spiritual." "Taoism," Okakura concludes, "furnished the basis for aesthetic ideals, Zennism made them practical."[6]

In Zen, D. T. Suzuki finds a characteristic expression of "the Chinese mentality"—one that can be "expressed most effectively in the Chinese language." He too stresses the element of spontaneity ("no speculation . . . ; only let things flow on as they would"; "keep Tao ever flowing with no obstructions") and the contrast with Western attitudes toward nature: "The idea of conquering Nature is something quite foreign to the Oriental, especially the Buddhist, way of thinking."[7]

For Alan Watts likewise, the contrasts between Eastern and Western attitudes toward nature are mirrored in their art. Whereas Oriental art is a spontaneous expression of nature, Western art is merely "representational." "The favorite subjects of Zen artists, whether painters or poets, are . . . natural, concrete, and secular things. . . . Even in painting, the work of art is considered not only as representing nature but as being itself a work of nature." The Zen painter's technique "involves the art of artlessness" or the "controlled accident"; "paintings are formed as naturally as the rocks and grasses which they depict." Western art forms, on the other hand, "arise from spiritual and philosophical traditions in which spirit is divided from nature, and comes down from heaven to work upon it as an intelligent energy upon an inert and recalcitrant stuff." The Western artist "conquers" his medium, and the scientific Western mind regards nature as an "order" from which "spontaneity" has been "screened out."

The "fundamental principle" of the universe, as Zen conceives it, however, is "relativity"; there is "no purpose because there is . . . no end to be attained." The "constant theme of Zen art," accordingly, is "the aimless life"; it expresses "the artist's own inner state of going nowhere in a timeless moment." Again, the Eastern artist paints "by not painting"—by an effective use of understatement, empty space, and reticence. "By filling in just one corner, [he] makes the whole area of the picture alive."[8]

Rudolf Otto stresses the "inner affinity" between Taoism and Mahayana Buddhism. Their "interpenetration" fostered "a mysticism of nature," and stimulated the art of Chinese and Japanese Zen.[9] For Holmes Welch, "the *purpose* of landscape painting" in China "has been to express the identification of the painter with nature." As an example he cites the opinion of Kuo Hsi that "the artist should identify himself with the landscape."[10]

Laurence Binyon likewise attributes the differences he finds between Eastern and Western art to their contrasting attitudes toward nature. The "essential difference between the art of the East and the West" is "rooted in philosophy of life, in mental habit and character. An opposition between man and Nature has been ingrained in Western thought. It is the achievements, the desires, the glory and the suffering of man that have held the central place in Western art; only very slowly and unwillingly has the man of the West taken trouble to consider the non-human life around him, and to understand it as a life lived for its own sake: for centuries he has but heeded it in so far as it opposed his will or ministered to his needs and appetites. But in China and Japan, as in India, we find no barrier set up between the life of man and the life of the rest of God's creatures. The continuity of the universe, the perpetual stream of change through its matter, are accepted as things of Nature, felt in the heart and not merely learnt as the conclusions of delving science. And these ways of thought are reflected in Eastern art. Not the glory of the naked human form, to Western art the noblest and most expressive of symbols; not the proud and conscious assertion of human personality; but, instead of these, all thoughts that lead us out from ourselves into the universal life, hints of the infinite, whispers from secret sources—mountains, waters, mists, flowering trees, whatever tells of powers and presences mightier than ourselves: these are the themes dwelt upon, cherished, and preferred." Hence "it is in landscape, and the themes allied to landscape, that the art of the East is superior to our own. The power of the art of the West excels in the human drama."

Western painting (Binyon continues) has been weakened by "the scientific aim" and by its encroachment on sculpture and architecture, usurping the sculptor's concern with "figures seen in roundness and relief" and the architect's concern with "ordered spaces and perspective." Oriental painting, on the other hand, "limits itself severely" and "leaves to sculpture and to architecture the effects proper to those arts."

Whereas Western artists copy nature, "all painters of the Asian tradition" aim at "the inner and informing spirit, not the outward semblance." Seeking to express the "essential character and genius" of whatever subject they have chosen, they rely on simplification and suggestion: "The more to concentrate on this seizure of the inherent life in what they draw, they will obliterate or ignore at will half or all of the surrounding objects with which the Western painter feels bound to fill his background. By isolation and the mere use of empty space they will give to a clump of narcissus . . . a sense of grandeur and a hint of the infinity of life."[11]

William Willetts also attributes the opposition between European realism and the "deeper" spirit of the Asian tradition to contrasting attitudes toward nature. Though "the category of Chinese painting called *hua niao*, 'flowers and birds,' is to some extent cognate with European still-life painting in subject-matter, yet spiritually the two have little or nothing in common. . . . Generally speaking, animals and plants are for Europeans nothing more than physical presences altogether devoid of any deeper psychological implication . . . , and consequently in depicting them no more is sought than external verisimilitude. . . . Asiatic peoples, on the other hand, have always invested natural life with a profound *mystique*." In his concern to portray the *li* or "governing principle" and "inherent nature" of each class of being, the artist sought to "identify himself with his subject, eliminate subjective and objective distinctions, and eventually capture and transmit something of that characteristic mode of being."[12]

3

In art criticism, then, we encounter the same difficulty we have met earlier in comparisons between Eastern and Western philosophy and religion—the tendency to generalize from insufficient evidence. Just as the comparative religionist tends to take Vedanta monism and absolute idealism as the archetype of Eastern thought, the comparative aesthetician tends to regard Taoist or Zen painting as the norm or exemplar of Asian art. Such an approach could never do justice to the diversity of Chinese painting, and it is manifestly inadequate as a yardstick for Oriental aesthetics as a whole.

There are, moreover, other weaknesses in this approach besides overgeneralization from an unrepresentative or involuntarily biased selection of data. In the first place, it is not true that "*all* painters" of "the Asian tradition" aimed at the "inner spirit" rather than the "outward semblance." Binyon's assertion that they did represents a rather exaggerated statement of a claim that many critics have nevertheless made for Oriental art. Some of these have been more cautious than Binyon in phrasing their claim, but the substance of their generalization has been essentially the same.

Unlike the Grail quest, any quest for "*the* Asian tradition" is apt to end by finding it. The quest terminates successfully through the valor and conviction of the Critic Errant—but he achieves his goal only by bold and slashing overstatements and sometimes no little violence to that distressed and naked demoiselle, the Truth. In Binyon's case the pursuit of Asia culminated in a sensitive and perceptive appreciation of Chinese painting— but only by the most daring stretch of the imagination can the latter be equated with Asian art as a whole.

Even his account of Chinese painting, moreover, shows no little exaggeration. The Chinese painters themselves contradict his assertion that "all" of them endeavored to portray the inner spirit. Far from it. On the contrary, the constant burden of their criticism is that, unlike the great masters of the past, the vast majority of their contemporaries flagrantly disregard Hsieh Ho's first principle; instead of grasping the spirit of the object, most painters merely aim at external likeness. In the opinion of these critics, moreover, even the masters themselves frequently fell short of perfection. Some indeed succeeded in grasping the spirit; but others excelled in applying color, others in rendering the form. The painters who excelled in all *six* of the canons were unfortunately very rare.

On this point Western observers have, it appears, confused theory and practice, art criticism with actual painting. Though the Chinese critics themselves usually placed primary stress on "Spirit-Rhythm, Life-Movement"[13] as an aesthetic norm, they consistently complained that most painters neglected this principle. We can scarcely dismiss this complaint as simply a rhetorical exaggeration. Like many other Western writers on Oriental art, Binyon has apparently accepted the critic's idea of what the artist *ought* to do as proof of what the artist actually and invariably *did*. He has taken theory as an index of practice.

Secondly, it is not strictly true that the Oriental painter and sculptor scrupulously avoided trespassing on each other's domain. Early Buddhist sculpture in the Far East frequently shows signs of having been modeled after paintings; in other cases religious paintings retain "sculpturesque" features probably derived ultimately from statuary. Binyon's argument that Western painting has been weakened by its "scientific aim" and its "encroachment on sculpture and architecture" may be applicable to the Renaissance (though one can regard this as an argument of strength rather than of weakness). Yet it hardly fits the Middle Ages.

Nor is the inference Binyon draws from this point convincing. Suppose we grant that, on the whole, Chinese painting "leaves to sculpture and to architecture the effects proper to these arts." Such a premise would seem to argue *against* his conclusion that the differences between European and Chinese painting inevitably reflect a fundamental difference between the "mental habit[s] and character" of East and West. We can scarcely take the absence (or alleged absence) of certain values in one art form as characteristic of the Chinese mentality, while arguing simultaneously that the same "Chinese mentality" has expressed them through other aesthetic modes. Though Chinese painting is not indifferent to plastic values—and still less to spatial arrangement and perspective—critics often use these as touchstones not only for contrasting European and Chinese aesthetics in particular, but also for differentiating the Western mind in general from the spirit of the East. In the same breath they dismiss plastic values and perspective as alien to the Chinese mind, yet praise the spatial sense manifested in Chinese architecture and the plastic values inherent in Chinese ceramics. In this respect it is noteworthy that Binyon underemphasizes an important genre in Chinese painting—the *architectural* pictures normally classified under the category of "places and buildings."

Hence, it is hardly fair to contrast Western and Eastern art in terms of an antithesis between "representation" and "expression" of nature. In actuality these terms are not so much antithetical as complementary. Even the most "spiritual" of Oriental painters believed that they were, in a sense, "representing" Nature (and the objects of nature) as well as expressing her. Even the most "scientific" of Renaissance artists usually felt that they were doing considerably more than "copying" nature. They were, in effect, creating a second nature endowed with the same forms and imitating the same ideas. In this way they came close to conceiving art as "a work of nature," even though they left the fuller development of this concept to a later generation. The romantic artist tended to identify himself still more closely with nature and natural feeling, and to regard his own art (poetry, painting, and especially music) less as "representative" than "expressive." For Schopenhauer, music—of all the arts—came closest to expressing the universal Will.

What the comparative critic really means in such a context is not so much the contrast between representation and expression as the opposition between "internal" and "external" representation, between essential and superficial resemblance. Once again, however, the opposition is more apparent than real, for the terms themselves are complementary rather than contradictory. Chinese and Western aesthetics emphasize both. Hsieh Ho's canons demand "conformity" with the object as well as "Spirit-Rhythm." Conversely, Western critics generally stress fidelity to the "essential form" or idea of an object; though they may emphasize verisimilitude, their concern with movement, vitality and personality in a work of art brings them close to the principles expressed in Hsieh Ho's first canon.

The sharp opposition between man and nature, which Binyon finds in Western thought, is certainly not characteristic of the Stoics and Neo-Platonists in classical antiquity, of the romantic poets of the eighteenth and nineteenth centuries, or of certain scientific (or pseudoscientific) traditions that played an important role in European thought in antiquity, the Middle Ages, and the Renaissance. The Stoics stressed the microcosm-macrocosm ratio, the intimate relationship between man and the universe he lived in: Man was a "little world made cunningly," a diminutive cosmos—nature in miniature. The universe, in turn, was man "writ large." Harmony with nature was, therefore, almost as important for them as for Confucians and Taoists. For the Neo-Platonists, the world was an "animal"—an organism animated by a world soul in which men and all other creatures "lived and moved and had their being." The romantics often verged on pantheism; all things were alive and instinct with the same living soul. Man was a part of nature, and his art an expression of nature—the "spontaneous overflow of powerful feelings." Most of the pseudoscientists—alchemists, astrologers, and (most lethal of all!) physicians—practiced a "natural magic," whose basic principle was the latent "sympathies" between man and nature.

Finally, like most art, Western art involves empathy—the "aesthetic" identification of the artist with his subject and the observer with the work of art. Most Western poetry—like poetry everywhere—is animistic and anthropomorphic. It invests inanimate objects—even if only metaphorically—with life and feeling; it endows them with human nature. What else is the "pathetic fallacy" than the projection of human sentiments onto natural phenomena? In such cases the distinction between man and

nature tends to disappear—and with it the sharp opposition between Eastern and Western aesthetic sensibility.

4

Most of the critical views we have examined thus far show a
decided bias toward Buddhist—or in a lesser degree, toward
Taoist—principles. Many a Western critic, in fact, has tended
to seek in Zen intuitionism the characteristic form of Oriental
aesthetics. By a series of non sequiturs (taking Chinese painting
as somehow representative of the entire "Asian imagination";
treating Buddhism as the dominant tradition in Chinese painting; emphasizing "Southern" Zen at the expense of other Buddhist sects; and, finally, overstressing the Taoist element in
Southern Zen), he manages to reduce Asian aesthetics to the
formula of spontaneity and sudden enlightenment. If there is a
Zen myth implicit in much recent art criticism, the responsibility
lies partly with the current Zen vogue in the West, partly with
the traditional categories of Far Eastern art history, and partly
with the persistence of anti-Confucian prejudices. The first of
these has engaged our attention already, in the discussion of
Oriental religion and philosophy. The second we shall consider
later in this chapter when we take up the theories of the Literary
Men. The third merits attention—partly because the current
overemphasis on Buddhist influences in art developed out of a
reaction against Confucian interpretations, and partly because
the reaction itself has gone too far. Since the beginning of this
century, when Ernest Fenollosa accused his contemporaries of
distorting Chinese and Japanese aesthetics through their Confucian bias, there has been a prevailing tendency to exaggerate
the Buddhist contribution to Far Eastern art and to underestimate that of Confucianism. Only very recently have art historians
begun to correct this imbalance.

For Fenollosa, the American scholar and art collector, who
resided in Japan from 1878 to 1890 and was subsequently curator

of the Department of Oriental Art in the Boston Museum of Fine Arts, most Sinologues were virtual accomplices in a mandarin conspiracy:

"How profoundly Chinese and Japanese civilizations in general, and art in particular, were gradually transformed by [the] quiet, pungent influence [of Buddhism] has never been written by any native scholar, and hardly even conceived by any European. . . . The standard works on Chinese life and culture almost ignore it. . . .

"The fact is that the whole influence of Confucian scholarship and influence, that is, the force of the whole Mandarin order, is implacably opposed to the spirit of Buddhism, and has been from the eighth century, and even before. This is why the views of Chinese history, and the estimate of relative values among institutions, derived through Chinese scholarship—and most of our Sinologues drink from that source—are entirely false in their prevailing attitude, in that Chinese scholarship, lying entirely in the hands of the Confucian literati, has always been violently partisan and antagonistic. . . . To write the history of the Chinese soul without seriously considering Buddhism would be like writing the history of Europe under the hypothesis that Christianity was a foreign and alien faith whose re-rooting in Western soil had been sporadic, disturbing, and on the whole deleterious."[14]

Fenollosa's anti-Confucian bias was as much political and social as aesthetic—though it is characteristic of him to phrase his indictment in aesthetic and spiritual rather than in purely political terms. In rereading his *Epochs of Chinese and Japanese Art,* one should bear in mind that it first appeared in 1912, the year of the fall of the Manchu dynasty and several years after his own death. His diatribes against the Confucian tradition should be interpreted in terms of this background; in this context they are, though not justifiable, at least understandable.

His attacks on the Confucian bureaucracy are, moreover, hardly more extreme than those of many Chinese "moderns" of his own generation. He raises many of the same charges against it, but broadens the indictment to include aesthetic as well as political offenses.

"What had happened in China," he declared, "was the complete loss of the early attempt in Ming to revive the anti-Confucian or Southern genius." Under the influence of "the conservative Confucian *literati*," Mongols and Manchus alike overthrew "that poetic Taoist and Buddhist idealism which has been the core of Chinese imaginative life. Of the more honest of those Confucians, it was no doubt a definite desire to make China into a moral machine, where every rite, ceremony, industry, and even thought should be conducted along pre-established formulae. Their ideal is uniformity; their standard is not insight but authority; their conception of literature is bounded by the dictionary; what they hate most is any manifestation of human freedom. Free thought with them was as horrid an anathema as with an eighteenth century New England Calvinist. . . . The modern Confucian government of China is a government of corrupt Puritans. . . ."

Or—to put it still more strongly—"the Mandarin class is China's Old Man of the Sea, a parasitic growth that chokes the life out of any effort at readaptation." It is the "hideous, cold, reptilian monster" that has given "the death crunch . . . to the Chinese soul."

This anti-Confucian bias is nowhere more evident than in Fenollosa's criticism of the Literary Men's painting (*wên-jên hua* or *bunjinga*). Though (like James Cahill) he recognized the strong Confucian element in this tradition, he turned it—characteristically—into an argument *against* the Confucians. The art of the literati was, in his opinion, altogether too Confucian. Repressive, formalistic, sterile, it represented another mandarin plot against the Chinese soul. Because "the whole Sung dynasty was a Chinese passionate protest against [the] crystallizing tyranny" of Confucianism, the "Tammany Mandarins" of the later Ming period dedicated themselves to eradicating its influence and substituting a "subversive . . . Confucian art, practically coterminous with . . . 'bunjinga.'" Mixed with "a barbarous Tartar and Thibetan Buddhism on the one hand, and with a Tartar realism and a Tartar love of crude ornament" on the other, this style "imposed itself upon the whole Manchu dynasty."

In the "free, blurry landscape art" of the four chief painters of the Yuan dynasty, the Confucians found a model—a style which "threw over all accurate knowledge of form, of varied effect in nature, to record only one style of feeling." A few "platitudes about old nature poetry were enough to quote. In such art and literature it was as if, because Shelley wrote a poem on a cloud, all future poets . . . should do the same thing."

For Fenollosa this art was "formless and woolly," and its very title ("literary") was enough to condemn it; for it was "rather a matter of thought and evolution than of visual imagination. It was as if we should write 'horse' under a child's drawing of a horse. To the merely literary mind, pictures are 'signs' of ideas— that is, another kind of 'word.' Of all that is involved in original line creation they know and care nothing." "In fact it can be said that the natural effect of the bunjinga theory is to obliterate the distinction between painting and handwriting. The drawn horse and the word 'horse' may be equally unpictorial."

In the Kanghsi period, he continues, the literati produced "a school of feeble landscape monochromes inherited from Ming. No longer understanding anything about line, its drawing is a travesty. Knowing nothing about notan, its spotting is cold and monotonous like the scrolls of written characters that were equally venerated. It is not unnatural that to the 'literary man' his poetical scroll and his symbolistic scrawl should hang side by side on the same wall." The *bunjinga* school triumphed "in the murder of Chinese art, and in the deification of the dead bones of formalism. . . ."[15]

Fenollosa's criticism—as dated as it is prejudiced—is largely conditioned by Western aesthetic ideals, the reaction against the traditional alliance of poetry and painting (embodied in the Horatian formula, *ut pictura poesis*) and the belief that art and society are so closely interconnected that a corrupt government must inevitably produce a degenerate art. The former bias makes him overlook the extent to which Chinese painting has been traditionally associated with poetry and calligraphy. The second blinds him to the merits of the Confucian tradition and leads him to read into "Confucian" painting all the vices of the Manchu dynasty. His remarks on the characteristics of *bunjinga* painting are not altogether inaccurate, however; he recognizes the qualities of the style, but judges them by criteria that are not strictly applicable. The final mark of his high-handed justice appears in the single illustration he reproduces in the text. Instead of a complete picture, he shows only a part—a fraction that really *does* appear "formless and woolly" and therefore supports his indictment. Indeed, he does not even bother to mention the title of the picture or the name of the artist; the illustration is simply an "Example of a 'Bunjinga' Landscape"![16]

Despite his protest against the high prestige of the Nanga— or *bunjinga*—school in Japan, his own views of Chinese painting were strongly influenced by Japanese archeologists. He saw Chinese civilization principally through Japanese eyes; and for all its personal eccentricity, his criticism retains a distinctly Japanese flavor. Today his consistent use of Japanese names for Chinese painters—Bayen for Ma Yuan, Rito for Li T'ang, Omakitsu for Wang Wei—sounds merely quaint. But it betrays the limitations of his approach to Chinese art.

Like Hearn, Fenollosa was highly subjective, intensely personal in his judgments; like Hearn, he reflected the attitudes and biases of his day. To blame him for these would be, in the literal sense of the word, impertinent. Despite his inaccuracies—and prejudices—he enriched immeasurably our understanding of the Far East. Just as Hearn possessed a rare and almost intuitive sympathy for Japanese culture (even though he never fully understood it), Fenollosa knew more about Oriental art than most Westerners and many Easterners of his generation—even though his judgments were marked by strong likes and dislikes. He despised the "literary man's painting" and applauded the meticulous but often uninspired craftsmanship of the Imperial Academy. He rapped the Buddhists sharply on the knuckles for "maundering on about 'the five noble truths'"—but he extolled Zen painting. He looked down on "plebeian art." He idolized the Kano school. He detested the Confucians. Nevertheless his very shortcomings as a critic make him all the more interesting as a writer; they contribute a distinctive flavor, if nothing else. His violent prejudices, like those of Dr. Johnson, sometimes possess an indubitable charm. Like Johnson, he is a prime example of a vanishing literary category—"the Critic as Curmudgeon."

5

Since Fenollosa's day the critical pendulum has swung to the opposite extreme; the imbalance in favor of Confucianism and to the disadvantage of Buddhism has been not so much rectified as reversed. His complaint—overstated even at the time he made it—has lost its original relevance; it may still serve, however, as an index of how profoundly critical attitudes have altered. Art historians have more than compensated for their earlier indifference to Buddhism; and many of them, in Europe and Asia alike, have greatly exaggerated the influence of Zen Buddhism in particular. Today, as a modern critic points out, it is "the role of Confucianism in the arts" which has suffered "neglect and distortion."[17]

In "most modern studies of Chinese painting," Dr. James Cahill observes, references to Confucian thought are "infrequent," "brief," and "unsympathetic." Critics tend to associate it with "dry academicism" in style or with a moralistic viewpoint equally arid— the doctrine that "by depicting exemplary themes" painting can "serve as a didactic tool or moralizing influence." Conversely, the same critics attribute to Taoism and Buddhism "all those views which involve the communication of intuitive knowledge, the operation of an aesthetic sense, or the embodiment of individual feeling."

In actuality, the "majority of poets and calligraphers" and "the great majority of painters who were philosophically committed at all . . . were Confucian scholars." Although the moralistic conception of art may have been the "dominant Confucian view in the Han dynasty," later Confucians recognized its aesthetic shortcomings and developed broader, more imaginative theories which gave greater scope to aesthetic values, subjective qualities, and the personality of the individual artist. Thus the "wên-jên *hua* theorists of the Northern Sung period"—the Literary Men who consciously painted as cultivated amateurs—succeeded in "finding for painting a means other than descriptive by which it might communicate the ineffable thoughts, the transient feeling, the very nature, of an admirable man, and so contribute to the moral betterment of those who see it." For these theorists "the import of the picture is primarily dependent not upon its subject, but upon the mind of its maker."

"The fundamental contention of the *wên-jên hua* theorists," in Cahill's opinion, "was that a painting is . . . a revelation of the nature of the man who painted it, and of his mood and feelings at the moment he painted it. Its expressive content therefore depends more upon his personal qualities and his transient feeling than upon the qualities of the subject represented." Painting is "a means of self-cultivation; and the products of this activity, as embodiments of the admirable qualities of cultivated individuals, serve a Confucian end in conveying those qualities to others."

In these views Cahill detects "Neo-Confucian attitudes toward the emotions and toward the proper modes of response to material things." Like the sage, the scholar-painter maintains his "inner equilibrium" and "essential composure." Avoiding "over-attachment" to natural objects, he is content merely to "lodge his mind" temporarily in them, without "allowing them, or his feelings toward them, to dictate the import of his pictures." Such Confucian virtues as sincerity and blandness controlled the creation and enjoyment of art. "A painting done by a cultivated man was a reflection of his sincerity." Like "the operations of Heaven and Earth," artistic creation was regulated by *li* (principle or natural order).

Though some of these ideals, such as "non-purposefulness" or "spontaneity," resemble Taoist and Ch'an Buddhist ideals, they are thoroughly in keeping with the eclectic character of Neo-Confucianism. As Cahill reminds us, "such ideas were by this time so thoroughly assimilated into Confucian thought that the Sung scholars had no need to turn to other sources for them."[18] A similar fusion of Taoist and Confucian principles characterized

the Six Essentials of Liu Tao-ch'un, who insisted not only that
"the brush should be handled with *tzu jan* (spontaneity)" but
also that "originality should not disregard the *li* (the principles
or essence) of things."[19]

"Confucianism," observes Dr. Sherman Lee, " . . . was not
merely a system of ethics for humans, but was a rational world
view of remarkable consistency. . . . Since the natural order or
principle (*Li*) pervades all things, all things are worthy subjects of attention. Further, since we can observe the fallibility of
man, the apparent infallibility of nature makes it *the* subject in
which *Li* can be shown in its purest form. The first full pictorial
expression of this rational attitude will be seen in the Northern
Sung period; but it was ever present in the minds of earlier
painters and critics. Thus the first most important of the six
pictorial canons listed by Hsieh Ho in the fifth century, 'anima-
tion through spirit consonance,' refers as much to a rational
correspondence of painting to principle as to mystic responsive-
ness to the Taoist Way of the Universe."[20]

In Miss Mai-Mai Sze's opinion, the prominence of *ssu*
(thought) in Ching Hao's Six Essentials probably reflects "neo-
Confucianist influence." The use of the term *yun* (rhythm) as
an alternate for *yun* (to revolve) in citing Hsieh Ho's first canon
may also "be taken as evidence of the Confucian viewpoint that
dominated art criticism." In her view, "this was inevitable, since
the background and training of painters and critics were basically Confucian," but the "results were both good and bad. . . .
Yun (harmony), the term that was used of sound and form, including rhythm, connotes a constructive and creative sense of
the harmony of the whole; but in application, owing to its
emphasis on order and correctness, it had the power to stifle that
most desired quality, *tzu jan* (spontaneity)."[21]

Such critics as these have helped to counterbalance the effects
of Fenollosa's antipathy to Confucianism and the Literary Men's
art. On the whole, however, the Confucian artists have found
few apologists and even fewer champions. In contrast to the
flood of volumes written by disciples of Zen, one would be hard

put to find a modern book on art composed by a "practicing" Confucian.

Though this bibliographical imbalance fosters an unbalanced conception of Far Eastern art, it is understandable. Though Confucianism may command their intellectual respect, Westerners do not accord it emotional assent. They do not turn to it as an answer to personal crises, as some of them have turned to Zen. Occidentals may study Confucianism, but they remain students, not converts. When they take up the study of Zen, however, they become, not infrequently, disciples or propagandists. To the art of the Far East they often bring the same preconceptions they bring to its philosophy. If they expect to encounter the "intuitive East" in Buddhist thought, they may also expect to meet it in Buddhist painting. Even though the attempt to "explain" Zen art and thought may seem like squaring the circle, even though the formidable bibliography on the subject seems to contract its basic principles, they remain undaunted by the paradox. From the exposition of the inexpressible they turn, in due course, to the iconography of the invisible.

6

Nevertheless the current overemphasis on Zen aesthetics cannot be blamed entirely, or even primarily, on the moderns. These have merely stumbled where Chinese art historians fell long before. Elements of the "Zen myth" (if we may call it that) have long been implicit in many of the fundamental categories of Far Eastern art criticism, and indeed in the aesthetic theories of the Literary Men themselves.

In the first place, the division between the Northern and Southern schools of Chinese painting—a conventional distinction in Far Eastern art history—derives from the division between Northern and Southern Ch'an (i.e., Zen), the former stressing gradual and the latter sudden enlightenment. As Osvald Sirén has observed, "this division of Ch'an Buddhism into two main schools became of particular importance to the art-historians in China," who took it as "the model for the presentation of the development of painting. . . . The parallelism between painting and philosophy was a construction made primarily to extoll the painters of the 'Southern School.' "

In the Ming period, the Chinese art historian Tung Ch'i-ch'ang made this distinction the "central topic" in his theory of land-scape painting, "the pivot around which his whole critical activity turns. The evolution of painting from the T'ang period down to his own time is considered in relation to this theory; the painters are arranged in the one or the other of the two camps in such a way that all those who, according to Tung Ch'i-ch'ang, repre-sent superior artistic qualities belong to the Southern, while the painters placed in the Northern school are denied all genius." To the Northern camp he assigned the members of the "so-called Chekiang school" and their "models and predecessors" in the Southern Sung Academy, "professional painters who were tied by formal rules and who lacked the 'gentleman spirit,' which expressed itself in a free and unprofessional creative activity."

In Sirén's opinion, this theory could hardly have been "estab-lished on the basis of actually existing stylistic differences." In fact, Tung and his group offered "very little evidence in this respect; their main argument is not formed by any kind of stylistic analysis but by philosophical speculations." Steeped in Ch'an Buddhism, they found it "natural to seek in the evolution of painting a similar division as that which had taken place in the history of Ch'an in the T'ang period. The characteristics of the Southern and the Northern schools of Ch'an were transferred to the Southern and Northern schools of painting, the former representing the free intuitive mode of creation, the latter a more formalistic intellectual approach to the problems of art."[22]

The division between Northern and Southern Ch'an also, ap-parently, influenced the history of Taoism. As Dr. Holmes Welch points out, the Taoist "Perfect Realization" sect similarly became divided into Northern and Southern schools, the one cultivating "life" and the other "nature"; the one seeking "physical im-mortality through *exterior* means," the other "seeking the realization of one's original nature by *interior* means." In his opinion, however, the distinction has been overstated, even if it is not largely arbitrary. The "classification into North and South," in turn, "was not based on geography, but arose by analogy with Ch'an Buddhism."[23]

Secondly, like the distinctions between Northern and Southern painting and Northern and Southern Taoism, the Literary Men's school has attracted a variety of myths. Tung Ch'i-ch'ang not only made "the term *wên-jên hua* . . . practically equivalent to the manner of the Southern school," but also regarded Wang Wei as the founder of both. This claim was "closely connected with the theory that he was the first to paint landscapes in the floating ink manner thereby suggesting atmospheric effects." Yet, as Sirén again points out, "the full development of this technique was accomplished only by Wang Hsia, who lived nearly a hundred years later. . . ."[24]

Recent criticism has also challenged other traditional claims of the Literary Men's school—notably its emphasis on the artist's amateur status and its tendency to understress the differences between Chinese and Japanese artists of this school.

Though the Literary Men claimed descent from the "Southern" school, "such distinctions [as several scholars observe] were very often quite arbitrary and meaningless." Though these painters were proud of their amateur status and scorned the professionals as mere technicians, it is "often extremely difficult to distinguish any difference in approach between the two streams of painting." Actually, as Professor Peter C. Swann suggests, "the distinction between professional and non-professional" is essentially economic and "seldom valid" for style.[25]

Theoretically (observes Professor Tokuzo Sagara) the Literary Man was a scholar-official of the mandarin class, who alternated between public and private life and "indulged in painting to satisfy his artistic urge." Eschewing the "artifice" and "technical devices" exploited by "professional artists of the art academy," he stressed spirit rather than technique—"a spirit becoming to a free and unfettered *bunjin*." As these ideas were introduced into Japan in the mid-Edo period, along with those of the Nanga (or "Southern") artists, the two became closely identified in Japan, just as they had long been associated in China. Nevertheless, as the social structure of Japan did not allow the existence of *bunjin* in the Chinese sense, the "most distinguished of the Nanga productions in Japan" are usually the works of career artists.[26] In Swann's opinion, moreover, the Japanese Nanga or *bunjinga* painters actually "contributed more original works than the Chinese."[27]

By overstressing the Buddhist and Taoist element in Far Eastern aesthetics, Western critics have not only slighted the Confucian tradition, but exaggerated the contrast between Asian and European concepts of nature and their significance for pictorial art. In art as in philosophy, criticism has tended to contrast Europe and Asia in terms of dualism and nondualism. It conceives Oriental art as an intuitive perception and spontaneous expression of the unity of subject and object; but it regards Western art as a labored, objective representation—as a "detached" art whose verisimilitude results from a fundamental distinction between subject and object.

For such criticism, Oriental art reflects the painter's awareness of his actual identity with the things he paints and his sense of oneness with nature, whereas Occidental art reflects his division from these objects and his alienation from nature. Upon this basic antithesis depends a whole cluster of related ideas— the contrast between internal and external resemblance, the dichotomy between expression and representation of nature, and the opposition between intuitive empathy and scientific detachment.

In the preceding pages we have traced the development of this "Buddhist stereotype" in Western art history and its impact on comparative criticism of European and Far Eastern art. In the next chapter we shall consider a further, but closely related aspect of the problem—the question of how far, if at all, Far Eastern art reveals an indebtedness to Buddhist theories of knowledge and reality.

xi

ART

AND PHILOSOPHY

――――――――――

. .

1

If art is indeed "a vision of reality," as Yeats declared, the artist's conception of reality and vision is significant for his art. If, as many critics assert, the Asian's views of knowledge and reality are fundamentally different from those of the West, one would expect this difference to be mirrored in his art forms. One would expect his literature and painting to reflect the unique qualities of his ontology and epistemology. One would expect to find in his architecture and music—in all of the arts—the same distinctions between conditioned and unconditioned reality, phenomenal and transcendental truth. His views on perception and inference, his conceptions of samadhi (superconsciousness) and satori (spiritual insight), his theory of "Suchness" (*Bhutatathata*) and "emptiness" (sunyata), his emphasis on immediate experience—all of these would, presumably, find expression in his aesthetic values. For art is "expression," if we believe Croce; "experience," if we agree with Dewey; and "cognition," if we follow the New Critics. Insofar as it is "aesthetic," or sensuous, it involves perception. Inasmuch as it is, in varying degrees, representational, it involves judgment or inference.

On the other hand, if Oriental views of the modes of knowledge and levels of reality do *not* differ radically from those of the West—if, in fact, they show striking resemblances in their epistemology and metaphysics—one may be skeptical about the profound spiritual or temperamental differences critics have discovered in Eastern and Western art. In the present chapter we shall be concerned not so much with similarities or differences between European and Asian art as with another facet of the "Buddhist stereotype" in Western art criticism—the tendency of many critics to overestimate the influence of Buddhist doctrines of knowledge and reality on Far Eastern aesthetics.

Buddhist theory draws a clear-cut distinction between direct and indirect knowledge—sense perception and rational inference—and an equally sharp division between the types of reality they cognize. The reality intuited by the senses is "instantaneous" —a succession of "point-instants." It is "kinetic"; "the essence of reality is motion." Though causality ("the interdependence of the moments following one another") may evoke "the illusion of stability or duration," these moments are really "forces or energies flashing into existence without any real enduring substance in them, but also without intervals or with infinitesimally small intervals." Both time and space, duration and extension, are unreal, and the universe is "a *staccato* movement." The only reality is "the efficient point-instant, all the rest is interpretation and thought-construction."[1]

This instantaneous reality is "dynamic" but it is also evanescent and impermanent; "the momentary thing represents its own annihilation." The "elements appear into life out of non-existence and return again into non-existence after having been existent" for a moment. "When a visual sensation arises . . ., there is absolutely nothing from which it proceeds, and when it vanishes, nought there is to which it retires."[2]

From another point of view, however, there is neither motion nor change nor evanescence; "just as annihilation, evanescence or change are not something real in superaddition to the thing changing or destroyed, but they are the thing itself,—just so is motion nothing additional to the thing, but it is the thing itself."[3]

To what extent does Oriental art reflect this view of reality? Mutability is undoubtedly a dominant motif of Far Eastern culture. Japanese No plays, Chinese elegiac verse, paintings of the seasons—all of these express the common theme of impermanency. The brevity of youth and beauty, the transiency of love and glory, the fragility of happiness—these are common themes in verse and romance. Chinese poetry is resonant with echoes of the past—vanished dynasties, half-forgotten warriors, and legendary beauties, the "pleasures of ruins." Japanese stage imagery evokes the poignancy of evanescence and the decay of noble houses, the parting of lovers symbolized by the shattered cherry blossoms and the falling *kiri* leaf.

For the Buddhists, as for Calderón and Shakespeare, life is a "dream" or a "play." The actors and their costumes are scarcely more substantial than the stage on which they play. The drama of Japanese life (as early Western observers saw it) was actually a No play, a poetic morality on the doctrine of impermanence. The stage and all its properties—houses, furnishings, costumes, implements of livelihood and means of adornment—were the most fragile and impermanent of materials: paper, straw, wood and bamboo. The substance of Japanese life was impermanence.

"Generally speaking," declared Lafcadio Hearn, "we construct for endurance, the Japanese for impermanency. Few things for common use are made in Japan with a view to durability. The straw sandals worn out and replaced at each stage of a journey; the robe consisting of a few simple widths loosely stitched together for wearing, and unstitched again for washing; the fresh chopsticks served to each new guest at a hotel; the light *shoji* frames serving at once for windows and walls, and repapered twice a year; the mattings renewed every autumn,—all these are but random examples of countless small things in daily life that illustrate the national contentment with impermanency."[4] So are the paper flowers that blossom briefly in water, the paper fan and the paper lantern, the bamboo cricket cage, the umbrella of oiled paper and bamboo, discarded after the shower.

Hearn continues: "Even in Japanese art—developed, if not actually created, under Buddhist influences—the doctrine of impermanency has left its trace. Buddhism taught that nature was a dream, an illusion, a phantasmagoria; but it also taught men how to seize the fleeting impressions of that dream, and how to interpret them in relation to the highest truth. And they learned well. In the flushed splendor of the blossom-bursts of spring, in the coming and the going of the cicadae, in the dying crimson of autumn foliage, in the ghostly beauty of snow, in the delusive motion of wave or cloud, they saw old parables of perpetual meaning."[5]

This doctrine, however, is neither distinctively Buddhist nor exclusively Japanese. It is no longer true that we in the West "construct for endurance." Instead, we build for "calculated obsolescence." Our houses are flimsy affairs; we do not intend them to last, and we erect them only to tear them down. We build not for centuries but for a few decades. We too build our civilization on paper, though less expertly than the Japanese—on paper or cellophane. Impermanency is as much a characteristic of our society as of Hearn's Japan—though we, of course, do not call it evanescence; instead, we term it progress.

The theme of mutability is as old as Western civilization itself —and the Greek and Hebrew cultures on which our society depends. On the one hand, we have Heraclitean flux, the *vita brevis* of Hippocrates, and the tragic insights of Homer and the Athenian dramatists. On the other, we have the elegiac melancholy that characterizes much Old Testament poetry. "All is vanity," and "all flesh is as grass." Man is "of few days"; "he cometh forth like a flower, and is cut down: he fleeth also as a shadow, and continueth not." If we look farther back, we can find the tragic sense of mortality in the literature of Sumer—in the epic of Gilgamesh.

The *ubi sunt* theme runs through Latin and Old English verse alike. "Where are the bones of Fabricius?" cries Boethius, and King Alfred transfers this lament to Weland. Man's "life on earth," declares one of King Edwin's councilors, is like a sparrow that flies out of the rain and snow into the king's fire-lit banqueting hall and out again, from winter into the winter, from storm into the storm. "Where now are the steed and the rider, and where the treasure-giver?" asks the Wanderer. "Here wealth is fleeting, friend is fleeting, and man himself is transitory." Medieval writers ring all the changes on the theme of the world's inconstancy; the complaint against Fortune remains for centuries one of the most fashionable of the literary genres. Villon descants on the vanished beauty of the aged Héaulmière and the "snows of yesteryear." Western art elaborates the Dance of Death—a motif that also belongs to the art of Tibet. Brueghel develops a Biblical image to portray the transiency of human life through the symbol of a hay wagon. Western poets employ the same images as Eastern writers to express the idea of impermanence— a bubble, a dewdrop, a cloud, a shadow, a dream, a shattered flower, the alternation of day and night, and the passing of the seasons. The motif of mutability receives its definitive statement from an English poet, Edmund Spenser, in his "Two Cantos of Mutabilitie" in *The Faerie Queene*.

The same theme runs also through Persian elegiac poetry, and its Victorian translators tend, if anything, to exaggerate it. It is in fact a global commonplace. Man has always been aware of his mortality and projected this awareness on the elements about him. It is not a peculiarly Buddhist insight nor is it exclusively Oriental.

There are, however, certain obvious differences in its context and its application. In the Christian West this motif was usually associated directly with the idea of Fortune (though this was a concept largely derived from Asia!) and indirectly linked with the idea of Providence. In the West, moreover, it was often specifically associated with ethical admonitions—warnings against ambition and avarice. "Why seek worldly rewards— wealth or fame or power?" many medieval writers were, in effect, arguing. "Like the world itself, these goods are transitory. Strive for imperishable rewards; seek eternal fame and incorruptible treasure in Heaven."

But this idea was not always taken so seriously. Not infrequently, it acquired a purely hedonistic significance; it became— in East and West alike—inseparably associated with the pursuit of sensual pleasure. The theme of impermanency became the *carpe diem* theme—an exhortation to "seize the day," to "gather . . . rosebuds while ye may" and extract the last ounce of pleasure from the passing moment.

In fact, the "fleeting world" became the mundane life—or indeed the life of the demimonde. The "floating world" of the Buddhist metaphor—mere flotsam and jetsam, a gourd floating on a stream—became the life of the "man of the world," the fashionable vices of the "man about town." This is the world of the ukiyoe prints—of Kabuki actors and Yoshiwara courtesans. Utamaro's Tokyo is essentially the same "floating world" as the Paris of Toulouse-Lautrec.

There are, to be sure, other affinities between Oriental art and the Buddhist theory of reality, but they appear to be largely fortuitous. The art of China and Japan is often intensely alive— animated by a high degree of movement and energy. Like the "reality" of the Buddhist logicians, it is "kinetic" and "dynamic." Not only is this true of beasts and birds and men. Landscapes are animated by waterfalls and rushing streams. The distorted forms of trees and stones show the force of the elements. The leaves of the iris and narcissus are twisted to suggest the organic force of their growth. The leaves of the bamboo reveal indirectly the movement of the wind. To a practiced eye, the very brush-strokes reveal the speed and the force of the hand that made them.

In a sense, therefore, a Chinese or Japanese painting approximates the Buddhist logician's conception of reality. Each brushstroke is "kinetic" and "dynamic" and corresponds to a "point-instant." The picture itself is the result of a succession of brushstrokes, just as reality consists in a succession of "point-instants." In both cases, moreover, the "interdependence" of the "moments following one another" produces the "illusion of stability," the illusion of an actual being. In reality, of course, neither exists.

Similarly, in its emphasis on energy and movement, Far Eastern painting comes close to the Buddhist philosopher's emphasis on "function" or activity as an essential part of the definition of any object. One would, logically, portray the wind as blowing, water as flowing, a bird as flying, a monkey as climbing, a horse as galloping—in fact, all objects in their characteristic activities.

Such a view is tempting, but since these characteristics of Chinese art antedate the introduction of Buddhism, it does not seem probable. At best it could merely provide rational support for practices already well-established in the native tradition or give clearer definition to the problems that faced a later generation of Buddhist or Taoist artists. Moreover, Western aesthetics placed a comparable emphasis on characteristic activity; this was a corollary of the principle of decorum.

Equally tempting are the analogies between the Buddhist denial of "stability" or "duration" and certain aspects of Chinese or Japanese art and music. If space and time, duration and extension, are unreal, why endeavor to portray them? Why trouble about the third dimension at all? Why bother about perspective to give landscape the appearance of space, or shading to give figures the appearance of solidity and stability—when this appearance is merely an illusion, when neither space nor stability actually exists? If Far Eastern painting often seems flat or "two-dimensional" in comparison with that of the West, it is because the artists themselves deny the reality of extension.

Many critics do, in fact, single out this aspect of Oriental painting as the feature that distinguishes it most sharply from that of the West. The absence of shading and perspective, they argue, points to a fundamental difference between Eastern and Western art, and this, in turn, exemplifies an equally basic distinction between the Oriental and Occidental temperament or "spirit." This distinction is one of the principal clichés in comparative criticism of Eastern and Western art; and, like other contrasts between Europe and Asia, it has been grossly exaggerated. Oriental painting does at times use gradations of color to suggest solid form even in monochrome paintings; and even in drawings based almost exclusively on line it does on occasion so manipulate the brush as to achieve degrees of shading in the same line and thus convey the idea of three-dimensional form. (The rendition of a pear or a bunch of grapes by almost any competent craftsman should illustrate this point.)

Finally, in the Buddhist conception of reality as a "staccato movement" of "point-instants," an observer could conceivably find parallels with Far Eastern music and the pointillist technique of several painters of the so-called "Southern School" in China. Yet as there is no evidence of direct influence, we must regard these analogies also as fortuitous.

2

Thus, despite its potentialities as the basis for an aesthetic theory, the Buddhist conception of instantaneous reality apparently exerted little influence on Far Eastern art. What of Buddhist epistemology? With its emphasis on sense perception as the source of direct knowledge and its stress on the "vivid" mental image produced in the observer, this too, one might expect, could provide a foundation for Oriental art. Yet in this case likewise one's expectation is disappointed.

In the first place, the appreciation of Oriental painting is not purely aesthetic. It demands an act of judgment as well as pure sensation. Unlike modern nonobjective painting, the traditional art of the Far East is objective; it depicts an object, and this demands an act of recognition—an act in which the mind intervenes and passes judgment on the sensation: "This is blue" or "This is a cat."

According to the Buddhist theory of perception, the moment of "pure sensation" (sense intuition) is immediately followed by a moment of "mental sensation" (intelligible intuition). A third "moment of cognition" stirs the memory. Then "the sensations fade away and the intellect constructs the abstract image according to its own laws."[6] This is the act of judgment, and it is the final stage in the process that converts pure sensation into knowledge.

Inasmuch as it evokes a "distinct image of the object," judgment is essential for knowledge. "(Pure) sense-perception," the Buddhist logician Dharmottara maintains, "becomes a (real) source of our knowledge only when it has elicited a judgment." This belongs properly to the understanding rather than the senses. Following the pattern "this is a cow," it unites sensation with conception, sense intuition with the "constructed image." It is a "thought construction."

Pure sensation, on the other hand, is not knowledge, since the observer is not conscious of the image; but it nevertheless bears a striking resemblance to the "undifferentiated" knowledge of the mystic. Indeed, Dharmottara argues that "in pure sensation . . . we are in touch with ultimate reality, with the uncognizable Thing-in-Itself." Another logician explains it more clearly and in greater detail:

> At the very first moment when an object is apprehended and it appears in its own absolute particularity, a state of consciousness is produced which is pure sensation. It contains nothing of that content which is specified by a name. Thereupon, at a subsequent moment, when the same object has been attentively regarded, the attention deviates towards the conventional name with which it is associated. After that, . . . the idea of its (enduring) existence and other (qualifications) arise; we then fix it in a perceptual judgment. [In the moment of pure sensation, however,] we can cognize (only) the bare presence of something undifferentiated by any of its qualifications.[7]

If Oriental art seriously aimed at "pure sensation," there would be some justification for stressing its "intuitive" and purely "aesthetic" character. But in fact it does not. Insofar as it is objective, it demands from its observer an act of judgment: the recognition that "this is a cow," "this is a cat," and so on. Instead of pausing at the "point-instants" which are the "ultimate reality" of "pure sensation," the spectator must take the further steps to invest them with name and form (namarupa) and cognize the "distinct image." Each step leads him nearer to knowledge but farther from pure sensation and intuition of reality.

In short, Oriental art, like most Western art, aims at the concept, the idea. It requires judgment in addition to sensation and "intelligible intuition."

In the second place, it frequently aims at the general rather than the particular, the universal rather than the individual. Here again it is essentially "conceptual" rather than "intuitive," according to the Buddhist theory of perception.

The object of direct knowledge, according to Dharmakirti, is the "extreme particular." "(Every) reality," his commentator explains, "indeed, has its real essence which is the particular (the unique) and a general (imagined aspect). . . . The directly perceived and the distinctly conceived are indeed two different things. What is immediately apprehended in sensation is only one moment. What is distinctly conceived is always a compact chain of moments cognized in a construction on the basis of sensation (e.g., 'this is blue'). And just this constructed synthesis of a chain of moments is (finally) realized by direct perception, because a unique moment can never be realized in a definite cognition."[8]

The particular is, in fact, the "exclusive object of sense-perception"; and it is responsible for producing a "mental image" in the observer—"a vivid (flash) of consciousness, if it is near, and a dim one, if it is . . . remote, but still amenable to the senses. . . ." This alone represents "ultimate reality."[9]

The Buddhist logician's conception of "general" and "particular" is rather more stringent than that of Western classical logic, as the former restricts the particular to pure sensation, not to the act of judgment. Nevertheless, even by Western criteria, the objects of Eastern art are often general rather than particular. If the artist paints a cat, he paints the "ideal" cat, not a particular animal. If he depicts a monkey, this is a "typical" monkey, not an individual example or even, as a rule, a particular species.

Furthermore, he often portrays objects from memory rather than from direct observation. Hence they are several steps removed from real "aesthetic" experience and the pure "intuition" of the senses. "When we mentally construct an absent object," Dharmottara declares, "we image it, we do not see it." Strictly speaking, such works are the product less of "seeing" than of "imagining"; and they result rather from "constructive (synthetic) thought" than from "direct cognition."[10]

Both Eastern and Western critics usually extol the "imaginative" and "intuitive" characteristics of Oriental art. By the classic Buddhist theory of knowledge, however, these two qualities are incompatible.

In fact, many of the characteristic virtues of Eastern art—the qualities usually emphasized by critics in Europe and Asia alike —actually remove it still further from pure sensation and "aesthetic" perception. Oriental painting and poetry (many critics insist —and with some justification) are allusive arts. Both prefer suggestion and nuance rather than direct presentation. To portray a mountain temple one depicts a solitary monk in the wilderness —nothing more. To suggest the autumn one portrays falling maple leaves; to suggest the winter one depicts plum blossoms in the snow. Moreover, these are often symbolic arts. They present abstract concepts concretely and indirectly through symbols. The crane and the pine and the deer denote longevity. Orchid and bamboo signify the virtuous man. Rocks and waves symbolize stability and flux.[11] Finally, both arts tend toward radical simplification and understatement. A single dot or an angular line may represent a distant bird. The blank space in a picture may represent an expanse of water or sky, a lawn, or a layer of mist. The entire meaning of a poem may be focused in a single poetic image. Far Eastern art relies, in large part, on symbolic resonance, on the eloquence of what is left unsaid; it makes its point by implication.

This criticism is, in large part, true. Nevertheless, in the strictest sense, these qualities are not purely "aesthetic." They pertain, on the whole, to imagination rather than pure sensation; they involve concepts and perceptual judgment. They are, by Dharmakirti's standards, direct knowledge, but they are not pure intuition. In other cases, however, they are not direct but indirect knowledge, for they demand an act of inference on the part of the observer. Confronted with the picture of a monk in the wilderness, the spectator must infer for himself the presence of the unseen monastery. This form of inference does not differ essentially from the standard example in Buddhist logical treatises—"where there is smoke there is fire."

Oriental painting is not, on the whole, "intuitive" in Dharma-kirti's sense of the word. It does not confine itself to sense impressions. On the contrary, it is representational. Like Western art, it depicts objects and imitates ideas.

Yet perhaps both Western and Oriental theorists have exaggerated the distinction between sense data and ideas. Perhaps perception and inference cannot be divorced as sharply as Plato and Dharmakirti thought they could. If the Gestaltists are correct, the very act of perception often involves an ideal "construction"; in a cluster of dots, the observer perceives a form, an idea —a triangle, a circle, a square. The same principle applies to Rorschach cards; one perceives a nonexistent bear or gourd or peony—or what not—in an inkblot. Pure perception or pure sensuousness in art is usually a myth. (Even in nonobjective paintings, the observer detects *patterns* of color and mathematical forms.)

Finally—in view of the exaggerated statements sometimes made about the intent and content of Oriental art—it seems necessary to emphasize an obvious truism. Regardless of what symbols or images it employs, Oriental art can portray neither "Suchness" nor "satori"—neither the ultimate "undifferentiated" reality nor the "undifferentiated" knowledge whereby it is apprehended. Since this lies beyond name and form (*namarupa*), it is beyond the reach of pen or brush; neither poet nor painter can express it. At most, he can merely suggest the "idea" either through poetic imagery or through visual symbolism—and the idea itself is, of course, painfully inadequate, a mental "construction" that obscures the truth. Images of the primeval Adi-Buddha, the cosmic Buddha Vairocana, or the Dharmakaya may be useful aids to meditation, but they are not intended as either representations or expressions of ultimate reality. Unfortunately, Western critics sometimes ignore this point. Thus Professor Northrop attaches the label "undifferentiated aesthetic continuum" to a painting of the Buddha. This designation would seem contradictory to most Buddhists, since it imposes name and form on what is by nature nameless, formless, and devoid of qualities. Indeed, it is one of the primary reasons why a Zen monk chopped up a Buddha image into firewood.

The apparently negligible influence of Buddhist epistemology seems all the more striking in contrast with Buddhism's profound impact on Oriental art in other respects. The legends of the Jatakas, episodes in the life of the Buddha as recorded by Ashvaghosha, the complex pantheon of Mahayana mythology, dominate Buddhist art from India to Japan. In fact, the spread of Indian styles and motifs in painting and sculpture through Central and South Asia into the Far East accompanies the spread of Buddhist doctrine. Indeed, the doctrines themselves find pictorial expression—the wheel of samsara and the wheel of dharma (the Law), karma and the rewards or penalties of the afterlife. Asian art is rich in these visible or tangible signs of Buddhist influence, but it does not show significant indebtedness to the Buddhist theory of knowledge.

Though the Buddhist epistemology possessed undeniable potentiality for an aesthetic theory, its actual influence on Asian art must remain purely conjectural. It does not seem to have had much impact on Buddhist art in India; and in China Taoism appears to have been far more significant—even in the case of Ch'an (or Zen) Buddhism. This would not be surprising, since both of these countries, unlike Tibet, had only a limited knowledge of Indian logic.

Though Taoism lacked many of the characteristic traits of Indian Buddhism—its philosophical subtleties, its complex theory of knowledge and perception, and its elaborate metaphysical speculations—they shared certain traits in common—a dedication to quietism, meditation, and nonviolence; a belief that ultimate reality was "unutterable" and transcended all qualifying attributes and contradictions; an emphasis on "the Void" and emptiness; and a tendency to interpret the phenomenal world in terms of a "universal flux." Yet they differed in their approach. Buddhism brilliantly demonstrated the doctrine of the Void, marshaling all the resources of logic; Taoism practiced it. Though Buddhist philosophy denied the existence of the soul,

Buddhist spirituality actually fell within the category of "soul mysticism"; Taoism, on the other hand, like Shinto, belonged to "nature mysticism." The two currents would, however, eventually meet in Zen.

However impressive the contribution of Buddhist legend, symbol, and myth to Far Eastern art, the impact of Buddhist theories of knowledge and reality is more difficult to trace. Several Western critics have insisted that Eastern art is oriented toward the general idea rather than the particular, and that this orientation is specifically Buddhist. Yet, as we have observed, Buddhist logicians often assign higher priority to knowledge of particulars rather than of universals. Though these logicians also entertained a conception of "instantaneous" reality that has affinities with the (later) Zen ideal of "instant enlightenment," it is difficult to demonstrate that the epistemology and ontology of the great Indian Buddhist logicians ever influenced Chinese and Japanese painting. The Zen artist's delight in "spontaneity" and his ideal of "catching Spirit (i.e., Tao) as it moves" actually derive from Taoism rather than from Buddhist logical theory. Even though several Western critics claim to find Buddhist principles of knowledge exemplified in Far Eastern painting, any positive indebtedness is still purely conjectural. One wonders, indeed, whether such interpretations have more validity than Stoic and Neo-Platonic readings of the *Odyssey* or medieval Christian allegorizations of Virgil and Ovid.

Thus far we have traced the myth of Asia in philosophy and religion and in the visual arts. In the final section of this book we shall examine its persistence in political and social theory.

PART FOUR

Politics

xii

THE

EASTERN DESPOT

━━━━━━━━━━━━━━

• •
•

1

The spiritual East—and yet the sensual East. The ascetic East—
and yet the gorgeous East. The militant East—but also the
decadent East. The cradle of civilization—yet also the heartland
of barbarism.

These violently contrasting images have grown too familiar to
surprise us. Having heard them since childhood, we accept them
as axiomatic, and exempt them from the laws of contradiction.
As with our other prejudices, we require our stereotypes of the
Orient to be expressive rather than consistent. Moreover, these
paradoxes are based on altogether different aspects of Asia—
different classes, different epochs, different countries, different
systems of government. We should not marvel, therefore, at still
another contradiction equally violent—the contrast between the
Oriental contemplative and the Oriental despot.

Like most clichés about the East, "Asiatic despotism" is a
term richer in overtones than in meaning. The Oriental despot
is, in fact, a tyrant of the imagination. He reigns with foremost
authority in the realms of fiction. The secrets of the seraglio,
the intrigues of eunuchs, the avarice of corrupt bureaucrats, the
extravagance of court ceremonials that barely fall short of idola-
try, the arbitrary cruelties of overcivilized princes and barbaric
conquerors, palace revolutions achieved by parricide—all of

these have loomed large in the imagination of the West. In the Black Hole of Calcutta, the Sepoy Mutiny, the massacre at Kandy, and similar atrocities, Europeans saw the characteristic perfidy and brutality of Oriental tyrants. In Marlowe's Tamburlaine, whose chariot was drawn by conquered kings ("pampered jades of Asia!") and who spurned a vanquished emperor as his footstool, they beheld not simply a dramatic emblem of Fortune but a vivid image of the Asiatic despot. In the Scriptures they encountered still more sinister examples of Oriental tyranny, despots who aggravated their crimes by affecting divine honors, violating the laws of humanity and the precepts of the true religion, or oppressing the holy community—the kings of Egypt and Assyria, Antioch and Babylon.

The fullest development of this myth belonged, however, not to the poet or the theologian but to the political economist and the historian. It was they who took this cliché with the greatest seriousness. It was they who developed it into a coherent theory, provided it with a rational explanation, and placed it—or attempted to place it—on a scientific basis. By their analysis of land tenure, taxation, and irrigation systems, their theories of surplus value, their insistence on the interrelationship between government and agriculture, and their arguments for the determinative influence of climate on society, they made the role of the Eastern despot seem historically and geographically inevitable. It is chiefly to their researches that the modern historian owes his ideas of the Orient's distinctive "hydraulic civilization," and it was largely on their foundation that the early Marxist constructed his myth of an anomalous Oriental society: a political and economic despotism—neither feudal, capitalist, nor proletarian—which did not seem to fit his categories of social evolution.

In their attitudes toward the governments of Asia, Western observers exhibit as great a diversity as in their opinions of Oriental religion and art. In the Persian monarchy, Herodotus and Aeschylus saw an absurd though dangerous autocracy that had wantonly sacrificed whole armies to gratify the overweening ambitions of one man. Yet in an earlier monarch of the same dynasty (Cyrus, the ancestor of both Darius and Xerxes), Xenophon recognized a political ideal from which the Greeks themselves had much to learn. The same diversity characterized eighteenth-century attitudes toward China. Where one French or British philosopher condemned its government as static, tyrannical, and corrupt, another extolled it as a rational and well-ordered state, a benevolent despotism that might advantageously serve as a pattern for modern European states.

For a spokesman of the Enlightenment, like Voltaire, the contrasts between Eastern and Western societies indicated the relativity of cultural values and the absurdity of national or sectarian intolerance. Confronted by such wealth of national or regional customs—some laudable, some reprehensible, many of them absurd—the citizen of the world contemplated them all with skeptical good humor. The only constant elements in human society were, apparently, the principles of justice and reason. All else seemed relative; neither the religion, the philosophy, nor the social conventions of any particular culture could serve as a universal and absolute standard of conduct or belief. Observing other societies with mixed amusement and admiration, the *philosophe* remained a detached spectator and accorded them the same observer's privileges—acknowledging their right to take a similar attitude toward his own culture and delighting in the notion of how quaint, how exotic, and how ridiculous French or British customs must seem to Chinese or Persian eyes.

A later generation of philosopher-historians, however, would contemplate these regional differences with rather less amusement and certainly far less skepticism. For the transcendental idealist of the late eighteenth and early nineteenth centuries, they represented different stages in the evolution of human society and distinct phases in the development of the "world process" and the manifestation of the "world spirit." For the tough-minded social historian, oriented toward Darwin or Marx, these phases obeyed scientific laws. Their causes were material, not spiritual; mechanical rather than purposive. They could best be accounted for, accordingly, on a mechanistic and materialistic basis—in terms of physical and economic laws. Already fashionable in the natural sciences, determinism reshaped the social sciences. Man's social evolution complemented his biological evolution and obeyed similar laws. A Darwinian preoccupation with heredity and environment encouraged some to exaggerate the importance of race and climate, while reliance on Marxian economic theory persuaded others to overstress the role that diverse methods of production and distribution had played in fostering cultural differences.

In varying degrees each of these theories made its own contribution to the myth of the Oriental despot. From Aristotle's contemptuous observations on Asian monarchy to the Marxist's equally disparaging view of Oriental society, "Eastern despotism" has been a familiar concept in the Western vocabulary. For many writers it has seemed so obviously true that it required no explanation. But others *have* tried to explain it, and it is the variety of their explanations that must concern us now.

2

Corruptio optimi pessima. "The worst of all corruptions is the corruption of the best." For Aristotle, the rule of one man was potentially the best and worst of all forms of government, since it held the greatest possibility for good or evil. "Just as a royal rule, if not a mere name, must exist by virtue of some great personal superiority in the king, so tyranny, which is the worst of governments, is necessarily the farthest removed from a well-constituted form." Among the Asiatics, Aristotle recognized a type of despotism that particularly befitted the Oriental disposition—a form of monarchy that "nearly resembles tyranny" but is nevertheless both "legal and hereditary." Since barbarians are "more servile in character than Hellenes, and Asiatics than Europeans," they do not "rebel against a despotic government. Such royalties have the nature of tyrannies because the people

are by nature slaves; but there is no danger of their being over-
thrown, for they are hereditary and legal." The characteristic
monarchy of "the barbarians" is, accordingly, a "hereditary
despotic government in accordance with law."[1]

Aristotle's authority as a political theorist helped to perpetuate
the notion of Asian servility; from the Renaissance down to our
own times most men with a classical education have been familiar with his view, even though some of them have questioned
it. He did not, however, try to explain its *cause*. With the eighteenth century, however, this became a problem of increasing
concern to political historians.

To Montesquieu, whose *De l'esprit des lois* was published in
1748, the primary causes of Eastern despotism were geographical
—or, more specifically, climatic. Unlike Europe, Asia lacked a
temperate zone, and the character and disposition of her peoples
exhibited the same fierce extremes as her climate. Temperament,
it would seem, varied in direct proportion to temperature. In
Europe "strong nations are opposed to strong"; in Asia strong
are opposed to weak. The "warlike, brave, and active people"
in Asia "touch immediately upon those who are indolent, effeminate, and timorous; the one must, therefore, conquer and
the other be conquered." This is the "grand reason of the weakness of Asia and of the strength of Europe; of the liberty of
Europe, and of the slavery of Asia." It is the reason why Rome
could subdue Asia with "ease and facility," but could conquer
Europe only with great difficulty. It is the reason why Asia has
been subdued thirteen times in the course of history: "eleven by
the northern nations, and twice by those of the south."

A second "physical cause" of Asia's slavery and Europe's
liberty was to be found in topography. Because Asia possesses
larger plains than Europe, she has herself been possessed by
greater empires. "Power in Asia ought . . . to be always despotic:
for if their slavery was not severe they would make a division
inconsistent with the nature of the country." In contrast to
Europe's "genius for liberty" Asia displays a "servile spirit,"
which its inhabitants have "never been able to shake off." In all

the histories of Asia it is impossible to find "a single passage which discovers a freedom of spirit"—impossible to "see anything there but the excess of slavery."[2]

Whereas Aristotle had opposed Asian despotism to Greek freedom and Montesquieu had opposed it to European liberty, Edward Gibbon, whose *History of the Decline and Fall of the Roman Empire* was published between 1776 and 1788, contrasted it with the "moderate and comprehensive policy" of Rome. "Domestic peace and union," he declared, "were the natural consequences" of Roman government. In the monarchies of Asia, on the other hand, "we . . . behold despotism in the centre and weakness in the extremities, the collection of the revenue or the administration of justice enforced by the presence of an army, hostile barbarians established in the heart of the country, hereditary satraps usurping the dominion of the provinces, and subjects inclined to rebellion though incapable of freedom." The "obedience of the Roman world," however, was "uniform, voluntary, and permanent."[3]

For the British economist, Richard Jones, whose *Peasant Rents: An Essay on the Distribution of Wealth and on the Sources of Taxation* was published in 1831, but continued to influence political and economic theory throughout the nineteenth century, a characteristically Asiatic system of land tenure was chiefly responsible for the continent's despotic governments. "Throughout Asia the sovereigns have ever been in the possession of an exclusive title to the soil of their dominions." The ruler himself is the sole proprietor, and the people "universally" his tenants. Though similar rights once prevailed in Europe, they were "soon moderated, and finally disappeared." In Asia, on the other hand, they have survived "undivided" and "unimpaired." This "universal dependence on the throne for the means of supporting life . . . is the real foundation of the unbroken despotism of the Eastern world, as it is of the revenue of the sovereigns, and of the form which society assumes beneath their feet."

The economic basis of Asian despotism was thus, in Jones's opinion, the system of ryot rents. "Produce rents paid by a laborer, raising his own wages from the soil, to the sovereign as its proprietor," these had traditionally been "peculiar to Asia," but had subsequently been "introduced by Asiatics" into European Turkey.

Throughout contemporary Asia (i.e., in 1831) the sovereign's claim to the soil rested on his rights as conqueror. China, India, Persia, Turkey—all of the great empires on the periphery of the continent had at one time or another been subdued by nomadic barbarians from central Asia. "Wherever these Scythian invaders have settled, they have established a despotic form of government, to which they have readily submitted themselves, while they were obliging the inhabitants of the conquered countries to submit to it." This autocratic system prevailed in "all the great empires of Asia," but exhibited "distinct modifications in each; arising from differences in the climate, soil, and even government. . . ." Monolithic though it be, even despotism was subject to change and variety.

The responsibility for enforcing this system—and perhaps for originating it—rested with the Tatars of Central Asia, whose hard lives had inured them to "habits of military submission." Throughout Asia they had "either adopted or established a political system which unites so readily with their national habits of submission in the people, and absolute power in the chiefs; and their conquests have either introduced or re-established it, from the Black Sea to the Pacific, from Pekin to the Nerbudda."

The economic and political effects of despotism, Jones insisted, had been almost invariably pejorative. It had consistently stunted the growth of capital, prevented the development of intermediate and independent classes, and—in short—paralyzed society. Great and little alike, in the despotic state, were "literally what they describe themselves to be, the slaves of that master on whose pleasure the means of their subsistence wholly depend." In the absence of powerful landed proprietors and independent townspeople, the sovereign encountered no check to his power anywhere in the society beneath him. Since he was "supreme proprietor of a territory cultivated by a population of ryot peasants," the whole population was compelled to look to him as the sole source of protection and subsistence. "He is by his position and necessarily a despot."[4]

In the opinion of William Mackinnon, whose *History of Civilization* (published in 1846) was frequently cited by later cultural historians and helped to shape Western opinion of Asian economics and politics, most Asian peoples had accepted despotic governments not through internal inclination, as many Western observers believed, but by external force. They obeyed tyrants not because they liked to obey but because they were compelled to. Nevertheless, for peoples so deficient in the "requisites of civilization" and so "besotted with immorality," this was probably the best form of government they could hope to have. "From the earliest times . . . to the present hour, the Asiatics have groaned under despotism of the most grievous kind, imposed on them by various conquerors"—Romans, Saracens, Turks, and Tatars. Except for a few nomadic tribes, "pure and unmixed despotism" was paramount over Asia; "slavery . . . of mind and body was universal." The "lives and property of whole communities" lay at the "entire disposal of their sovereign"; even the "form of religion he dictated was implicitly professed."

The causes of Oriental despotism, Mackinnon believed, were both economic and moral. In nearly all Asiatic governments the sovereign himself was regarded as the legal "proprietor of the land." The cultivators were thus utterly dependent on a master who could at will "deprive them of food" and arbitrarily dismiss or replace them. This right was the real basis and "formal foundation of his absolute power." Even more important than economics were ethical factors. "Whence does it happen that such a population has . . . been . . . steeped in ignorance, barbarism, and slavery?—that man has been treated not as a human being? Simply because the essential requisite for civilisation, moral principle, has been wanting. The eternal law of justice has been lost sight of. . . ."[5]

John Stuart Mill, in turn, whose *Principles of Political Economy* was published in 1848, emphasized the degree to which the luxury, monumental architecture, and public works of Oriental empires had depended on the sovereign's control over his production and distribution of wealth. By stripping food surpluses from the actual cultivators and redistributing it among government functionaries and royal favorites, he was able to finance the extravagances of the royal household, maintain his palace guards and his armies in the field, carry out whatever works of public utility (tanks, wells, irrigation canals) his "liberality and enlightened self-interest" might suggest—or, alternatively, invest in such monumental and "durable" edifices as the Pyramids and the Taj Mahal.

Since the regime usually stripped the cultivators of everything except the bare "necessaries" of life, it was able to make "a show of riches quite out of proportion to the general condition of the society." Hence the European's "inveterate" but usually erroneous "impression . . . concerning the great opulence of Oriental nations." This radical and systematic appropriation of surplus wealth by the government was "characteristic of the extensive monarchies which from a time beyond historical record have occupied the plains of Asia."[6]

For Thomas De Quincey, the barbaric and despotic character of the Orient was nowhere more evident than in that humiliating act of deference—the kowtow. Writing on "The Chinese Question in 1857," he castigated the Manchu court for demanding so slavish a form of homage ("genuflexions, prostrations, and knockings of the ground nine times with the forehead") from a British ambassador. Nevertheless this "hideous degradation of human nature has always disgraced the East." Even in the days of Darius and Xerxes "this very abject form of homage" was already firmly established, and Persia herself had undoubtedly inherited it from still older courts, the throne rooms of Nineveh and Babylon. The "Moloch vassalage" that the Chinese despot had attempted to impose on the West was characteristic of Oriental society. "That no Asiatic state has ever debarbarised itself is evident from the condition of WOMAN at this hour all over Asia. . . ."[7]

Later in the century a series of influential writers—journalists, editors, authors of universal histories, philosophies of history, and histories of civilization—attempted to trace the causes of

Asian despotism to psychological or geographical characteristics, to heredity or environment, to physical or metaphysical laws. For Henry Thomas Buckle, whose *History of Civilization in England* (published between 1857 and 1861) was highly regarded during the latter part of the nineteenth century, the despotic character of Oriental societies—like that of pre-Columbian America—had been largely determined by natural forces. It resulted primarily from "certain physical causes" (notably climate and soil) that had favored the accumulation of wealth but had hindered a "just subdivision of it." Like Mexico and Peru, India and Egypt were unable to diffuse "even that scanty civilization which they really possessed." They shared the same "utter absence of any thing approaching to the democratic spirit," the same "despotic power on the part of the upper classes, and the same contemptible subservience on the part of the lower." The "peculiarities of climate, and of food" in India were responsible for that country's "redundant" labor market, its "unequal distribution of wealth," and its "corresponding inequality of social and political power." "Pinched by the most galling poverty," the majority of the Indian people had always remained "in a state of stupid debasement, broken by incessant misfortune, crouching before their superiors in abject submission, and only fit either to be slaves themselves or to be led to battle to make slaves of others."

The very fertility of the country had paradoxically increased the abject condition of the people. The very "cheapness and abundance of the national food" had made interest rates and rents excessively high, and wages excessively low. Thus by "physical laws utterly impossible to resist," the majority of the Indian population had been doomed to accept "abject, eternal slavery" as their "natural state."[8]

Another historian of civilization, Amos Dean—an American lawyer and prolific writer whose *History of Civilization* was published in 1868–69—regarded Asiatic society as "in the extremest degree, despotic; fettering body, mind and soul." In India religion and morality had led to "general inaction," and the caste system had transformed "the entire social fabric into a bed for Procrustes." Government and religion, exhibiting their "worst possible forms," exercised a perpetual tyranny over the human mind; Asian government had reduced man to a slave, Asian religion had made him a mere "creature of destiny." Oriental history was simply "an unbroken succession of despotisms."

In Europe alone, Dean continued, do we first encounter freedom, the "great and chief element of activity in man." To turn from Asia to Greece was to "proceed from inertia to action; from where man was nothing to where he is everything; from despotism to democracy. . . ."[9]

Meredith Townsend, editor of *The Spectator* (of London), was long a resident of India, edited a journal there entitled *The Friend of India* in the 1850's, and had considerable influence on Britain's Indian policies. Though admittedly more sympathetic to Asian values and institutions, he also traced the roots of Oriental despotism to the religious attitudes of the East. The "keynote of the Asiatic mind" was a "habitual and willing submission to the supernatural, even when the decrees of the supernatural are not utilitarian." This attitude was largely responsible both for the "separateness of Asia" and for its despotic governments. "There is . . . in the Asiatic mind a special political and a special social idea. It is not by accident that the European desires self-government, and the Asiatic to be governed by an absolute will. The European holds government to be an earthly business . . . and accordingly he either governs himself directly, or he frames a series of laws which nobody, not even the King, is at liberty to break through." The Asiatic, on the other hand, "holds that Power is Divine, and that a good king ought to be enabled to 'crush the bad and nourish the good,' . . . without check or hindrance." Hence throughout history the Asiatic "invariably sets up a despotism, and when . . . the despot strikes him down, bows to the decree. . . ." Even under an oppressive and unjust government he refuses to "quarrel with God's representative on earth."[10]

With Hegel and Marx, Oriental despotism acquired philosophical significance; it belonged to the dialectic of history.

Hegel's *Philosophy of History* was, by his own confession, a theodicy, "a justification of the ways of . God," in which he attempted to demonstrate that "Reason directs the World" and that "Universal History" is essentially "the exhibition of Spirit in the process of working out the knowledge of that which it is potentially." In his view, accordingly, Oriental despotism was a necessary phase in the evolution and self-revelation of the cosmic Spirit in realizing the ideal of liberty. For "the History of the world is none other than the consciousness of Freedom." In its progress toward this ideal, the World Spirit had passed successively from China through India and Persia to Greece, Rome and finally to "the German world."

"The Orientals," Hegel maintained, "have not attained the knowledge that Spirit—Man *as such*—is free; and because they do not know this, they are not free. They only know that *one is free*. But on this very account the freedom of that one is only caprice; ferocity—brutal recklessness of passion, or a mildness and tameness of the desires, which is itself only an accident of Nature—mere caprice like the former. That *one* is therefore only a Despot; not a *free man*." Hence "the Eastern nations knew only that *one* is free; the Greek and Roman world only that *some* are free; while *we* know that all men absolutely (man *as man*) are free." Oriental despotism thus belonged to the childhood of human society, Greco-Roman polity to its youth and maturity, and modern European government to its old age.[11]

A curious feature of this theory was its mixture of new philosophical methods and old geographical myths. The framework of Hegel's historical dialectic belonged to German transcendentalism, but its content reflected the old tradition that the course of civilization and empire moves from east to west, following the course of the sun. This belief had been conventionally associated with astrological superstition and with the Biblical motif of the Four Monarchies (the transition of empire from Babylon and Assyria to Persia, and thence to Greece and Rome). One is not surprised to find it in Dante or even in Sir Walter Raleigh—but it is strange to encounter it as late as Hegel.

Hegelian idealism and Marxist materialism were poles apart, but both systems shared the conception of history as a dialectical process. Society evolved, they insisted, by creating and resolving contradictions. In both systems Oriental despotism constituted an inevitable stage in man's social development; it was historically—and indeed metaphysically—determined.

For Hegel, however, the forces that created Oriental despotism were spiritual and purposive; for Marx, they were mechanical and material. For Hegel, Asian autocracy was a necessary precondition of Western society—an earlier stage in the development of the same social organism. It bore the same relation to Western society as the child to the old man or the caterpillar to the butterfly. It was not a different line of development so much as an earlier phase in the same line of development.

For Marx, on the other hand, and for many of his disciples, it represented an altogether different species, genetically distinct from Western society. Responding to the pressure of class conflicts, Europe had developed progressively from feudalism through capitalism toward socialism. It had not, however, passed through a despotic stage comparable to that of Asia. Despotism remained, therefore, a social phenomenon primarily characteristic of Oriental societies and—as certain later writers maintained—the ancient empires of Mexico and Peru.

"In the 1850's," declares Karl Wittfogel, author of *Oriental Despotism: A Comparative Study of Total Power* (1957) and a leading authority on "hydraulic civilization," "the notion of a specific Asiatic society struck Marx with the force of a discovery." Building largely on the foundation left by British classical economists—Richard Jones, Adam Smith, James and John Stuart Mill—Marx contrasted the institutions of Asian and European societies, along with their modes of production and distribution. In his opinion, both India and China possessed characteristically "Asiatic" institutions. Arguing that "climate and territorial conditions" had made "irrigation by canals and water works the basis of Oriental agriculture," Marx traced the origin of the Oriental form of society to the "need for government-directed water works." Characteristic of the "Asiatic mode of production" was the "'dispersed' condition of the 'Oriental people' and their agglomeration in 'self-supporting' villages (combining small agriculture and domestic handicraft). . . ." The Oriental state was essentially a system of "general slavery."

In his youth Lenin held similar views. Refusing to equate European and Asiatic institutions, he too denounced "the cursed heritage of bondage of the *Aziatchina* and the shameful treatment of man" it entailed. He too stressed "the peculiarity of 'the Oriental system,' the 'Asiatic system,' and the stagnation of the Orient." Distinguishing the Asiatic mode of production from the ancient, feudal and "modern bourgeois" systems of the West, he defined "Asiatic despotism" as a "totality of traits" with special "economic, political, and sociological characteristics."

Throughout the 1920's prominent Soviet officials continued to develop the notions of a specifically Asiatic society and an "Asiatic mode of production." As late as 1925 the Hungarian economist Evgeny Varga maintained that the basis of Chinese society was to be found in "government-controlled productive and protective water works" and that China's real ruling class was the bureaucracy of "scholarly administrators" rather than the landowning class.

Under Stalinist influence, the theory of a specifically Oriental society was condemned in 1931—partly on the grounds that it might encourage Asian nationalists to "reject the doctrinal authority of the Comintern" and that it represented the capitalist West as "capable . . . of constructive action." Instead of "Asiatic" and "semi-Asiatic" societies, the orthodox now spoke of "feudalism." Outside Russia, however, the "Asiatic-hydraulic interpretation of Oriental civilization" survived well into the 1940's.

Despite the influence of the "Asiatic-hydraulic" theory on such writers as Chi Ch'ao-ting and the Indian Marxist R. P. Dutt, the majority of Asian socialists and communists have (in Karl Wittfogel's opinion) been indifferent to Marx's views on Asiatic society. In discussing Chinese political and economic history, Mao Tse-tung has usually preferred to label the traditional society "feudal" rather than "Oriental."[12]

The concept of Asian despotism is, however, far from dead.

Despite official disfavor on the part of the Comintern and indifference on the part of Asian socialists, the theory of the "Oriental society" is still a controversial issue in the academic—if not in the political—forum. Wittfogel still insists on the "peculiarity" of this "non-Western semi-managerial system of despotic power" and on the need for interpreting "Communist totalitarianism as a total managerial, and much more despotic, variant of that system." His recent publications in this field follow many of the same principles that guided him in the early 1930's, when he attempted "to determine the peculiarity of Chinese economics as part of a peculiar Chinese (and 'Asiatic') society."[13] In his later studies, nevertheless, he stresses the need for a new terminology. The terms "hydraulic society" and "hydraulic civilization" express more accurately, in his opinion, the "peculiarities of the order under discussion" than do the traditional labels "Oriental" and "Asiatic."

Other scholars, however, are skeptical of Asian despotism. As Wolfram Eberhard observed in 1957, many of the "Oriental societies" frequently regarded as despotic actually contained "within themselves institutional checks on the power of the ruler." Such "societal checks" existed in Mesopotamia and, to a limited extent, in pre-Moslem India, but were not clearly operative in Islamic monarchies or in ancient Egypt. In Mesopotamia "the priests had great power in checking the actions of the king, and, as long as such a system prevailed, despotism was impossible." The Indian system "provided for the possibility of criticizing the ruler when he violated *dharma*" (moral and social law), but offered "few possibilities" for criticizing his "political actions." The Egyptian monarch could not, theoretically, "act arbitrarily," as he was obligated to maintain justice and "right order." Nevertheless, as an "embodiment of god," he was not subject to criticism, and despotism remained a distinct possibility under this system. In Islamic society, finally, "moral checks existed in the religion," but "no institutional framework provided for an efficient check on the ruler by the citizens." In such a society, "despotism (defined as unchecked personal rule) could develop."

Did "similar checks exist in China. . . ?" asks Eberhard. "Was the Chinese emperor a despot? A god-king? A combination of temporal and spiritual ruler?" Was the Chinese gentry, in turn, merely "a group of bureaucrats and 'scholars' which depended solely upon the emperor and derived its economic and political power from him. . . ?" Or did the gentry possess "economic and political power resulting from its own structure?" In the Han period, Eberhard believes, the scholar-officials found an institutional check to the emperor's despotic power in the interpretation of omens and portents. As some of these divine warnings and admonitions could be—and were—fabricated, it was possible to exert pressure on the emperor to alter his policy or his conduct.[14] Similarly, for the "idealistic scholar-officials" of the Sung dynasty, as Dr. James Liu observes, even the "ultimate power of the emperor" ought, theoretically, to be subordinated to Confucian principles. In attempting to "translate their political theory into reality," such officials "relied mainly upon persuasion exerted on the emperor."[15]

Professor de Bary has likewise stressed the role that Confucianism played in "softening and humanizing . . . Chinese despotism, through its continuing efforts to restrain the exercise of absolute power by moral suasion and to reform the governmental structure itself." An outstanding example of this ideal was the seventeenth-century political treatise *A Plan for the Prince*. Written by the Confucian theorist Huang Tsung-hsi, this work is an "analysis and condemnation of Chinese despotism, which had reached its peak in the Ming dynasty." Proposing sweeping reforms in the imperial household and the state—reducing the number of the emperor's wives, curbing the power of the court eunuchs, redistributing the land, altering the administration of taxes—Huang also insists on placing moral restraints on the prince's sovereignty by surrounding him with virtuous and capable advisers. "Thus, in contrast to the despot whose power is absolute and before whom all men, even the highest ministers, are no more than slaves, the Prince would be surrounded and supported by a hierarchy of merit and learning." Proposing to curb imperial despotism by a scholarly meritocracy, Huang perceived the basic legal issue as a choice "not between men and laws but between true law and the unlawful restrictions of the ruler."[16]

3

Thus, from Aristotle to Lenin, the notion of "Oriental despotism" has haunted Western political theory—even though writers have varied widely in their views of its nature and causes. But what, after all, do we mean by this term? Does it signify the same thing when applied to China and to India, to Turkey and to Persia? Does Asia possess its own peculiar species of absolutism distinct from those of Europe and pre-Columbian America? What are its causes? its functions? the reasons for its development and decline? Does the power structure of Communist China bear, as some observers believe, a definable relation to that of its bureaucratic and "despotic" predecessors? How valid are such terms as "Oriental society" and "hydraulic civilization"?

That Western writers still disagree on such basic questions as these may be attributable in part to their fields of specialization—to the necessity of concentrating, in so broad and unmanageable a field, either on a single society in depth or else on one particular aspect of several societies. (In spite of their global scope, many otherwise valuable studies of "hydraulic society" seem to fall under the second category. Their definition of despotism seems, accordingly, too narrow, and their approach to the problems it raises too limited.) Equally, if not more, significant, however, is the equivocal nature of this term. François Quesnay, physician, political economist, and founder of the physiocratic school, long ago called attention to the ambiguity of the word "despotism," and even today many writers still treat it as virtually synonymous with absolute monarchy, dictatorship or tyranny. For other observers, the element of personal rule is less significant than the managerial function of a highly centralized bureaucracy and the extent of government control over land tenure, production, and distribution.

However we define it, it is not a purely Asiatic phenomenon. In Africa and America, Karl Wittfogel finds hydraulic societies comparable to those of Asia. The despotic or semidespotic power wielded by the emperors of Rome—and still earlier by Alexander of Macedon—can hardly be dismissed as an Oriental import. It may indeed have been associated with Oriental trappings, but these, like so many other Asiatic imports during the Hellenistic and Roman periods, were largely superficial. They adorned, but did not conceal, the armor beneath the imperial robes; the brutal realities of a military dictatorship were still apparent under the insignia of legitimate authority. Even the "despotic" East offers few apologies for absolute power so radical as Hobbes's *Leviathan.* Nor were the Western Sinophiles of the seventeenth and eighteenth centuries unprejudiced observers; most of them viewed Chinese institutions against a background of European political theory. Their vision had been conditioned by Western theories of absolute monarchy and benevolent despotism.

Though unfair, Montesquieu's somewhat cynical suggestion— that European missionaries found Chinese despotism attractive because they themselves obeyed an authoritarian discipline and because they hoped to further their own ends in China and India by capturing the ear of the sovereign—nevertheless contains a partial truth. Western attitudes toward Eastern governments do, in part, reflect alterations in Western political theory. It is significant that the unfavorable criticism of China, which became increasingly prominent during the latter part of the eighteenth century, coincided with growing hostility to royalist absolutism in Europe.

European attitudes to China over the past three centuries have been more than ambivalent; they have been sharply contradictory. Leibniz[17] admired the Chinese system of government, and Turgot (eighteenth century political economist, comptroller general of France, and author of *Reflections on the Formation and Distribution of Wealth*) was deeply interested in its agricultural methods and policies. For many philosophers of the Enlightenment this was a benevolent despotism, which the absolute monarchs of the West might advantageously emulate.

John Webb, author of *An Historical Essay Endeavoring a Probability That the Language of the Empire of China Is the Primitive Language* (1669), urged Charles II to imitate the Chinese emperors, and in the next century the king of France consciously followed the example—or at least the ceremonial plow—of Sons of Heaven in Cathay.

Father Louis LeComte, French missionary in China whose *Nouveaux mémoires sur l'état présent de la Chine* appeared in 1696, emphatically distinguished China's absolute monarchy from tyranny. Though the laws gave the emperor "unbounded Authority," they also constrained him to rule with "moderation and discretion." Tyrannical and oppressive government did not proceed from "the absoluteness of the Princes' power," but from the "Princes' own wildness."

Étienne de Silhouette, French financier, comptroller general, and writer on politics, whose *Idée générale du gouvernement et de la morale des Chinois, tirée particulièrement des ouvrages de Confucius* was published in 1729, observed that though "the authority of the emperor is despotic," he cannot violate the laws without "injuring his own powers." François Marie de Marsy, who wrote the first eleven volumes of the *Histoire moderne des Chinois, des Japonnois, des Indiens, des Persans, des Turcs, des Russiens* (1755–1778), held that though the Chinese government was "completely despotic," it was not tyrannical.

François Quesnay distinguished in *Le despotisme de la Chine* (published in 1767) between "legal" and "arbitrary or illegal" despots. The former were absolute monarchs, the latter merely "tyrannical and arbitrary" rulers. "Observing that the term despotism had been applied to the government of China, because the sovereign of that empire took into his own hands exclusively the supreme authority," Quesnay maintained that the Chinese empire was a benevolent despotism. Its "political and moral constitution" was based on "a knowledge of the Natural Law." Far from regarding his power as "arbitrary and superior to the laws of the nation," the Chinese constitution both "deters the sovereign from doing evil and assures him in his legitimate administration, supreme power in doing good." Thus the imperial authority proved "a beatitude for the ruler and an idolized rule for the subject."[18]

Nevertheless other voices were distinctly less favorable to the Chinese government. "It is the cudgel that governs China," wrote Father Du Halde, French Jesuit whose *Description géographique, historique, chronologique et physique de l'Empire de la Chine et de la Tartarie Chinoise* appeared in 1735.[19] "There is no power on earth more despotic than that of the Emperor of China," observed the English authors of the *Universal History from the Earliest Account of Time to the Present* (1735-65) which was compiled anonymously but has been ascribed to G. Sale, G. Psalmanazar, A. Bower, and several other authors.[20] "Our missionaries inform us that the government of the vast Empire of China is admirable," declared Montesquieu, "and that it has a proper mixture of fear, honor, and virtue. . . . But I cannot conceive what this honor can be among a people who act only through fear of being bastinadoed." China is "a despotic state, whose principle is fear."[21]

For better or for worse, it is the government of China that has exerted the strongest influence on modern Western conceptions of Oriental despotism. Yet these stereotypes have also been shaped by other Eastern societies—India, Turkey, Persia, and even the nomads of Central Asia.

For several eighteenth- and nineteenth-century theorists— Montesquieu, Richard Jones, Mackinnon—the chief responsibility for the despotic systems of Asia seemed to lie less with the relatively civilized peoples along the fringes of the continent than with their fierce conquerors from the steppes—the Mongol and Tatar hordes, the Huns and the Scythians, and other militant tribes of Central Asia. Had not such barbarians as these repeatedly overrun the settled kingdoms of the Far and Middle East and threatened Europe itself? Had they not invaded Rome and Byzantium, Peking and Delhi—and ridden "in triumph through Persepolis"? Arabic sultanates and the eastern Roman Empire had fallen before the Turks. The descendants of Genghis Khan had established dynasties in Persia and China; and the heirs of Tamerlane reigned in India. It seemed natural to blame the enslavement of Asia on its nomadic conquerors.

Montesquieu regarded the "people of Tartary"—Asia's "natural conquerors"—as "themselves enslaved." Mackinnon traced the despotic power of the Mogul emperors back to their ancestor Tamerlane. The emperor Akbar had demanded adoration "as a deity." "The Mogul," declared Father Catrou, French Jesuit and author of *Histoire générale de l'Empire du Mogol* (1702), "is the sole proprietor of the entire soil, and the only heir of his people." "Nothing can be more simple than the springs that move this great empire. The emperor is the soul of the whole. As his rule is as absolute as his right over the soil, the whole authority is concentrated in his person alone, and properly speaking, there is but one master in Hindoostan. All the rest are more entitled to be regarded as slaves than subjects."[22]

The theory that Asiatic despotism originated in the steppes and was subsequently imposed by force of arms on the civilized societies to the east, south, and west seemed to provide a single cause for the apparent similarities in the autocratic empires of the Orient. It combined two popular but very different stereotypes of the despotic East—the militant barbarians of Central Asia and the static, bureaucracy-ridden civilizations of India, China, and Persia.

The same theory was partly responsible for the widespread conception of Russia as a "semi-Asiatic" society that had derived its despotic structure from its Mongol conquerors. Richard Jones believed that only the power of the aristocracy had restrained the Czar from exercising the "unlimited despotism" characteristic of the Orient. From "this influence, even the absolute government of the Russian Emperor receives an unacknowledged but powerful check, sufficient to distinguish it from an Asiatic despotism. . . ."[23] Many of the early Marxists condemned Russian society as still semi-Asiatic and the Czarist regime as a somewhat hybridized version of Asiatic despotism. Some of them sedulously avoided applying the term "feudal" to conditions in Russia, preferring to stress the analogy with Asia rather than with medieval Europe. They deplored the prevalence of "Asianism" (*Aziatchina*) under the Czar, and even after the Revolution warning voices emphasized the dangers of an "Asiatic restoration"—the re-establishment of the old state despotism under the new regime.[24]

4

That Asian statesmen themselves could be keenly aware of the political and economic hazards that attended absolute rule is abundantly demonstrated by the writings of Confucian scholar-officials. In analyzing its dangers they could, moreover, rely exclusively on their own historical and philosophical traditions without having to borrow examples and principles from other societies. Huang's critique of despotism, for instance, was firmly grounded on Confucian principles; it was a distinctly Chinese analysis of Chinese political institutions. With the subsequent spread of Western economic and political ideas, however, such critiques became increasingly cosmopolitan. Their authors frequently regarded their own governments, past or present, through Western as well as "Oriental" eyes.

Much as Russian revolutionaries urged their countrymen to overthrow the semi-Asiatic despotism of the Czars, Chinese revolutionaries and nationalists exhorted their compatriots to end the despotic rule of the Manchus and the absolutist principles that sustained it. T'an Ssu-t'ung complained that the Manchus had converted Confucian doctrines into an instrument of oppression; the emperor relied on such principles not merely to control men's bodies but also to "control their minds." "We must shatter at a blow the despotic and confused governmental system of some thousands of years," cried Liang Ch'i-ch'ao; "we must sweep away the corrupt and sycophantic learning of these thousands of years." Urging the overthrow of the "tyrannical" Manchu dynasty and its "autocratic form of government," Hu Han-min insisted on "rooting out the elements of absolutism." Absolute monarchy is "unsuitable to the present age," and "political observers determine the level of a country's civilization by inquiring whether its political system is despotic or not." During "several thousand years of absolute government," declared Tsiang T'ing-fu, the "historic task of the Chinese monarch was to destroy all the classes and institutions outside the royal family which could possibly become the center of political power."[25]

After the Meiji Restoration in 1868, Japanese conservatives and liberals debated the pros and cons of absolute and constitutional monarchy. "In enlightened countries," observed Kido Koin, ". . . a sovereign . . . does not hold sway in an arbitrary fashion." "The idea that the nation is the passive object of the ruler's government," declared Minobe Tatsukichi, ". . . makes the nation something inanimate and devoid of energies and therefore is contrary to a completely sound national spirit." On the other hand, many conservatives and nationalists regarded representative government as derogatory to imperial authority and contrary to the traditional "national polity."[26]

Indian leaders likewise exploited the commonplace of Oriental despotism. According to Dadabhai Naoroji, British rule had freed India from the "oppression caused by the caprice or avarice of despotic rulers." This "new lesson that kings are made for the people, not people for their kings . . . we have learned amidst the darkness of Asiatic despotism only by the light of free English civilization." M. G. Ranade, on the other hand, applied to India's economy under the British raj the very terms that European economists had applied to Oriental societies. "The land is a monopoly of the State." The state "claims to be the sole landlord and is certainly the largest capitalist in the country."[27]

From classical Greece to modern Asia, from French Jesuits to Russian Marxists, the notion of Oriental despotism has undergone numerous, and sometimes paradoxical, variations. Aristotle could argue that it demonstrated the servile character of Asiatics and their fitness for absolute rule; within the last century, however, Asian reformers could turn the same cliché into an argument for independence from foreign overlords—indicting the Manchu dynasty, and indeed the British raj, as Oriental despots. European revolutionaries could level similar charges against their own monarchs, accusing the Czar of Russia of exercising a semi-Asiatic despotism inherited from the Tatars.

Western attitudes toward the "Eastern despot" ranged from indignation to admiration. Early travelers—merchants and official ambassadors—were impressed by his wealth and magnificence; early missionaries by the efficiency of the political and economic system he commanded; French physiocrats by his central bureaucracy and its control over agriculture and public works. Others were appalled by the burdens this system imposed on the peasantry, by its affront to economic and political freedom, and by the moral corruption it appeared to have fostered in the monarch himself and his entourage. Milton, as we have seen, associated the "gorgeous East" and its "barbaric pearl and gold" with tyranny,[28] and John Stuart Mill maintained that the alleged "opulence of Oriental nations" was merely a veneer, disguising the ugly realities of universal poverty.

In their conceptions of the causes of Oriental despotism Western observers have been just as divided. Some have attributed it to temperament, some to race and climate, some to the system of land tenure, some to methods of production and distribution.

The "Eastern despot" is essentially a European concept; and the story of its fortunes belongs properly to the history of European thought rather than to that of Asia. Nevertheless, for all their inadequacies, its critics and apologists sometimes based their judgments on conscientious observation of Asian institutions.

In the next chapters we shall examine another aspect of Asian government. This too concerns the problems of effective central administration—and state management—but from a different angle. In particular, we shall consider some of the difficulties that currently confront several of the newly independent countries of South and Southeast Asia in attempting to integrate older, diverse, and sometimes hostile communities into modern national states.

xiii

ASIAN DIVERSITY AND
THE COMMUNAL PROBLEM

• •
•

1

For the Westerner, his first personal encounter with East and Southeast Asia may also become a personal crisis. Exposing his stereotypes to the test of experience, it compels him to revise cherished preconceptions. Discarding such vulgar clichés as "the mystic East" and "the inscrutable Orient," he also abandons the more sophisticated "Quarrel of Continents" and the myths of "Europe" and "Asia." He realizes (if he is an American) that the penalty of an affluent society is a standardized culture and that, in comparison with these, his own is indeed a historyless civilization.

The most immediate challenges are the two elements most notably lacking in his own society—antiquity and variety. Beholding like Ulysses so many peoples and cultures, so many "cities of men," he is struck not merely by their divergence from his own; he is, if anything, more impressed by their greater differences among themselves. Asia seems an unbroken human continuum, in which history and prehistory are still preserved intact, like fossil insects in amber or mammoths in Arctic ice. Yet these are *living* fossils. Here, if anywhere, "time past" is truly "contained in time present." Elsewhere antiquity seems static; here it is dynamic, for the past is still in movement.

Vertically—between past and present—he finds apparent con-

tinuity. Horizontally—between one tableau and another—he sees
little except *dis*continuity, and he can record this impression
only in the idiom of the travelogue. Fire rituals in the Jain
temples of Sravanabelgola. Shinto dances at the shrine of Ama-
terasu Omikami in Ise. Trapezoidal sails of Chinese junks mo-
tionless in the Pearl River, the red lights of oil lamps mirrored
in the moonlit estuary. Towers of silence at Bombay. Morning
puja at the temple of the Golden Lily at Madura. Igorots with
head axes and loincloths shopping for sacrificial pigs in the
village market above the rice terraces of Banaue. A Hindu wor-
shiping the rising sun beside a tank in the ruined Mogul palace
at Mandu. The ancient Jewish synagogues at Ernakulam. The
Nestorian altar on St. Thomas' Mount near Madras. An aged
Tibetan setting up prayer flags on Tiger Hill at sunrise, invoking
the gods of Kanchenjunga. Yellow-robed monks with begging-
bowls paddling the canals of Bangkok at dawn. Sarong-clad
men and women at Angkor Wat driving their water buffaloes at
twilight over the lichen-covered causeway of the Khmers. All
these are incredibly old, yet in no way obsolete. The past seems
contemporaneous—and infinitely diverse.

In comparison, the marks of Western influence in the cities
seem monotonously uniform. Everywhere Oriental variety
clashes violently with Western standardization.

As he moves from country to country, scenes shift as abruptly
as in a Chinese opera. An entire cast enters and departs, while
another—just as exotically costumed—comes onstage with altogether different orchestration and choreography. The dagobas
and viharas—shrines and temples and monastic buildings—of
Siam replace the torii and pagodas—Shinto portals and Buddhist
towers—of Japan, then yield to India's gopuras; and these
ornate and many-tiered temple gateways yield, in turn, to
mosques. Yet always there remains one corner of the stage that
does not change. The familiar backdrop of bank, office building,
and Government House—the tourist's triad of railroad station,
airport, and hotel—remains virtually the same, although modified occasionally by different vegetation, banyan or deodar, palm

tree or pine. The ghost of his own civilization still stalks him, as inseparable as his shadow.

He is, of course, grateful for the contrast. It enables him to train his camera on scenes of exotic squalor by day, yet enjoy the amenities of an international hotel by night. Yet, if he is not unwise, it will trouble him. In the variegated antiquity of the East, the diversity so eminently adaptable to color film—and, by contrast, the standard comforts of his Western hostelry—he may recognize the symptoms of a chronic disease.

For these are, in fact, salient features of the communal virus endemic in southern Asia. So various and so ancient are the social groups (whether racial or linguistic, cultural or religious) now coexisting within the same national boundaries—so new and unfamiliar the political and economic concepts thrust upon them by central governments—that they pose grave difficulties for effective administration. The resulting tensions between indigenous traditions and national policy not only hamstring central authority but, in extreme cases, imperil its very existence.

At the moment of writing, communal tensions are rife throughout southern Asia. In Vietnam the friction between Buddhist and Roman Catholic communities continues to jeopardize national security. India faces communal dissensions on two fronts: In the east Mizo tribesmen have been fighting for independence; in the west Sikhs and Hindus have been rioting over the future of the Punjab and the question of a Punjabi-speaking state. In Indonesia the older native populations have risen against the overseas Chinese. Farther afield, in Japan, a Korean immigrant has avenged an insult to his nationality by slaying several Japanese and holding others as hostages. In the Mauritius Islands, off the African coast, open conflicts have broken out between the Creole and Indian communities. Still farther afield—in the Fiji Islands, in Kenya and South Africa and even in Great Britain—communal tensions have developed, with increasing bitterness, between South Asian settlers (Indian or Pakistani) and the indigenous populations.

Such problems are not, obviously, peculiar to South and

Southeast Asia. They are, however, particularly critical in these areas, and in the following pages I shall be concerned primarily with the societies of this region rather than with Asia as a whole. Furthermore, in most instances these problems are by no means new. They have challenged native or colonial administration for centuries. In recent years, however, they have been aggravated by the transition from colonial status to national sovereignty. In effecting this transition, most new governments have faced a dual task—the immediate end of consolidating national unity and the more distant objective of approximating the political and economic standards of the West. Both goals demand a dramatic reorientation of deep-rooted local traditions, a radical "transvaluation of values."

Asia's material destiny depends largely on a small Western-educated intelligentsia, whose social objectives derive usually from European rather than native tradition. To realize these values, Asian leaders cannot merely impose them like a veneer on the surface of Eastern societies; they must reorganize the societies themselves—and from the foundations upwards. Hence they have transferred to Asian soil the historic tensions between East and West. The conflict between native and alien traditions has become another "Quarrel of Ancients and Moderns"—a political struggle between the older communities of Asia and their new "Westernized" governments.

The challenge is the task of transforming a cultural mosaic into a monolith, heterogeneous communities into a national state. Or (to adapt Hobbes's imagery) a matter of converting the Hydra into Leviathan.

2

Cultural historians, like scholastic philosophers, are sometimes overfond of classifications. Not infrequently they approach Asia's communal tensions as though these could be neatly divided into four categories—cultural, religious, racial, linguistic. But, even if it is possible to isolate and distinguish these ideas in theory, they are nevertheless closely interrelated in actuality. Such concepts as "culture" or "race" are, in fact, so vague that one can scarcely consider them entirely apart from religion and language. Both of the latter may contribute to a sense of "cultural" or "racial" homogeneity, and vice versa. The historic culture of India is inconceivable apart from Hinduism, yet the latter still reflects the influence of prehistoric racial tensions which exist in a somewhat different form today—either as linguistic rivalry or as caste hostility.

Religious communalism is like the authority of a divorce court; it can join or put asunder. It has split prewar India into two distinct nations—Hindustan and Pakistan—yet it also provides virtually the sole bond between East Bengal and West Pakistan, strikingly different in race and language and separated by a thousand miles of alien territory. Similarly, the common bond of the Hindu religion and civilization provides one of the strongest incentives to the political unity of Hindustan. Religious communalism underlay the massacres that attended this partition and the minor clashes that have since occurred in both countries. It has created and then prolonged the Kashmir crisis; and the latter in turn has heightened communal tensions in both Pakistan and Hindustan. Within the state of Kashmir it has fostered friction between Hindu and Moslem communities within the subprovinces of Jammu (which is predominantly Hindu) and Kashmir (which is largely Moslem) and created tensions between Moslems and Buddhists in the subprovince of Ladakh.

Surgery is a drastic remedy—a bloody and by no means infallible cure. The amputation of two of its limbs has merely weakened the subcontinent instead of healing it. Its communal fevers are still rife. Partition has established an armed truce between Hindu and Moslem, but has not resolved their conflicts. Moreover, it has left unsolved the problems of minority sects. In Hindustan the government has clashed repeatedly with elements of the Sikh community, and more recently Sikhs and Hindu extremists have come to blows over the Punjabi issue. In

Pakistan the Ahmadiya sect has frequently suffered persecution at the hands of the Sunni majority.

Constitutionally, India is a secular state; unlike Burma and Pakistan—or England and Spain, for that matter—she has no religious establishment. Both Moslems and Hindus are represented in the central government. Other religions have long been tolerated—Christians, who trace their spiritual lineage to St. Thomas; a Jewish community that can claim continuity of residence for nearly two millennia; Parsees, who dominate the commerce of Bombay; Jains, whose religion dates from a contemporary of Gautama; Buddhism, which recently experienced a striking revival in its homeland after centuries of eclipse; Sikhs, whose religion began as a *via media* between Hinduism and Islam but has developed strong communal loyalties all its own.

Yet the fact remains that the majority of India's population are Hindus—over 85 percent, according to the most recent census. This community of religion confers a certain degree of national unity, but it nevertheless presents serious obstacles to the official ideal of a secular, democratic state. Gandhi's tolerant attitude toward Moslems led to martyrdom at the hands of a Hindu fanatic. Orthodox Hindus still agitate for legislation against cow slaughter. The sense of caste is too strong to be legislated out of existence; thus, in spite of their *legal* equality, many Harijans remain in practice "untouchable." Hinduism is as patient, as pliant, as stubbornly tenacious, as Uncle Remus' Tar Baby. To remold it in the image of a progressive state will require unusual finesse; for its passivity is deceptive. Like the image of tar, it possesses a certain inert viscosity that can bring the nimblest and most agile of politicians to a halt. Like Br'er Rabbit, the civil official who rashly hustles it may find himself stuck fast.[1]

3

Linguistic and racial communalism has been less violent than religious conflict, but it has nevertheless embarrassed national and provincial governments in both India and Pakistan. The decision to establish Hindi—a northern dialect ultimately derived from Sanskrit—as the official language of the country has outraged the peoples of southern India; they find English an easier medium than a northern-Indian tongue, and some of them (notably the Tamils) already possess impressive literary traditions in their ancestral languages. Extremists have demanded an autonomous southern state—"Dravidia"—as a foil to "Aryan" Hindustan in the north.

Such opposition is not, however, confined to the Dravidian tongues. Several northern-Indian peoples also resent the adoption of Hindi. Moslems have inherited a distinguished literature in Urdu, a form of Hindustani enriched by an Arabic and Persian vocabulary and employing the Arabic script. Bengalis argue, with some justification, that their own literary heritage is far richer than that of the proposed tongue.

Unfortunately, the linguistic issue has not been limited to the question of a national language. Some of the bitterest regional antagonisms have sprung from popular pressure to reorganize the provincial states on the basis of language. Less than two decades ago Tamils and Telugu speakers were rioting over the fate of the city of Madras. The latter insisted on incorporating it into Andhra—a linguistic state carved out of Hyderabad. The former demanded that it be retained as the capital of Madras State. This regional agitation resulted in open violence and a hunger strike to the death by one of the Telugu leaders.

A similar conflict arose over the state and city of Bombay. In November 1956, when the provinces of India had been reorganized into fourteen states, Bombay State consisted largely of two language groups—Gujarati and Marathi—besides the multiracial, polyglot population of its capital. Both of the principal groups agitated for partition, but both laid claim to the city of Bombay. Despite government opposition to the formation of any additional linguistic states, popular pressure eventually prevailed, and in May 1960 the state of Bombay was divided into two smaller states—Gujarat and Maharashtra, the city falling to the latter.

Of the thirteen "official" languages recognized by the Indian government, only Punjabi has missed the distinction of becoming the established tongue of a separate state—a fact that lies at the root of the long-standing friction between Sikhs and Hindus in the East Punjab. Since reorganization on a linguistic basis would leave the state with a Sikh majority, the language problem has become a source of religious friction. For years representatives of both communities have vied with one another in fast and counterfast, seeking to bring pressure on the central government. The recent decision in favor of a Punjabi-speaking state has touched off riots and communal friction not only in the Punjab itself but in Delhi and other cities of northern India.

Besides these political tensions, the diversity of tongues poses formidable difficulties for education, for literature, and for government administration. In primary schools a child is entitled to instruction in his mother tongue. As there are at least thirteen major languages and over a hundred dialects (the exact number varying with one's basis of classification), this means that the nation must publish textbooks in thirteen or more different tongues. It also means that in multilingual cities there must be separate schools or classes with different mother tongues. To instruct Tamils, Hindustanis, Bengalis, and Marathas in the same subject, a school must have four different teachers for the same course—or at the very least an instructor fluent in all four tongues. A schoolhouse in the larger cities sometimes bears a more than superficial resemblance to the tower of Babel.

The deadline for establishing Hindi as the official tongue has been repeatedly postponed, and each new deadline has precipitated a new linguistic crisis, attended with communal rioting and protests against the government. In actuality, despite official policy, little progress has been made in diffusing Hindi. English still remains the most convenient medium for persons of different linguistic background—Tamil and Bengali, Gujarati and Kanarese—to converse. It is scarcely surprising, therefore, that many of the best writers of modern India (R.K. Narayan, Nirad Chaudhuri, Khushwant Singh, Ved Mehta—not to mention Europeans like Ruth Prawer Jhabvala or Indian *émigrés* like

Dom Moraes, Santha Rama Rau, and Aubrey Menen) have chosen English as their medium in preference to Hindi or any other Indian language or dialect.

Nor have India's neighbors been spared similar tensions. Friction between East and West Pakistan has had profound effects on the nation's politics and economy. Not only has it led to serious rioting between Bengali and West Pakistani industrial workers, but for many years it impeded efforts to frame an effective constitution and establish a stable democratic government.

The Burmese government, in turn, has had to contend not only with a large indigenous Indian population, but also with the demand for autonomy by various minority groups—Karens, Nagas, quasi-Chinese tribes of the Shan States. Ceylon has experienced continual friction between the Sinhalese community and the large Tamil minority. Other Asian commonwealths have already splintered on the rock of communal faction. The unstable empire that was Indochina disintegrated into its traditional components—Laos, Cambodia, Annam—with grave consequences for all three. More recently, the Malay Federation split into irreconcilable linguistic and cultural blocs—Malay and Chinese.

4

Most of these communities are far older than the states to which they now belong. Their antiquity presents a formidable obstacle for any new government and any legislative attempt to alter their traditional patterns of behavior from above and thereby supplant communal with national loyalties. Their diversity resists the efforts of any central authority to integrate them into a single national framework.

In one respect these communal tensions offer a striking contrast to those of other underdeveloped continents, such as Africa and South America. In Asia they are confined almost entirely to older native populations. Outside Hong Kong and other surviving colonies, few truly European communities remain in the East. Although several Eurasian groups have developed a sense of communal identity—Anglo-Indians, Hispano-Filipinos, families of mixed Dutch or English or Portuguese ancestry in Ceylon, and certain residents of the former French and Portuguese enclaves incorporated into Hindustan—most of Asia's communal groups antedate the era of European expansion. Their conflicts originated long ago, far back in the precolonial past.

Oriental societies are by no means inexperienced in meeting such crises. Even though some of their remedies have proved notably abortive, others have worked more or less satisfactorily, and radically transformed society in the process. The most obvious example—India's caste system—though fortunately obsolescent, still dominates the structure of her society. Complex and often inconsistent like so many of her institutions, it evolved in response to the communal crisis precipitated by the so-called "Aryan" invasion—a crisis usually described as "racial" but strongly characterized by cultural, religious, and even linguistic factors. The conquerors met the problem by incorporating part of the native population into their own social and religious framework while rigidly excluding other elements—subsequently known as the "scheduled" castes and tribes. In the process they profoundly altered their own culture, modifying the imported Vedic religion by indigenous practices and beliefs, fusing Indo-Aryan and Dravidian elements into a common culture that still unites Hindus from Kashmir to Assam and from Nepal to Travancore. Later, in its expansion through Southeast Asia and the Malay Archipelago and northwards into Nepal and Tibet, Hinduism demonstrated the same capacity for synthesis, an ability to embrace other peoples of radically diverse language and stock. The religion still survives in Bali and among the Chams of southern Vietnam; and even where the faith itself has vanished its cultural impact remains. The *Ramayana* still lives in the dance dramas and puppet shows of "Farther India," entertaining Moslem and Buddhist alike with the mythology of the Hindu.

Nevertheless, though India's religious synthesis provided a solution to one type of communal crisis, it soon provoked others.

The increasing rigidity of Brahmanism multiplied subcastes and pitted the ruling castes against each other in a struggle for power. Legend credits the hero Parasurama—an incarnation of Vishnu—with preserving Brahmin supremacy and decisively defeating the Kshatriya caste. In reaction to Brahmanist orthodoxy two new religious movements (Buddhism and Jainism) sprang up about the same time—both bearing the imprint of Indian philosophical speculation of the sixth century B.C., both founded by Kshatriya princes in the province of Bihar, and both protesting against the inflexibility of the Brahmanist code—its ritualism, its social hierarchy, its exaggerated emphasis on speculation ("the vanity of theorizing," as Gautama complained). (The term Brahmanism—often loosely defined—is usually applied to philosophical speculations concerning the Absolute—Brahman—set forth in the Upanishads and to the rituals prescribed in the Brahmanas. Hinduism is usually regarded as evolving at a somewhat later date and embracing popular devotions as well as priestly lore.) Both Buddhism and Jainism cut across caste lines; yet ultimately, instead of undermining the caste system, they merely created two additional communities within a caste-ridden society.

Buddhism competed successfully with Hinduism not only on its native soil but throughout Southeast Asia and Tibet as well. Jainism never spread so widely; it could challenge its Hindu rival only within India and even there on a very limited scale. Yet even these victories were temporary. Hindu reaction and Islamic zeal eventually expelled the Buddhist religion from its native soil. Virtually extinct in the country of its birth except for a few lamaist communities along the frontiers of Tibet, it had to wait its 2,500th anniversary to achieve even a partial comeback. Under Moslem persecution Jainism experienced a similar decline; today its adherents number fewer than 1,500,000. Hinduism outlived its rivals (albeit somewhat modified by their thought and sensibility) only to confront a more militant competitor—the proselyting armies of Islam.

The new invaders introduced more violent forms of communalism. Most of them held orthodox Sunni beliefs and at-

tempted to impose on India's pluralistic society the uniformity
of Islamic law. Nevertheless both rulers and subjects occasionally
made notable efforts to bridge the gulf between Hindu and
Moslem communities. Akbar displayed keen personal interest in
Hinduism as well as in Christianity. His solutions, however, were,
on the whole, private rather than public. Unwilling to embrace
the religions themselves, he could—and did—espouse their
daughters. With wives of Hindu, Moslem, and Christian al-
legiance, he achieved in the seraglio an eclectic solution he could
never accomplish in the state. His universalist faith—Din-i-Ilahi
—was short-lived and scarcely survived his own reign. His
efforts to lower communal tensions came to naught. His heresies
outraged the faithful, and his successors completely reversed his
policy of toleration and compromise.

Although mystics like the Moslem weaver Kabir might emphasize their common ground with Hinduism, such cases were
fairly rare. Attempts to reconcile the creeds often resulted in
greater antagonism. Though Nanak Shah, the first guru (teacher
and leader) of the Sikhs, stressed a personal, monotheistic creed
that respected both religions as different but converging paths
to the same God, Moslem persecution eventually turned his
followers into bitter opponents of Islam. Paradoxically, most
efforts to resolve communal frictions in South Asia have either
established new communal groups or heightened existing tensions.

5

Asia's borrowings from the West are, for the most part, material rather than spiritual. In importing Europe's technical
achievements she has no intention of sacrificing her own cultures. From the West she does not seek a religion or a civilization, but a standard of living. For this end she may willingly
alter her economic and political traditions, but not her mind and
faith.

The tension between native tradition and foreign innovation

naturally assumes different forms in various countries and at unequal rates. Such disproportionate development is especially evident in the striking contrast between India and Japan. The former was almost the first Oriental country to experience the impact of the modern West. The latter was virtually the last. Yet India has often shown reluctance to adopt Western techniques, whereas Japan has carried them further than any other Asian country.

The paradox can be partly explained by India's former colonial status and by the social inertia so frequently associated with Hinduism. Even more significant, however, is the relative homogeneity of the Japanese. As islanders they possess—like their geographical counterparts in Britain—many of the cohesive virtues of insularity. They possess a common language and common ethnic ties. They have retained the same imperial dynasty for about two thousand years. Their religions tend to overlap rather than clash; the same man can be simultaneously Shintoist, Buddhist, and even Confucian. In contrast with India's linguistic and racial diversity, dynastic changes and religious conflicts, Japanese culture appears unified, monolithic.

It was much easier, accordingly, for the Japanese to adapt themselves to the modern state, once their political leaders had committed them to such a policy. The sense of nationhood already existed; all that was really necessary was to modernize the political and economic pattern. And this was precisely what the country set out to do in the era of the Meiji Restoration. To Western eyes, many aspects of the Japanese state between 1868 and the present undoubtedly seem medieval and anachronistic, but in actuality they represent a more or less conscious effort at modernization. The state Shinto, which was so prominent a feature of prewar Japan and today seems so archaic even in Tokyo itself, was a fairly late development—an attempt to buttress the new system of government with the authority of a much older religion. A complex blend of animism, ancestor worship, and natural piety, traditional Shinto was deeply and firmly rooted in the feeling for country and clan. It worshiped the living forces of nature—vegetation spirits, animal spirits, spirits of mountain and stream, spirits of departed forebears—attributing soul and sentience even to objects we regard as inanimate. Through these associations with locality and family it could easily be converted into a national patriotic cult. As an instrument of the state it served to disguise the extent of political innovation—the restoration of imperial rule after a long series of shogunates, the suppression of the clans and their powerful daimyo (feudal lords), the dispersal of the ancient warrior class or samurai, the imitation of Western ideas and techniques, the shifting from an insular to a global perspective. These were radical changes in the established society; and to render them acceptable to a conservative and self-conscious people, the new leaders clothed them in the familiar trappings of tradition.

In India and in many other Asian countries, however, the problem of constructing a modern state has assumed very different proportions. Unlike its Japanese counterpart, the Indian state is a recent creation, with little political continuity and with few roots in the traditional past. Its real predecessor is the British raj—not the empires of Ashoka and Akbar. Only very rarely has the subcontinent enjoyed political unity—for very brief periods indeed and usually by the agency of foreigners. The present state is in many respects an artificial creation, collected more or less haphazardly by the East India Company and subsequently given a more rational structure by the British vice-regency. That the state possesses its present political boundaries, that it is a secular democracy instead of a Mogul theocracy, that its society is predominantly Hindu rather than Moslem—all of these features are indirectly due to its direct succession from the raj.

India's dilemmas are characteristic of many other countries of southern Asia—Burma, Ceylon, Thailand, Indonesia, Malaya. Throughout this region the architects of the twentieth-century state are building their structure on a fault line, the line of cleavage between "two worlds—one dead, the other struggling to be born." Under the very foundations of the modern edifice, the strains and tensions of far older societies are still present, still powerful, still in movement. Like buried giants, they are restless and imperil the entire superstructure.

Asian governments must maintain a precarious equilibrium—an extremely delicate balance between native traditions and Western techniques. They must somehow reconcile the political and economic requirements of the modern state with the religious and cultural demands of far more ancient communities. This is a feat requiring no mean skill. The new leaders of the Orient may not be holy ascetics, treading the razor's edge to the Absolute. They may have little firsthand knowledge of the craft of juggling or of the Indian rope trick. But they must, all the same, master the art of another Asian acrobat—the tightrope walker.

xiv

COMMUNALISM AND
THE NATIONAL STATE

. .

1

"Asia," declared an Anglo-Indian writer, "is not going to be civilized after the methods of the West. There is too much Asia and she is too old." This prognosis was fast becoming obsolete when Kipling made it, and it is flagrantly anachronistic today. For Asia, we all recognize, is rapidly transforming herself. From Japan to Ceylon, her historic civilizations are undergoing a sea change, and it is precisely by, through and because of the "methods of the West" that they are doing so. This interplay of Eastern traditions and Western techniques is, indeed, one of the most striking features of the modern Orient. The twain *are* meeting, and the signs of this fusion are evident throughout the East.

The process may occur gradually or violently; the reaction is potentially benign or dangerous. In the alchemy of history it may transmute cow dung and sacred ashes to gold—or produce a nuclear explosion.

Emblematic of this metamorphosis is the great dam near the ruined city of Vijayanagar in southern India—or Chandigarh, the new capital of the East Punjab, designed by the French architect Le Corbusier. But it is equally apparent in minor, yet not insignificant, details. The neon lights of Tokyo blazon the latest commercial slogans in the most ancient ideograms. From

298

an Istanbul minaret the high voice of a muezzin exhorts the faithful to prayer in the traditional formulas—but the words are "recorded," incised on a gramophone disk and broadcast over loudspeakers. In Kamakura, the temple of Amida has become a tourist café, where signboards invite the passerby to "Drink, dine, and dance at the Hotel Buddha." At Sravanabelgola, Jain pilgrims to the sanctuaries of their saints face an embarrassing crisis of conscience. Though their religion forbids them to take the life of any creature—whether fly or flea, moth or microbe— the interests of public health demand that they be inoculated en masse—vaccinated, sprayed, and dusted liberally with DDT. The secular government of modern India, it seems, places greater faith in antiseptics and antibiotics than in mantras and ritual purification.

These details, unimportant in themselves, are significant as pointers. They represent the transformation of Asia "after the methods of the West," the tension between innovation and tradition.

2

No single agent is responsible for this metamorphosis. The former colonial regimes, local commercial interests, Western advisers, sometimes the historic institutions themselves, have all played a part in creating the new Asia. Yet the major responsibility rests with the new national governments and the small minority trained in Western ideologies and methods. It is these who are rejuvenating a venerable but sometimes senile society.

This is dangerous sorcery, however; and whether they have really mastered it remains to be seen. To rejuvenate her patients, Medea first slew them and dissected them. Some of them regained life and youth—but not all. Political gerontology is scarcely less violent. Rejuvenating the Orient often means slaying the past— nor is it by any means certain that all of the patients will recover.

The attempt to create a modern state frequently brings the new administration into open conflict with far older communities.

Though the only real solution to such communal problems is integration—welding subnational (or international) groups into a national structure—the very pursuit of unity can foster new tensions between government and people. To unite the severed members of old societies under a new head is a surgical feat that must tax even Medea's skill.

In the first place, a government must commit itself to either a communal or non-communal formula of statehood. For prototypes of both, one need hardly look beyond the confines of India. If the Maurya emperor Ashoka chose the latter, the Mogul emperor Aurangzeb committed himself just as wholeheartedly to the former. Either alternative can conceivably succeed in curbing internal dissension and thus securing national stability, but neither can be altogether free from communal pressure.

To achieve a non-communal solution, a nation must rely on an established framework of values that most of its component groups already hold in common. Yet in many Eastern states such a framework does not exist, and it is hard to supply it. A democratic government cannot impose one arbitrarily (by borrowing or adapting the principles of the dominant community) without abandoning its non-communal character. But the attempt to realize a pluralistic society can never win the support of all communal groups. Religious jealousies have constantly harassed, if not jeopardized, the secular state. In Indonesia, the extremist Dar Ul Islam Movement has continually sought to overthrow the central government and establish a theocratic state in conformity with Moslem law. In India, Hindu extremists have opposed legislation to reform marriage laws and the caste system, resisted efforts to reach an understanding with Pakistan over Kashmir, and violently protested most concessions to other religious minorities, whether Moslem or Sikh.

Nevertheless, despite her Hindu majority, India has officially committed herself to a pluralist formula, rejecting the pattern of a Hindu theocracy for that of a secular state. That she has chosen Ashoka's lion-capital for her national insignia is not fortuitous. Iconographically, it provides a concrete symbol of national unity over and above communal loyalties. By his conquests this early chakravartin (or "world ruler") succeeded in welding the subcontinent into a single empire that roughly comprehended the national boundaries of today. Then, by embracing Buddhism and the doctrine of nonviolence (ahimsa), he provided yet another sentimental tie with the founders of modern Hindustan. The fact that he was a Buddhist has enhanced his value as a national symbol, as it sets him above the communal loyalties of modern India. Neither Moslems nor Hindus can regard him as peculiarly their own; unlike Akbar or Prithvi Raj, he belonged to the nation, not a sect. But his primary significance for the present regime lies in his official policy of toleration for all religions. In this respect he established a symbolic precedent for the modern non-communal state.

However, many Asian countries lack the sense of national identity that might enable them to transcend communal consciousness. Torn by religious or racial or linguistic tensions, they are forced to create a sense of nationhood out of nothing—or, at best, out of chaos.

The artificiality of existing boundaries heightens the problem. Many of these follow the lines of older Oriental empires that embraced peoples of very different ethnic and cultural backgrounds. Others are the legacy of Western colonialism. European empires in the Orient were often acquired gradually and piecemeal—partly from other Occidental powers, partly from Asian kingdoms. Their boundaries, accordingly, often bore little relation to true ethnic differences. Official frontiers rarely followed the older, invisible boundaries of race or religion, culture and language. When these former colonies achieved their independence, they inherited the external paraphernalia of nationhood—legitimate governments and official boundaries, civil and military services, central administrations—but not, necessarily, national identity. The task of creating unified nations out of different communities—of developing national souls to animate the physical structure of statehood—remained a challenge for the new governments to meet as best they could.

Other emergent states have faced similar problems after shaking off colonial rule; the thirteen American colonies are an obvious example. But the situation is only roughly analogous and the actual basis for potential unity altogether different. The peoples of India, for instance (or the populations of Pakistan, Burma, Indonesia, or the Philippines), are far more diverse in race, language, and religion than those of eighteenth-century America. On the other hand, they possess one apparent advantage—though it may, in the long run, turn out to be a handicap. In many instances they have inherited their national structures from former colonial powers; the American states, on the contrary, were forced to evolve their own national organization. Yet in one respect the parallel remains—in both cases the nation has had to be its own demiurge; in a very real sense it has been compelled to create itself. No divine command intervening to fashion it out of chaos and "circumscribe its being," each country has had to grapple with the problems of order and chaos, unity and diversity, on its own initiative—voluntarily integrating its component communities into a national society. Despite such efforts, however, nationality in many Asian states is still rather a legal fiction than a social reality. The political cosmos is scarcely less complex than the physical universe; and in the New Asia the act of creation is still incomplete.

Apart from overt communal tensions, the central governments of the East face formidable physical and psychological obstacles in their pursuit of national unity. To integrate their subnational communities into the national framework would be difficult under any circumstances; geographical and social barriers increase the difficulty. Moreover, the relative autonomy formerly enjoyed by certain minorities under colonial rule presents an additional challenge. Finally, nearly all communal groups naturally resent the imposition of new values and resist the new ways of behavior legislated from above. They are, understandably, reluctant to sacrifice their traditional patterns or jeopardize their sense of unique identity for the sake of closer national integration and a standardized national culture.

The geographical obstacles to effective administration are as obvious as the lines on a relief map—barriers of mountain and jungle in Burma, Thailand, and Vietnam; sheer distance in

Hindustan; the isolation of East from West Pakistan by the entire width of the subcontinent; in Indonesia and the Philippines the multitude of islands. Moreover, in many areas communications are still too undeveloped to permit efficient exercise of central authority. Much of the present diversity of Asia can be attributed specifically to purely physical obstacles which impede movement and social intercourse.

Social barriers—dramatic contrasts in wealth or literacy, disparate degrees of technical advancement, conflicting political objectives—also retard the movement toward unity. Many of these class and professional differences have become so closely interwoven with the cultural and religious fabric of Asian society that they can scarcely be altered without destroying it. Others are more recent and date from the contrast of modern educational, economic, or political patterns with more ancient institutions. One may point, for example, to the economic problems created in India by competition between manual and machine labor in manufacturing cotton textiles. Though the machine can produce cheaper cloth, this would endanger the market for hand-woven fabrics; hence its production had to be rigidly curtailed by law.

Several South Asian governments face the problem of extending central authority to areas hitherto subjected to lax or indirect supervision by colonial administrations. In exercising jurisdiction over the princely states, the governments of Hindustan and Pakistan alike have had to establish new relationships with them in regard to education, public health, and other aspects of public welfare. Such transitions can entail appreciable changes in local standards of living; before independence these had sometimes been markedly superior or inferior to the national average.

The transfer of sovereignty from European powers to the new native governments also meant that minorities found themselves occupying a different status vis-à-vis the majority. Instead of standing on equal or higher ground under the Olympian aegis of "Government House," they now held an apparently disadvantageous position. Central control seemed to threaten political domination by the majority group, and to jeopardize the special privileges hitherto enjoyed by the minority. Their language and culture might, they feared, be subordinated to the demands of national uniformity. Their religion might be overshadowed by other faiths. Racially, they might be absorbed by larger communities. This dread of domination or repression by more powerful groups sometimes underlies the more violent manifestations of communal friction—the reluctance of many Moslems to form part of a united—but largely Hindu—India; the alarm of the Hindu community in Jammu at the possibility of Moslem domination either in an autonomous—but predominantly Moslem—Kashmir or under the more direct control of Pakistan; tensions between Sikhs and the Indian government; the Karen rebellion in Burma; the demands for independence by Naga and Mizo tribesmen; the restlessness of numerous communities in the Malay Archipelago under central control from Java.

Finally—aside from latent communal jealousies or overt conflict—the fundamental diversity of peoples and cultures within the same nation has been a continual stumbling block to effective administration. India must somehow integrate into the same national framework such highly educated minority groups as Parsees and Jains and such backward tribal peoples as Bhils and Gonds. Indonesia faces similar problems with its Dayaks, Ceylon with its Veddas, and the Philippines with the Igorots and other isolated mountain tribes. Linguistic diversity presents administrative problems unparalleled in the West—even in such multilingual states as Switzerland. Because of the very number of languages and dialects in his country, it is impossible for an educated Indian or Filipino or Indonesian to master more than a fraction of the various idioms spoken by his compatriots. The problem of communication is further complicated by the fact that many of these tongues belong to entirely different linguistic families, as different in phonetics and grammar and syntax as in vocabulary.

Thus even when communal groups manage to coexist amicably without marked antagonism, other factors tend to estrange them. Linguistic differences in particular impose serious restrictions on the forces that could best foster a sense of national unity—education, the press, literature, and commerce.

3

The potentiality for disintegration along communal lines thus constitutes the "tragic flaw" of many Oriental governments. This internal vulnerability necessarily has international implications, affecting relations with neighboring countries, with Western nations, and with Communist powers.

Since communal loyalties often transcend national boundaries, communal crises easily become international. The status of Moslem communities in India, the Philippines, or China engages the sympathies of Pakistan, Indonesia, Iran and other Asian states with predominantly Moslem populations. The welfare of Christian communities in India, Indochina, and Ceylon concerns their coreligionists in the Philippines and the West. China cannot remain detached from the large overseas Chinese settlements in Southeast Asia—Malaya and Burma and Indonesia, Thailand, the Philippines, and Vietnam. Neither North nor South Korea is indifferent to the problems of the Korean minority in Japan. India cannot ignore the status of Hindus in Pakistan, Ceylon, and Africa. Several of the most sacred shrines of the Sikh community are located in the West Punjab across the Pakistani border—and thus complicate India's relations with her neighbor. Buddhist communities in Ladakh and within Sikkim and Bhutan have been profoundly affected by developments in Chinese-occupied Tibet—even apart from the conflicting claims of both India and China to much of their territory. Purely internal communal problems can easily provoke diplomatic tensions or military conflicts between national states.

Communal tensions have rendered many Oriental countries unusually vulnerable to outside intervention. Short of armed invasion or conspiracy, they constitute Asia's greatest weakness, and they are largely responsible for her exaggerated sensitivity to Western "colonialism" and her vulnerability to Communist subversion.

By long experience, most Oriental peoples have grown painfully suspicious of foreign motives and acutely aware of the dangers of global politics. The possibility that outside powers might exploit communal differences for their own purposes has seemed very real—nor is this fear unjustified in the light of the last two centuries. The lingering distrust of the West and the current attractions of neutralism both spring in part from the fear that rivalries between non-Asian power blocs would be extended to the East and Asian pitted against Asian in the interests of Western powers. This has been a recurrent motif in Asian criticism of European policy in the past; indeed, as early as the sixteenth and seventeenth centuries it led to the expulsion of foreigners and the suppression of Christianity in Japan. Today it is intensified by the internal weakness of most Asian states— and by the spectacle of more than one country devastated by civil wars and divided by contrary commitments to Communist and Western powers.

For most independent states in southern Asia the major threats to national security are (in their own eyes) colonialism, Communism, and communalism—though neither their governments nor their public have agreed on the relative gravity of these political perils. At their Colombo meeting in 1954 the prime ministers of India, Ceylon, Pakistan, Burma, and Indonesia were divided as to whether the colonial or Communist danger was the more urgent. The one national hazard on which all could agree —and which all of these countries faced in varying degrees— was the communal problem, the threat of disintegration along the lines of religious, cultural, or regional loyalties.

For several decades European "imperialism"—an epithet now transferred indiscriminately to American policy—has been the whipping boy of Asian nationalists. Today, without discarding this convenient propaganda device as a political or diplomatic tool, some Oriental countries have become increasingly aware that the major threat to their independence is of Asian rather than Western origin. The Chinese invasion of India and the abortive Communist coup in Indonesia have, in particular, alerted both of these countries to their danger and—temporarily at least—increased the unpopularity of the Peking government in southern Asia. The presence of large groups of overseas Chinese in many Southeast Asian countries, the possibility of Communist-inspired dissidence among minority groups, and the infiltration of terrorists and guerrillas from the borders of Communist-held territory have awakened many of these states to a sense of their vulnerability.

Communal frictions offer an easy target for expansionist powers in this area—a ready opportunity to weaken the nations of southern Asia internally, to retard the establishment of strong central governments, and to stunt the development of responsible, integrated states. A firmly rooted sense of national identity, capable of transcending communal loyalties, seems essential if the commonwealths of this region are to survive.

Yet this can hardly be taken for granted. In many cases it still remains to be achieved, through a long, gradual, and inevitably painful process of integration. It is true, of course, that in the past different communal groups frequently combined their efforts and resources in pursuit of national independence. Today it is equally true that many of them still recognize that cooperation within a single national framework is vital for their mutual welfare and, indeed, for their very existence. Many have, accordingly, resisted the temptation to agitate for complete autonomy—and acquiesced in accepting the old colonial boundaries as national boundaries, the old colonial administrative organizations as bases for national administration. Nevertheless, the mere awareness that unity is expedient is not enough; it is not an adequate substitute for a real sense of national identity. In most instances nationhood is still a process of evolution, and neither the new Asian governments nor the Western powers can afford to overlook this fact.

For the former, the problem is fraught with exasperating ambiguities. Communal agitations today bear—all too frequently

—an embarrassing family resemblance to the movements for national independence a few decades ago. Communal leaders often appeal to the same principles, echo the same slogans, or imitate the same techniques that an earlier generation had employed against the British, the French, or the Dutch. Such martial echoes may sound discordant—out of tune as out of time —but, for some ears, they still retain their original power. They still carry overtones of patriotism even when (paradoxically) directed *against* the national government. Few officials can be altogether unconscious of the irony that turns against their own administrations the very political weapons—the very motives and ideals—they themselves helped to sharpen.

The task of controlling these communal movements is a delicate one. It will require all the proverbial skills of Oriental diplomacy —the penchant for subtlety and indirection, the delight in paradox and contradiction, the combination of firmness and flexibility, the symbolic virtues of bamboo and pine. Communal loyalties are subjective and psychological; the problem of integrating them into a national spirit is likewise psychological. They are ambivalent—both a potential asset and an imminent threat— and demand, accordingly, a certain ambiguity of approach, an unusual expertise and finesse. While too lax a rein may possibly run the risk of anarchy, too tight a rein is, surely, even more dangerous. By too rigid an exercise of central control, or too reckless a display of zeal, the pursuit of national unity can easily defeat itself. By estranging the various communal groups or pitting them against one another, it can result merely in disruption rather than harmony. To foster a valid sense of national identity, the central governments must approach the communal problem obliquely and indirectly, by compromise, rather than frontally and directly, by coercion. For this endeavor the Confucian mean—the rule of moderation—is indispensable, but even this is insufficient. Like Chinese painting, the art of government requires the knowledge of yin as well as yang; if they are to survive, the new states of South and Southeast Asia must take a leaf out of Lao-tse.

4

In the light of these communal problems, Western powers, in turn, should take a fresh look at "Asian nationalism"—a phenomenon that dismays the Occidental today almost as much as it alarmed his ancestors a century ago. The difference in his reaction is one of quality rather than degree; unlike his grandfather's generation, the educated Westerner does not *fear* Asia, nor does he distrust it; he is merely disappointed by its apparent failure to live up to the social and political ideals of the West. His dismay springs not from xenophobia but from a disillusioned liberalism. Like many an Asian intellectual, he had regarded "independence"—*swaraj* or *merdeka*—as a panacea for all evils. In Europe as in Asia, it had long been—and rightly—a goal of liberal opinion. The "liberation" of Asia *ought*, therefore, to represent a triumph of liberalism. And in a sense it does—though only partially and ambiguously.

Fortunately, politicians, like generals, are not logicians; in the field of international relations, as of combat, one requires quick decisions, and it is a great advantage to be fearless of an equivoque, reckless of a non sequitur, and heedless of the dangers of a hypothetical syllogism. Once the liberal goal had been achieved, once Asia had at last achieved her independence, Western observers (journalists, sporadic tourists, special correspondents, and diplomatists, who should have known better) were shocked that the new governments failed to implement the Western liberal platform. Instead of rebuilding Bloomsbury in Delhi and Jakarta, they fell embarrassingly short of enlightened European opinion. Indeed, even by conservative standards, they were sometimes distressingly reactionary.

"Asian nationalism" (for nearly two decades the phrase has been a cliché) was one of many phenomena that distressed Western liberals. Most of these were "well-wishers" toward the East; by habit as well as disposition they were conditioned to sympathy. Yet, in their eyes, nationalism was patently an anachronism; and—like their ancestors, the spokesmen of an earlier Enlightenment—they deplored the failure of the "noble savage" to abide by their own standards. Being charitable men, they usually attributed this regrettable development to resentment against the colonial past; they deplored it, but would courteously overlook it. Few saw it in perspective—against the background of the communal problem.

For it is largely in terms of the danger of communal disintegration and the "correlative objective" of national integration that the West must consider Asian nationalism. If it is indeed anachronistic in the West, it is still a necessary phase in the evolution of many Oriental societies. Indeed, the very concept of the nation-state is, in some instances, a legacy from European politics. Thus we in the West might do well to acknowledge the potential value of Asian nationalism as well as its dangers. There is surely a valid mean for nationalist sentiment between the extremes of communal disintegration on the one hand and a chauvinistic "Asiatic" imperialism on the other. The possibility of either extreme should not obscure the importance of the median, the "middle way." For many, if not most, of these states, an intelligent and restrained nationalism is essential for internal strength and stability. Only a sense of national identity can give them the necessary unity of spirit to meet the communal crises that could disrupt them internally. However old-fashioned it may seem to the modern West, only a well-established awareness of "nationhood" can create new and integrated societies out of Asia's ancient and diverse communities—fostering the will and capability for resisting aggression from without and disintegration from within.

NOTES

PREFACE

1. A more complicated version of this story appears in the *Udana* (VI, 4), part of the Pali canon of Buddhist scripture. See *Some Sayings of the Buddha*, trans. F. L. Woodward, pp. 285–88. (I am indebted to Mrs. Barbara Hutchins for this reference.) Another version of this tale is described by Romila Thapar, *A History of India*, Vol. I, p. 65.

2. E. W. F. Tomlin, *The Oriental Philosophers*, p. 14.

3. See Arthur O. Lovejoy, *The Great Chain of Being*, p. 14.

CHAPTER I

1. For the nomenclature of these societies I have followed Professor Arnold J. Toynbee's *A Study of History*. For the sake of simplicity, however, I have omitted at this point his subdivisions of these and other societies, the question of their derivation from older civilizations, and his dual classification of the successors of the "Hellenic society"

as Eastern Orthodoxy and Western Christendom.

2. Leonard Bloomfield, *Languages*, pp. 69–71.

3. For utopianism and the West, see F. S. C. Northrop, *The Meeting of East and West*, p. 291.

4. *Cf.* Hugh Tinker, *South Asia: A Short History*, pp. 32–34, on the fate of the Burmese kingdom and the eventual outcome of Tipu Sahib's conquests in Mysore and Malabar. Asian militarism and imperialism were not dead (a Burmese general "was ordered to march upon Calcutta and bind the British Viceroy in chains"!), but when they challenged European interests they had little chance of success. Not until the Russo-Japanese War did an imperialistic Asian state successfully confront an imperialistic European power.

5. For discussion of this "quarrel of continents" see Toynbee, Vol. VIII, Annex IX.C (i), " 'Asia' and 'Europe': Facts and Fantasies." For a study of the impact of Asia on Europe from 1500 to 1800 and the European view of Asia at the time, see Donald F. Lach, *Asia in the*

Making of Europe: The Century of Discovery. C. Northcote Parkinson has given an entertaining account of this "quarrel" in *East and West.*
6. *The Collected Writings of Thomas De Quincey,* ed. David Masson, Vol. III, pp. 441–43.
7. *Cf.* O. R. Gurney, *The Hittites,* p. 56, on Hittite references to the Land of Assuwa; "Assuwa is most probably to be located on the west coast of Asia Minor, and it has been suggested that the name is actually the original form of the word Asia, for the Roman province of Asia was precisely in this region." In *Ugarit and Minoan Crete,* p. 32, Cyrus H. Gordon, commenting on the classical myth of Europa and her brother Cadmus, observes that " 'Europa' and 'Cadmus' are an appropriate pair of Semitic names, meaning 'West' and 'East' respectively."

CHAPTER II

1. Several Moslem spokesmen insist that theocracy is "absolutely foreign to Islam." *Cf. Sources of Indian Tradition,* ed. William Theodore de Bary *et al.,* Vol. II, pp. 292–93, 318–19. This objection is valid if one accepts their definition of theocracy as specifically "a government by ordained priests, who wield authority as being specially appointed by those who claim to derive their rights from their sacerdotal position." In a broader sense, however, we may regard as theocratic any government (whether of church or state or both) which accepts as its supreme authority a supernaturally derived code of moral or social laws and attempts to regulate the behavior of the community (and of the individual) by this code.

2. The current emphasis on Indian spirituality has overshadowed the secular aspects of Indian culture as reflected in the *Arthashastra* and the *Kamasutra.* In Dandin's sixth-century novel *The Ten Princes,* written in Sanskrit, the tale of "Vishruta's Adventure" is an object lesson in the vital importance of "political science" in governing a kingdom. The education of a prince (as the same novel describes it) involves a singular mixture of the sacred and profane, ranging from scripture to romances and ethics to gambling.
3. This distinction is roughly comparable to Professor Zaehner's genetic classification of these religions as "Indian" and "Semitic." See R. C. Zaehner, *The Comparison of Religions.* We shall consider Taoism and Confucianism in a later chapter.
4. Many of the passages quoted in this chapter will be found in M. Monier-Williams, *Hinduism,* or in Swami Vivekananda, *Bhakti-Yoga.* Quotations from the *Bhagavad-Gita* have been taken from the translation by Swami Paramananda, in *The Wisdom of India and China,* ed. Lin Yutang.
5. See Daisetz Teitaro Suzuki, *Outlines of Mahayana Buddhism,* pp. 21, 221–22; Edward Conze, *Buddhism: Its Essence and Development, passim.*
6. Romila Thapar, *A History of India,* Vol. I, pp. 86–88.

CHAPTER III

1. *Barlaam and Josaphat, English Lives of Buddha,* ed. Joseph Jacobs, p. xi. Italics mine.
2. See William W. Appleton, *A Cycle of Cathay: The Chinese Vogue in England During the*

Seventeenth and Eighteenth Centuries, pp. 37, 39.

3. Cf. J. Hackin et al., Asiatic Mythology, pp. 352–58.

4. For a detailed and illuminating analysis of the modifications experienced by Buddhism as it passed from Indian soil to that of Tibet, China, and Japan, see Hajime Nakamura, Ways of Thinking of Eastern Peoples, revised English translation, ed. Philip P. Wiener.

5. Fung Yu-lan, A Short History of Chinese Philosophy, ed. Derk Bodde, p. 318.

6. Ibid., p. 21.

7. See Holmes Welch, Taoism, The Parting of the Way, revised edition, p. 124.

8. Fung Yu-lan, pp. 8–9, 22.

9. Welch, p. 111.

10. Ibid., p. 134; Fung Yu-lan, p. 3.

11. Cf. J. Hackin et al., pp. 252–384.

12. Fung Yu-lan, pp. 231–40.

13. The view that Western mathematics acquired its zero symbol indirectly from India through the Arabs is still widely accepted, even though it has been challenged in recent years. Thus Otto Neugebauer, The Exact Sciences in Antiquity, second edition, pp. 26–27, argues that a zero sign had been introduced into Babylonian mathematics before 500 B.C. and that the Arabic zero symbol was "simply taken from Greek astronomical manuscripts." The same author also cites evidence for "a direct contact of Hindu astronomy with Hellenistic tradition" and suggests that various Mesopotamian influences probably reached India "through the Greek and Persian civilization of the Sasanian period" (pp. 166, 186).

14. See André Malraux, Antimémoires, p. 199.

15. See Sources of Indian Tradition, ed. William Theodore de Bary et al., Vol. II, p. 370.

16. See Sources of Japanese Tradition, ed. William Theodore de Bary et al., Vol. II, p. 326.

17. See Malraux, p. 360.

18. Fung Yu-lan, pp. 323–24.

19. Foreign Affairs, Vol. 46 (1967), pp. 78–94.

20. See Malraux, p. 546.

21. H. G. Creel, Chinese Thought from Confucius to Mao Tse-tung, pp. 191–92, 197.

22. Joseph R. Levenson, " 'History' and 'Value': The Tensions of Intellectual Choice in Modern China," in Studies in Chinese Thought, ed. Arthur F. Wright, pp. 151–52.

23. Sources of Chinese Tradition, ed. William Theodore de Bary et al., Vol. II, pp. 48, 50, 52–54.

24. Sources of Japanese Tradition, ed. William Theodore de Bary et al., Vol. II, p. 100. Cf. Sources of Chinese Tradition, Vol. II, p. 82; Chinese Thought and Institutions, ed. John K. Fairbank, p. 229. "Chinese studies for the essential principles and Western studies for their practical application."

25. Sources of Chinese Tradition, Vol. II, p. 65.

26. Wright, Studies in Chinese Thought, p. 155.

27. Ibid., p. 156.

28. Joseph R. Levenson, Liang Ch'i-ch'ao and the Mind of Modern China, p. 7n.

29. Wright, pp. 158–59.

30. Levenson, pp. 2–3, in Sources of Chinese Tradition, Vol. II, pp. 185–86.

31. Sources of Chinese Tradition, Vol. II, pp. 191–92.

32. Sources of Japanese Tradition, Vol. II, pp. 100, 285, 288.

33. Ibid., pp. 351, 373, 383, 389, 399.

34. *Sources of Indian Tradition,* Vol. II, pp. 67–68, 98–100.
35. *Ibid.,* pp. 163–64.
36. *Ibid.,* pp. 257, 259.
37. See Malraux, p. 200.
38. *Sources of Indian Tradition,* Vol. II, p. 239.
39. *Ibid.,* pp. 209–10.
40. Malraux, pp. 341, 350.
41. *Sources of Indian Tradition,* Vol. II, pp. 358–61.

CHAPTER IV

1. See J. Hackin *et al., Asiatic Mythology,* p. 28.
2. F. S. C. Northrop, *The Meeting of East and West,* pp. 294, 374–75; *cf.* pp. 305–16.
3. F. Th. Stcherbatsky, *Buddhist Logic,* Vol. II, p. 142.
4. *Ibid.,* Vol. I, p. 26.
5. *Ibid.,* Vol. I, p. 285.
6. See Cicero, *De Inventione,* trans. H. M. Hubbell, pp. 99–123; *Rhetorica ad Herennium,* trans. Harry Caplan, pp. 107–13. Cicero attributes the five-part syllogism to the followers of Aristotle and Theophrastus. Modern scholars suggest Stoic influence and stress the "rhetorical adaptation of syllogistic reasoning" in the five-fold syllogism (or epicheirema) of Hermagoras.
7. Stcherbatsky, Vol. I, pp. 315–17. See especially pp. 295–319 for an extended discussion of differences between Indian and European theories of the syllogism.
8. Stcherbatsky, Vol. I, pp. 70, 79, 315; Vol. II, pp. 12–13.
9. George Thibaut, trans., *The Vedanta Sutras of Badarayana,* Part I, pp. 316–17, 355. *Cf.* p. 314, "In matters to be known from Scripture mere reasoning is not to be relied on."
10. *Ibid.,* pp. 19, 363.

11. *Ibid.,* Part I, p. 363; Part II, p. 35.
12. *Ibid.,* Part I, pp. 61–64.
13. Thibaut, Part II, pp. 155, 166, 401–02.
14. Thibaut, Part I, p. 190; Part II, p. 402.
15. *Ibid.,* Part I, p. xxx. *Cf.* pp. xci, c.
16. Like the term *lila, maya* has often been interpreted in too narrow or pejorative a sense. For discussion of this point, see S. Radhakrishnan, *The Hindu View of Life,* pp. 45–50 and *passim.*
17. R. C. Zaehner, *The Comparison of Religions: Religion East and West,* classifies these two groups of religions as "Indian" and "Semitic."
18. Benjamin Farrington, *Greek Science,* Vol. II, pp. 88–89.
19. See Edward Rosen, "Renaissance Science as Seen by Burckhardt and His Successors," in *The Renaissance,* ed. Tinsley Helton, pp. 77–103.
20. Gustave E. von Grunebaum, *Medieval Islam,* second edition, p. 342. The author is speaking specifically of Western Europe and Islam, but the same analogy may be applied to the Greek-speaking East.
21. George Sarton, *Appreciation of Ancient and Medieval Science During the Renaissance,* pp. 145–46.
22. *Ibid.,* pp. 16 ff.
23. Derek J. de Solla Price, "Automata and the Origins of Mechanism and Mechanistic Philosophy," in *Automata in History,* pp. 16–17.
24. Silvio A. Bedini, "The Role of Automata in the History of Technology," in *Automata in History,* p. 29.
25. Rosen, pp. 77–103.
26. Sarton, p. 158.
27. Grunebaum, p. 338.
28. *Ibid.,* pp. 245–46, 339–40. In *Ibn Khaldun's Philosophy of History*

Muhsin Mahdi challenges "the traditional view of Ibn Khaldun's fatherhood of modern social science and cultural history" as "not completely satisfactory."

29. Sarton, p. 172.

30. Francis Bacon, The Advancement of Learning, ed. J. E. Creighton, p. 366.

31. China's failure to develop these and other technological inventions or scientific discoveries more fully has been discussed passim in Joseph Needham's monumental but still incomplete study, Science and Civilization in China.

32. Lynn White, Jr., Medieval Technology and Social Change.

33. Ibid., p. 131.

34. Sarton, p. 160.

CHAPTER V

1. E. W. F. Tomlin, The Oriental Philosophers, p. 21.

2. Edward Conze, Buddhism: Its Essence and Development, pp. 12, 15.

3. Fung Yu-lan, A Short History of Chinese Philosophy, ed. Derk Bodde, pp. 1–6.

4. F. Th. Stcherbatsky, Buddhist Logic, Vol. I, p. 8.

5. Ibid., pp. 114 ff., 198 ff., 226 ff., and passim.

6. See the prefatory essay in D. T. Suzuki, Zen Buddhism, ed. William Barrett, pp. ix–x.

7. See Lynn White, Jr., Medieval Technology and Social Change, pp. 15–16, 35, 81, 86, 93, 97, 99, 104, 116, 119, 130–32, 140–41, 151–52.

8. Conze, p. 12.

9. Ibid., pp. 140–42.

10. Ibid., pp. 142–43.

11. Cf. Eric R. Dodds, The Greeks and the Irrational, pp. 68–69, on ecstatic prophecy in the cult of Apollo, on Rohde's confusion of "Apolline mediumship" and "Dionysiac experience," and on Nietzsche's "impressive antithesis . . . between the 'rational' religion of Apollo and the 'irrational' religion of Dionysus."

12. S. Radhakrishnan, Eastern Religions and Western Thought, second edition, pp. 134, 152–55.

13. Ibid., pp. 162, 171–77, 185, 192–98, 203–04, 215, 230, 240–41.

14. Voltaire himself includes a variation of this etymology in his Philosophy of History.

15. Heinrich Wölfflin, Classic Art: An Introduction to the Italian Renaissance, p. 246.

16. Though formerly etymologized as "secret sessions," the term upanishads is currently interpreted as "connections" or "equivalences" (between "microcosm and macrocosm"). Cf. Louis Renou, Indian Literature, trans. Patrick Evans, pp. 7–8; H. W. Bailey in Literatures of the East, ed. Eric B. Ceadel, p. 111.

17. Hans Jonas, The Gnostic Religion, second edition, p. 17.

18. Ibid., p. 252.

CHAPTER VI

1. S. Radhakrishnan, The Hindu View of Life, pp. 13, 16.

2. S. Radhakrishnan and C. A. Moore, eds., A Source Book in Indian Philosophy, p. xxvii.

3. S. Radhakrishnan, Eastern Religions and Western Thought, second edition, p. 21.

4. Bhagavad-Gita, trans. Swami Paramananda, in The Wisdom of India and China, ed. Lin Yutang, Chapters 6, 12.

5. These personal deities may not, by the strictest Vedanta and Mahayana doctrines, be ultimately

"real"; nor are they truly "without"—external to the observer. Nevertheless they are "manifestations" of reality. The "Highest Self" (as Shankara puts it) manifests itself thus for the purpose of "devotion." Such theoretical distinctions have, however, relatively little influence on popular worship.

6. Radhakrishnan, *Eastern Religions,* p. 64.
7. Rudolf Otto, *Mysticism East and West,* trans. Bertha L. Bracey and Richenda C. Payne, p. 225.
8. Radhakrishnan, *Eastern Religions,* p. 65.
9. Otto, p. 183.
10. Radhakrishnan, *Eastern Religions,* pp. 30, 48–50.
11. *Ibid.,* p. 75.
12. Otto, p. 5.
13. *Ibid.,* pp. 123, 126–27, 136, 187, 223.
14. *Ibid.,* p. 183. *cf.* p. 179.
15. *Ibid.,* p. 167.
16. F. Th. Stcherbatsky, *Buddhist Logic,* Vol. I, p. 20.
17. Otto, p. 162.
18. *Ibid.,* pp. 162, 166.
19. *Ibid.,* p. 163.
20. *Bhagavad-Gita,* Chapters 2, 11. *Cf.* Chapter 12.
21. Otto, p. 95.
22. See *Traditional India,* ed. O. L. Chavarria-Aguilar, p. 111.
23. *Cf. Meister Eckhart,* trans. Raymond B. Blakney, p. xi.
24. Patanjali, *Aphorisms,* trans. Swami Vivekananda, in *The Wisdom of India and China,* ed. Lin Yutang, p. 127.
25. *Ibid.,* p. 78. *Cf.* p. 80.
26. George Thibaut, trans., *The Vedanta Sutras of Badarayana,* Vol. I, p. 15; Vol. II, p. 171.
27. *Ibid.,* Vol. II, pp. 402–03.
28. *Ibid.,* Vol. I, pp. 18, 101.
29. *Ibid.,* Vol. I, p. 35.
30. *Ibid.,* Vol. II, p. 161.

31. *Ibid.,* Vol. I, pp. 23–25, 34.
32. *Ibid.,* Vol. I, pp. 185–86; Vol. II, pp. 139, 163, 408. Italics mine.
33. *Ibid.,* Vol. I, p. 32; Vol. II, p. 62.
34. D. T. Suzuki, *Outlines of Mahayana Buddhism,* pp. 95, 100–09.
35. *Cf.* Suzuki, p. 46; Edward Conze, *Buddhism: Its Essence and Development,* p. 172.
36. Suzuki, p. 263; Conze, p. 172.
37. Suzuki, p. 46.
38. Stcherbatsky, Vol. II, pp. 30–33. *Cf. ibid.,* p. 30n.; Vol. I, p. 162.
39. *Cf.* Stcherbatsky, Vol. II, pp. 31–32, for Vinitadeva's emphasis on the "decisive moment" when "the meditating man suddenly acquires the faculty of transcendental intuition" and "changes completely," realizing "the Relativity (*sunyata*) and unreality of the phenomenal veil concealing absolute Reality" and understanding that samsara and nirvana are the same.
40. Stcherbatsky, Vol. I, pp. 21, 162.
41. *Ibid.,* p. 32n.

Chapter VII

1. John Leighton, *On Japanese Art: A Discourse Delivered at the Royal Institution of Great Britain,* pp. 3–10.
2. Lafcadio Hearn, *Glimpses of Unfamiliar Japan,* ed. U. Miyagi, pp. 67–69.
3. *Ibid.,* pp. 1–27.
4. Laurence Binyon, *Painting in the Far East,* third edition, revised, pp. 3–5.
5. *Ibid.,* p. 6.
6. *Ibid.,* p. 7.
7. Sir Thomas Arnold, *Painting in Islam,* p. 70.
8. *Ibid.,* pp. 66–68. The story re-

sembles the alleged contest between Apelles and Zeuxis; *cf.* the versions in Pliny and in Sir Thomas Browne.

CHAPTER VIII

1. Gorgias of Leontini (485?–370? B.C.). Though excessive use of the "Gorgian figures" could result in an ornate or "gorgeous" style, there is apparently no connection between the two words. The medieval French *gorgias* (from which the English "gorgeous" was derived) is still regarded as of uncertain origin. In the Renaissance the latter term (in the sense of "magnificent" or "adorned with rich or brilliant colors") was extended to phraseology and literary coloring. The *Oxford English Dictionary* (*s.v.* gorgeous) cites several late sixteenth-century examples of this usage—"gorgeous and fine woordes," "gorgeous neattnes of Ciceroe's speach," etc. It is possible that this application of the term "gorgeous" to rhetorical ornament may have been partly influenced by its verbal resemblance to "Gorgian figures."
2. *Cf.* Cicero, *Orator,* trans. H. M. Hubbell, p. 325; Quintilian, *Institutio Oratoria,* trans. H. E. Butler, Vol. III, pp. 187–89; Vol. IV, pp. 459–61. For Renaissance conceptions of the Asiatic and Attic styles, see George Williamson, *The Senecan Amble,* and Morris William Croll, *Style, Rhetoric, and Rhythm: Essays,* ed. J. Max Patrick.
3. See William Willetts, *Chinese Art,* pp. 298, 323–39.
4. *Cf.* Jean Seznec, *The Survival of the Pagan Gods,* trans. Barbara F. Sessions, p. 241n.
5. Richard D. Lane, *Masters of the Japanese Print,* p. 206, suggests that the French postimpressionists, threatened by the encroachment of

photography on "their traditional function," found in Japanese prints a partial solution to their problems —"first, the abandonment of surface realism, and then the reduction of nature to a decorative pattern of only two dimensions." See also Tokuzo Sagara, *Japanese Fine Arts, passim.*
6. Hugo Munsterberg, *The Arts of Japan,* pp. 109, 160. Italics mine.

CHAPTER IX

1. Sir Thomas Arnold, *Painting in Islam,* pp. 66, 69.
2. See William Cohn, *Chinese Painting,* second revised edition, plates 136, 145–46.
3. *Ibid.,* pp. 32, 79, 81.
4. William Willetts, *Chinese Art,* p. 595.
5. Hugo Munsterberg, *The Arts of Japan, An Illustrated History,* pp. 43, 92, 98, 100, 150.
6. Ananda K. Coomaraswamy, *The Transformation of Nature in Art,* second edition, pp. 9–15.
7. *Ibid.,* p. 15.
8. Oswald Spengler, *The Decline of the West,* trans. C. F. Atkinson, pp. 174–75, 190–91, 203.
9. *Ibid.,* pp. 239–42.
10. *Ibid.,* pp. 224–27.
11. *Ibid.,* p. 219.
12. *Saddharma Pundarika or the Lotus of the True Law,* trans. H. Kern, pp. 3, 7, 15, 32, 146, 154–55.
13. Mircea Eliade, *Cosmos and History: The Myth of the Eternal Return,* second edition, trans. Willard R. Trask, pp. 116–17.
14. *Ibid.,* pp. 108, 113–16.
15. Edward Conze, *Buddhism: Its Essence and Development,* p. 49.
16. Heinrich Zimmer, *Myths and Symbols in Indian Art and Civilization,* ed. Joseph Campbell, p. 6.
17. Conze, p. 155.

18. Cohn, p. 17.

19. Basil Gray, *Buddhist Cave Paintings at Tun-huang*, p. 72; see plates 51B, 54A, 55, 64A.

20. *Ibid.*, pp. 56, 66; for other instances of organization in depth, *cf.* pp. 24–34, 56–59, 64, 66.

21. Coomaraswamy, p. 30.

22. Willetts, p. 376.

23. *Ibid.*, p. 376.

24. Erwin Panofsky, "Artist, Scientist, Genius: Notes on the 'Renaissance Dämmerung,' " in *The Renaissance: Six Essays*, pp. 128, 133, 140–42.

25. Earl Rosenthal in *The Renaissance*, ed. Tinsley Helton, p. 67.

26. Coomaraswamy, pp. 33–34.

27. *Ibid.*, p. 29.

28. Panofsky, p. 124.

29. Heinrich Wölfflin, *Classic Art: An Introduction to the Italian Renaissance*, p. 4.

30. Ernest F. Fenollosa, *Epochs of Chinese and Japanese Art*, new and revised edition, Vol. II, pp. 13, 18.

31. Sherman E. Lee, *Chinese Landscape Painting*, second edition, p. 6.

32. *Ibid.*, p. 5.

33. Willetts, p. 558.

CHAPTER X

1. Langdon Warner, *The Enduring Art of Japan*, p. 101.

2. Henry P. Bowie, *On the Laws of Japanese Painting*, pp. 8, 12.

3. Ernest F. Fenollosa, *Epochs of Chinese and Japanese Art*, new and revised edition, Vol. II, p. 14. Italics mine.

4. F. S. C. Northrop, *The Meeting of East and West*, pp. 305–06.

5. Chiang Yee, in *Ideological Differences and World Order*, ed. F. S. C. Northrop, p. 66.

6. Okakura, Kakuzo, *The Book of Tea*, pp. 31–45. *Cf.* Bowie, pp. 46–47 on the "value of suppression in design."

7. D. T. Suzuki, *Zen and Japanese Buddhism*, pp. 3, 24, 27, 141.

8. Alan W. Watts, *The Way of Zen*, pp. 169–75.

9. Rudolf Otto, *Mysticism East and West*, trans. Bertha L. Bracey and Richenda C. Payne, p. 166.

10. Holmes Welch, *Taoism, The Parting of the Way*, revised edition, p. 159.

11. Laurence Binyon, *Painting in the Far East*, third edition, revised, pp. 11–25.

12. William Willetts, *Chinese Art*, pp. 584–87.

13. Hsieh Ho's first canon (*Ch'i Yün Shêng Tung*) has been variously translated. *Cf.* William Cohn, *Chinese Painting*, second revised edition, p. 11; Osvald Sirén, *The Chinese on the Art of Painting*, pp. 18–25; Ernest F. Fenollosa, *Epochs of Chinese and Japanese Art*, Vol. II, p. 83; Laurence Binyon, *Painting in the Far East*, third edition, revised, pp. 11, 72; Michael Sullivan, *Introduction to Chinese Art*, p. 98; Holmes Welch, *Taoism*, revised edition, p. 160; Ananda K. Coomaraswamy, *The Transformation of Nature in Art*, p. 20; Sherman Lee, *Chinese Landscape Painting*, second edition, revised, p. 17; Peter C. Swann, *The Art of China, Korea, and Japan*, p. 37 and *passim.*; Benjamin Rowland, Jr., *Art in East and West*, p. 20; Mai-mai Sze, *The Way of Chinese Painting*, p. 177 and *passim.*

14. Fenollosa, Vol. I, pp. 28–29.

15. Fenollosa, Vol. II, pp. 142–54.

16. *Ibid.*, p. 146.

17. James F. Cahill, "Confucian Elements in the Theory of Painting," in *Confucianism and Chinese Civilization*, ed. Arthur F. Wright, p. 77.

18. See Cahill, pp. 77–98. See also Cahill's *Chinese Painting*.
19. Mai-mai Sze, *The Way of Chinese Painting*, p. 54.
20. Sherman Lee, *Chinese Landscape Painting*, second edition, pp. 3–4.
21. Mai-mai Sze, pp. 55–57.
22. Osvald Sirén, *The Chinese on the Art of Painting*, pp. 102–03, 131–32.
23. Holmes Welch, *Taoism*, revised edition, pp. 147–48.
24. Sirén, p. 146.
25. See Peter C. Swann, *The Art of China, Korea, and Japan*, pp. 179–80.
26. Tokuzo Sagara, *Japanese Fine Arts*, pp. 107–11.
27. Swann, p. 179.

Chapter XI

1. F. Th. Stcherbatsky, *Buddhist Logic*, Vol. I, pp. 80–87.
2. *Ibid.*, pp. 92–95, 111.
3. *Ibid.*, p. 98.
4. Lafcadio Hearn, *Glimpses of Japan*, ed. U. Miyagi, p. 73.
5. *Ibid.*, p. 77.
6. Stcherbatsky, Vol. I, pp. 205–06; cf. p. 211 on "empirical perception."
7. *Ibid.*, p. 152. Cf. pp. 151, 154.
8. Stcherbatsky, Vol. II, pp. 33–34.
9. *Ibid.*, pp. 35–36.
10. *Ibid.*, p. 45; cf. p. 37.
11. Langdon Warner, *The Enduring Art of Japan*, pp. 86–89.

Chapter XII

1. *The Basic Works of Aristotle*, ed. Richard McKeon, pp. 1198–99, 1207. Cf. p. 1219.
2. Charles de Secondat, Baron de Montesquieu, *The Spirit of Laws*, trans. Thomas Nugent, revised edition, Vol. I, pp. 266–69.
3. Edward Gibbon, *The Decline and Fall of the Roman Empire*, ed. Dero A. Saunders, p. 66.
4. Richard Jones, *Peasant Rents: An Essay on the Distribution of Wealth and on the Sources of Taxation, 1831*, pp. 5, 97–101, 124.
5. William Alexander Mackinnon, *History of Civilization and Public Opinion*, third edition, Vol. II, pp. 186–91.
6. *Collected Works of John Stuart Mill*, Vol. II, *Principles of Political Economy*, ed. J. M. Robson, pp. 13–14.
7. *The Collected Writings of Thomas De Quincey*, ed. David Masson, Vol. XIV. pp. 357–59.
8. Henry Thomas Buckle, *History of Civilization in England*, Vol. I, Part I, pp. 53–58, 80.
9. Amos Dean, *The History of Civilization*, Vol. I, pp. 693–95.
10. Meredith Townsend, *Asia and Europe*, third edition, pp. 30–32.
11. Georg Wilhelm Friedrich Hegel, *The Philosophy of History*, trans. J. Sibree, pp. 12–19; see especially Part I "The Oriental World," pp. 111–222. Cf. J. B. Bury, *The Idea of Progress: An Inquiry into Its Origin and Growth*, pp. 254–55.
12. Karl A. Wittfogel, *Oriental Despotism: A Comparative Study of Total Power*, pp. 273–83, 400–09, 445.
13. *Ibid.*, pp. iii–iv. For China as an Oriental society, see also John King Fairbank, *The United States and China*, new edition, pp. 47–51, 324. In his important essay "Oriental Society" in *The Concept of Ideology and Other Essays*, pp. 62–93, George Lichtheim re-examines the development of Marx's and Engels' views on "the subject of

Oriental society" and the problem of how far their remarks on this subject are "reducible to a consistent pattern."

14. Wolfram Eberhard, "The Political Function of Astronomy and Astronomers in Han China," in *Chinese Thought and Institutions,* ed. John K. Fairbank, pp. 33–70, 345–52.

15. James T. C. Liu, "An Early Sung Reformer: Fan Chung-yen," in *Chinese Thought and Institutions,* pp. 105–31.

16. William Theodore de Bary, "Chinese Despotism and the Confucian Ideal: A Seventeenth-Century View," in *Chinese Thought and Institutions,* pp. 163–203.

17. *Cf. Leibniz, Selections,* ed. Philip P. Wiener, pp. xlix–li, 596–99, on Leibniz's admiration for Chinese mathematics, moral philosophy, and "political and social administration"; and Donald F. Lach, "Leibniz and China" in *Journal of the History of Ideas* (1945), pp. 453 f.

18. Lewis A. Maverick, *China—A Model for Europe,* pp. 12, 18, 30, 36, 141, 225, 264.

19. Montesquieu, Vol. I, p. 123n.

20. Maverick, p. 225.

21. Montesquieu, Vol. I, pp. 122–25. For European attitudes toward China's government and civilization, see also the following studies: William W. Appleton, *A Cycle of Cathay: The Chinese Vogue in England During the Seventeenth and Eighteenth Centuries;* Virgile Pinot, *La Chine et la formation de l'esprit philosophique en France* (1640–1740); Geoffrey F. Hudson, *Europe and China: A Survey of Their Relations from Earliest Times to 1800.*

22. Mackinnon, Vol. II, pp. 187–90.

23. Jones, p. 51. *Cf.* pp. 20–22.

24. Wittfogel, pp. 369–412.

25. *Sources of Chinese Tradition,* ed. William Theodore de Bary *et al.,* Vol. II, pp. 89, 97, 102, 131.

26. *Sources of Japanese Tradition,* ed. William Theodore de Bary *et al.,* Vol. II, pp. 143, 160–61, 228, 242, and *passim.*

27. *Sources of Indian Tradition,* ed. William Theodore de Bary *et al.,* Vol. II, pp. 114, 119, 140–41.

28. *Cf.* Merritt Y. Hughes, "Satan and the 'Myth' of the Tyrant," in *Ten Perspectives on Milton,* pp. 165–95.

CHAPTER XIII

1. The story has an Indian parallel in the tale of "The Monkey and the Pitch-Trap." See F. L. Woodward, trans., *Some Sayings of the Buddha,* pp. 242–44.

SELECT BIBLIOGRAPHY

• •
•

Appleton, William W., *A Cycle of Cathay: The Chinese Vogue in England During the Seventeenth and Eighteenth Centuries.* New York, 1951.

Aristotle, *The Basic Works of Aristotle,* ed. Richard McKeon. New York, 1941.

Arnold, Sir Thomas, *Painting in Islam.* New York, 1965.

Art Treasures from Japan, Los Angeles County Museum of Art. Tokyo, 1965.

Art Treasures of Japan, ed. Yashiro Yukio. Tokyo, 1960.

Ashton, Sir Leigh, and Gray, Basil, *Chinese Art.* London, 1951.

Asin, Miguel, *Islam and the Divine Comedy,* trans. and abridged by Harold Sunderland. New York, 1926.

Aston, W. G., *A History of Japanese Literature.* London, 1933.

Automata in History, William Andrews Clark Memorial Library. Los Angeles, 1964.

Bacon, Francis, *The Advancement of Learning,* ed. J. E. Creighton. New York, 1944.

Balazs, Étienne, *Chinese Civilization and Bureaucracy,* trans. H. M. Wright, ed. Arthur F. Wright. New Haven and London, 1967.

Barthold, V.-V., *La découverte de l'Asie, histoire de l'orientalisme en Europe et en Russie,* trans. B. Nikitine. Paris, 1947.

Basham, A. L., *The Wonder That Was India.* London, 1954.

Becker, Carl L., *The Heavenly City of the Eighteenth-Century Philosophers.* New Haven, 1932.

Benedetto, L. V., *The Travels of Marco Polo,* trans. Aldo Ricci. New York, 1931.

Binyon, Laurence, *Painting in the Far East,* third edition, revised. New York, 1959.

Bluntschli, J. K., *The Theory of the State*, trans. D. G. Ritchie *et al.* Oxford, 1885.

Blyth, R. H., *Haiku*. Tokyo, 1950–1952.

Boer, T. J. de, *The History of Philosophy in Islam*, trans. Edward R. Jones. New York, 1967.

Bossuet, Jacques Bénigne, *Discours sur l'histoire universelle*. Paris, 1836.

Bouquet, A. C., *Comparative Religion*, third and revised edition. Harmondsworth, Middlesex, 1950.

Bowers, Faubion, *Japanese Theatre*. London, 1934.

Bowie, Henry P., *On the Laws of Japanese Painting*. New York, n.d.

Brandt, Conrad, Schwartz, Benjamin, and Fairbank, John K., *A Documentary History of Chinese Communism*. London and Cambridge, Mass., 1952.

Brière, O., S.J., *Fifty Years of Chinese Philosophy, 1898–1948*, trans. Laurence G. Thompson, ed. Dennis J. Doolin. New York and Washington, 1965.

Brower, Robert H., and Miner, Earl, *Japanese Court Poetry*. Stanford, 1961.

Browne, E. G., *A Literary History of Persia*. Cambridge, 1928.

Bruce, J. Percy, *Chu Hsi and His Masters: An Introduction to Chu Hsi and the Sung School of Chinese Philosophy*. London, 1928.

Buckle, Henry Thomas, *History of Civilization in England*. New York, 1913.

Burke, Edmund, *The Speeches of the Right Honourable Edmund Burke on the Impeachment of Warren Hastings*. London, 1885.

Bury, J. B., *The Idea of Progress: An Inquiry into Its Origin and Growth*. New York, 1955.

Butler, Dom Cuthbert, *Western Mysticism*. New York, 1924.

Cahill, James F., *Chinese Painting*. Cleveland, 1960.

The Cambridge History of India. Cambridge, 1922–.

Ceadel, Eric B., ed., *Literatures of the East*. London, 1953.

Chao, Nai-Tuan, *Richard Jones: An Early English Institutionalist*. New York, 1930.

Chavarria-Aguilar, O. L., ed., *Traditional India*. Englewood Cliffs, N.J., 1964.

Chiang Yee, *The Chinese Eye*. London, 1935.

The Chinese Classics, trans. James Legge, second edition. Oxford, 1893–1895.

Chu Hsi, *The Philosophy of Human Nature*, trans. J. Percy Bruce. London, 1922.

Cicero, *De Inventione*, trans. H. M. Hubbell. London and Cambridge, Mass., 1949.

—— *Orator,* trans. H. M. Hubbell. Cambridge, Mass., and London, 1939.

Clyde, Paul H., *The Far East: A History of the Impact of the West on Eastern Asia,* third revised edition. New York, 1958.

Cohn, William, *Chinese Painting,* second revised edition. New York, 1950.

Conze, Edward, *Buddhism: Its Essence and Development.* New York, 1959.

—— *et al.,* eds., *Buddhist Texts Through the Ages.* New York, 1964.

Coomaraswamy, Ananda K., *Christian and Oriental Philosophy of Art.* New York, 1957.

—— *History of Indian and Indonesian Art.* New York, 1965.

—— *The Transformation of Nature in Art,* second edition. New York, 1956.

Creel, H. G., *Chinese Thought from Confucius to Mao Tse-tung.* New York and Toronto, 1953.

Croll, Morris William, *Style, Rhetoric, and Rhythm: Essays,* ed. J. Max Patrick. Princeton, 1966.

Crozier, Brian, *South-East Asia in Turmoil.* Baltimore, 1965.

Dandin's Dasha-Kumara-Charita, The Ten Princes, trans. Arthur W. Ryder. Chicago, 1960.

Dasgupta, Surendranath, *A History of Indian Philosophy.* Cambridge, England, 1922–1955.

Davids, T. W. Rhys, *Buddhism, Its History and Literature.* London, 1923.

Day, Clarence Burton, *The Philosophers of China, Classical and Contemporary.* New York, 1962.

Dean, Amos, *The History of Civilization.* Albany, N. Y., 1868.

De Bary, William Theodore, *et al.,* eds., *Sources of Chinese Tradition.* Introduction to Oriental Civilizations. Records of Civilization, Sources and Studies, edited under the auspices of the Department of History, Columbia University. New York and London, 1965.

—— *Sources of Indian Tradition.* Introduction to Oriental Civilizations. Records of Civilization, Sources and Studies. New York and London, 1966.

—— *Sources of Japanese Tradition.* Introduction to Oriental Civilizations. Records of Civilization, Sources and Studies. New York and London, 1965.

De Quincey, Thomas, *The Collected Writings of Thomas De Quincey,* ed. David Masson. Edinburgh, 1890.

De Vries, Jan, *Heroic Song and Heroic Legend,* trans. B. J. Timmer. London, New York, Toronto, 1963.

Dodds, E. R., *The Greeks and the Irrational.* Berkeley, 1951.

Draper, John William, *History of the Intellectual Development of Europe,* revised edition. New York, 1878.

Duchesne-Guillemin, Jacques, *The Hymns of Zarathustra,* trans. M. Henning. Boston, 1963.

Dutt, Vidya Prakash, *China and the World: An Analysis of Communist China's Foreign Policy.* New York and Washington, 1966.

East, W. Gordon and Spate, O. H. K., eds., *The Changing Map of Asia: A Political Geography.* London, 1950.

Eckhart, Meister, *Meister Eckhart,* trans. Raymond B. Blakney. New York, 1941.

Elegant, Robert S., *The Dragon's Seed: Peking and the Overseas Chinese.* New York, 1959.

—— "China's Next Phase." *Foreign Affairs,* Vol. 46 (1967), pp. 137–50.

Eliade, Mircea. *Cosmos and History: The Myth of the Eternal Return,* trans. Willard R. Trask. New York, 1959.

—— *The Sacred and the Profane,* trans. Willard R. Trask. New York, 1961.

Eliot, H. M., and Dowson, J., eds., *The History of India as Told by Its Own Historians.* Cambridge, 1931.

Fairbank, John King, *The United States and China,* new edition. New York, 1962.

—— ed., *Chinese Thought and Institutions.* London and Chicago, 1957, 1967.

Farrington, Benjamin, *Greek Science.* Harmondsworth, Middlesex, 1949.

Fenollosa, Ernest F., *Epochs of Chinese and Japanese Art,* new and revised edition. New York, 1963.

Ferguson, W. K. *et al., The Renaissance: Six Essays.* New York, 1962.

Foster, William, ed., *Early Travels in India, 1583–1619.* London and New York, 1921.

Fujisawa, Chikao, *Zen and Shinto: The Story of Japanese Philosophy.* New York, 1959.

Fung Yu-lan, *A Short History of Chinese Philosophy,* ed. Derk Bodde. New York and London, 1966.

—— *The Spirit of Chinese Philosophy,* trans. E. R. Hughes. Boston, 1962.

Geertz, Clifford, *The Religion of Java.* London, 1964.

Gettleman, Marvin E., ed., *Vietnam: History, Documents, and Opinions on a Major World Crisis.* Greenwich, Conn., 1966.

Ghirschman, Roman, *Persian Art, the Parthian and Sassanian Dynasties, 249 B.C.—A.D. 651,* trans. Stuart Gilbert and James Emmons. New York, 1962.

Gibbon, Edward, *The Decline and Fall of the Roman Empire*, ed. Dero A. Saunders. New York, 1962.

Giles, H. A., *A History of Chinese Literature*. London, 1901.

Goodrich, L. Carrington, *A Short History of the Chinese People*. New York, 1943.

Gordon, Antoinette K., *The Iconography of Tibetan Lamaism*, revised edition. Rutland, Vt., and Tokyo, 1959.

Gordon, Cyrus H., *The Common Background of Greek and Hebrew Civilizations*. New York, 1965.

———— *Ugarit and Minoan Crete*. New York, 1967.

Gray, Basil, *Buddhist Cave Paintings at Tun-huang*. Chicago, 1959.

Griswold, Alexander B., Kim, Chewon, and Pott, Peter H., *The Art of Burma, Korea, Tibet*. New York, 1964.

Grousset, René, *La Chine et son art*. Paris, 1951.

———— *The Civilizations of the East*, trans. Catherine Alison Phillips. New York and London, 1931.

———— *The Rise and Splendour of the Chinese Empire*, trans. Anthony Watson-Gandy and Terence Gordon. London, 1952.

Grube, Ernst J., *The World of Islam*. New York and Toronto, 1966.

Grunebaum, Gustave E. von, *Medieval Islam*, second edition. Chicago, 1961.

Gurney, O. R., *The Hittites*. Baltimore, 1962.

Hackin, J. *et al.*, *Asiatic Mythology*, trans. F. M. Atkinson. New York, 1963.

Hall, D. G. E., *History of South-east Asia*, third edition. New York, 1968.

Harle, J. C., *Temple Gateways in South India*. Oxford, 1963.

Hearn, Lafcadio, *Glimpses of Japan*, ed. U. Miyagi. S.l., n.d.

———— *Japan: An Attempt at Interpretation*. New York, 1904.

Hegel, Georg Wilhelm Friedrich, *The Philosophy of History*, trans. J. Sibree. New York, 1956.

Helton, Tinsley, ed., *The Renaissance*. Madison, Wisconsin, 1964.

Hitti, P. K., *The Arabs: A Short History*. London, 1948.

Hourani, G. F., *Arab Seafaring in the Indian Ocean in Ancient and Early Medieval Times*. Princeton, 1951.

Hsia, C. T., *A History of Modern Chinese Fiction, 1917–1957*. New Haven and London, 1962.

Hudson, Geoffrey F., *Europe and China: A Survey of Their Relations from Earliest Times to 1800*. London, 1931.

Hume, R. E., *The Thirteen Principal Upanishads*, second edition. Oxford, 1931.

Hughes, E. R., *The Invasion of China by the Western World*. New York, 1938.

Hughes, Merritt Y., *Ten Perspectives on Milton*. New Haven and London, 1965.

Humphreys, Christmas, *Buddhism*. London, 1958.

India: Paintings from Ajanta Caves, UNESCO World Art Series. New York Graphic Society, Paris, 1954.

Jacobs, Joseph, ed., *Barlaam and Josaphat, English Lives of Buddha*. London, 1896.

Japanese Painters of the Floating World, ed. Martie W. Young and Robert J. Smith. Ithaca, N.Y., and Utica, N.Y., 1966.

Jenyns, Soame, *A Background to Chinese Painting*. New York, 1966.

Jonas, Hans, *The Gnostic Religion*, second edition, enlarged. Boston, 1963.

Jones, Richard, *Peasant Rents: An Essay on the Distribution of Wealth and on the Sources of Taxation, 1831*. New York and London, 1895.

Kahin, George McT., ed., *Major Governments of Asia*. Ithaca, N.Y., 1958.

Kaltenmark, Odile, *Chinese Literature*, trans. Anne-Marie Geoghegan. New York, 1964.

Keene, Donald, *Japanese Literature: An Introduction for Western Readers*. London, 1953.

Keith, A. B., *A History of Sanskrit Literature*. New York, 1928.

—— *Religion and Philosophy of the Vedas and Upanishads*. Cambridge, Mass., 1925.

Kidder, J. Edward, Jr., *Japanese Temples, Sculpture, Paintings, Gardens and Architecture*. Tokyo and Amsterdam, 1967.

Kimble, George H. T., *Geography in the Middle Ages*. London, 1938.

Kitagawa, Joseph M., *Religions of the East*, enlarged edition. Philadelphia, 1968.

Kramrisch, Stella, *The Art of India*, third edition. Greenwich, Conn., 1965.

Lach, Donald F., *Asia in the Making of Europe: The Century of Discovery*. Chicago, 1964.

—— and Flaumenhaft, Carol, eds., *Asia on the Eve of Europe's Expansion*. Englewood Cliffs, N.J., 1965.

Lai Ming, *A History of Chinese Literature*. New York, 1966.

Lancman, Eli, *Chinese Portraiture*. Rutland, Vt., 1966.

Lane, Richard D., *Masters of the Japanese Print*. Garden City, N.Y., 1962.

Latourette, Kenneth Scott, *The Chinese: Their History and Culture*, third edition, revised. New York, 1946.

—— *The History of Japan*. New York, 1947.

—— *A Short History of the Far East*. New York, 1957.

Law, B. C., *A History of Pali Literature*. London, 1933.

Lee, Sherman E., *Chinese Landscape Painting*, second edition. Cleveland, 1962.

The Legacy of India, ed. G. T. Garratt. London, 1937.

The Legacy of Islam, ed. Sir Thomas Arnold and Alfred Guillaume. London, 1931.

Legge, James, trans., *The I Ching, The Book of Changes*. New York, 1963.

Leibniz, Gottfried W. von, *Leibniz, Selections*, ed. Philip P. Wiener. New York, 1951.

Leighton, John, *On Japanese Art: A Discourse Delivered at the Royal Institution of Great Britain*. London, 1863.

Levenson, Joseph R., *Liang Ch'i-ch'ao and the Mind of Modern China*. Berkeley and Los Angeles, 1967.

Levy, Reuben, *Persian Literature: An Introduction*. Oxford, 1923.

Lewis, Bernard, *The Arabs in History*. London, 1950.

Li Chien-nung, *The Political History of China, 1840–1928*, trans. and ed. Ssu-yu Teng and Jeremy Ingalls. Stanford, California, 1967.

Lichtheim, George, *The Concept of Ideology and Other Essays*. New York, 1967.

————, "What Is Left of Communism." *Foreign Affairs*, Vol. 46 (1967), pp. 78–94.

Lin Yutang, ed., *The Wisdom of India and China*. New York, 1942.

Liu, James J. Y., *The Art of Chinese Poetry*. Chicago, 1966.

Liu, Wu-chi, *An Introduction to Chinese Literature*. Bloomington, Ind., and London, 1966.

Lovejoy, Arthur O., *Essays in the History of Ideas*. Baltimore, 1948.

———— *The Great Chain of Being*. New York, 1960.

Macauliffe, M. A., *The Sikh Religion*. Oxford, 1909.

McCrindle, J. W., *Ancient India as Described in Classical Literature*. Westminster, 1901.

MacFarquhar, Roderick, *The Hundred Flowers Campaign and the Chinese Intellectuals*. New York, 1960.

Mackinnon, William Alexander, *History of Civilization and Public Opinion*, third edition. London, 1849.

Mahdi, Muhsin, *Ibn Khaldun's Philosophy of History*. Chicago, 1957.

Majumdar, R. C. *et al.*, *Advanced History of India*, second edition. New York, 1950.

Malraux, André, *Antimémoires*. Paris, 1967.

Marx, Karl, *Capital: A Critical Analysis of Capitalist Production*, trans. Samuel Moore and Edward Aveling, ed. Frederick Engels. London, 1912.

Matthew, Helen G., ed., *Asia in the Modern World*. New York, 1963.

Maverick, Lewis A., *China—A Model for Europe*. San Antonio, Texas, 1946.

Michener, James A., *Japanese Prints from the Early Masters to the Modern*. Rutland, Vt., and Tokyo, 1960.

Mill, John Stuart, *Collected Works of John Stuart Mill*, ed. F. E. L. Priestley and J. M. Robson. Toronto, 1963–.

Mission to Asia: Narratives and Letters of the Franciscan Missionaries in Mongolia and China in the Thirteenth and Fourteenth Centuries, ed. Christopher Dawson. New York, 1966.

Monk, Samuel H., *The Sublime*. Ann Arbor, 1960.

Monier-Williams, M., *Hinduism*. Calcutta, 1951.

Montesquieu, Charles de Secondat, Baron de, *The Spirit of Laws*, trans. Thomas Nugent, revised edition. London and New York, 1900.

Moon, Penderel, *Gandhi and Modern India*. New York, 1969.

Moore, Charles A., *The Chinese Mind: Essentials of Chinese Philosophy and Culture*. Honolulu, 1967.

———— *The Indian Mind: Essentials of Indian Philosophy and Culture*. Honolulu, 1967.

———— *The Japanese Mind: Essentials of Japanese Philosophy and Culture*. Honolulu, 1967.

Morley, John, *Rousseau*. London, 1873.

Müller, F. Max, ed., *Sacred Books of the East*. Oxford, 1879–.

Munsterberg, Hugo, *The Arts of Japan*. Rutland, Vt., and Tokyo, 1957.

Myrdal, Gunnar, *Asian Drama: An Inquiry Into the Poverty of Nations*. New York, 1968.

Nakamura, Hajime, *Ways of Thinking of Eastern Peoples: India, China, Tibet, Japan*, ed. Philip P. Wiener. Honolulu, 1964.

Nakamura, Tanio, *Sesshu*. Kodansha Library of Japanese Art. Rutland, Vt., and Tokyo, n.d.

Needham, Joseph, *Science and Civilization in China*. Cambridge University Press, 1954–1962.

Neugebauer, O., *The Exact Sciences in Antiquity*, second edition. New York, 1962.

Nicholson, R. A., *A Literary History of the Arabs*. London, 1907.

Nicolson, Marjorie Hope, *Mountain Gloom and Mountain Glory*. New York, 1963.

Northrop, F. S. C., *The Meeting of East and West*. New York, 1946.

———— ed., *Ideological Differences and World Order*. New Haven, 1949.

Okakura, Kakuzo, *The Book of Tea*. Tokyo, n.d.

Osgood, Cornelius, *The Koreans and Their Culture*. New York, 1951.

Otto, Rudolf, *Mysticism East and West*, trans. Bertha L. Bracey and Richenda C. Payne. New York, 1962.

Paine, Robert Treat and Soper, Alexander, *The Art and Architecture of Japan*. Baltimore, 1955.

Panikkar, K. M., *Asia and Western Dominance*. London, 1953.

Parkinson, C. Northcote, *East and West*. New York, 1965.

Peffer, Nathaniel, *The Far East: A Modern History*. Ann Arbor, 1958.

Penrose, Boies, *Travel and Discovery in the Renaissance, 1420–1620*. New York, 1962.

Phillips, E. D., *The Royal Hordes: Nomad Peoples of the Steppes*. New York, 1965.

Piggott, Stuart, *Prehistoric India*. Harmondsworth, Middlesex, 1962.

Pinot, Virgile, *La Chine et la formation de l'esprit philosophique en France (1640–1740)*. Paris, 1932.

Priest, Alan, *Aspects of Chinese Painting*. New York, 1954.

Pritchard, James B., ed., *The Ancient Near East: An Anthology of Texts and Pictures*. Princeton, 1958.

Prodan, Mario, *Chinese Art: An Introduction*. New York, 1958.

Quintilian, *Institutio Oratoria*, trans. H. E. Butler. Cambridge, Mass., and London, 1921–1966. 4 vols.

Radhakrishnan, S., *Eastern Religions and Western Thought*, second edition. London, 1940.

——— *The Hindu View of Life*. London, 1948.

——— *Indian Philosophy*. London, 1923–1927.

——— and Moore, C. A., eds., *A Source Book in Indian Philosophy*. Princeton, 1957.

Ramsay, David, *Universal History Americanised; or, an Historical View of the World*. Philadelphia, 1819.

Rawlinson, H. G., *India: A Short Cultural History*, fourth revised edition. New York, 1965.

Raynal, Guillaume T. F., *A Philosophical and Political History of the Settlements and Trade of the Europeans in the East and West Indies*. Edinburgh, 1804.

Reichwein, Adolf, *China and Europe, Intellectual and Artistic Contacts in the Eighteenth Century*. New York, 1925.

Reischauer, Edwin O., *Japan Past and Present*. New York, 1946.

——— *The United States and Japan*. Cambridge, Mass., 1950.

——— and Fairbank, John K., *East Asia: The Great Tradition*. Boston, 1960.

Renou, Louis, *Indian Literature*, trans. Patrick Evans. New York, 1964.

——— *Religions of Ancient India*. London and New York, 1953.

Rhetorica ad Herennium, trans. Harry Caplan. Cambridge, Mass., and London, 1954.

Ross, Nancy Wilson, *Three Ways of Asian Wisdom: Hinduism, Buddhism, Zen and Their Significance for the West*. New York, 1966.

Rousseau, Jean-Jacques, *Discours sur les sciences et les arts*, ed. George R. Havens. New York and London, 1946.

Rowbotham, Arnold H., *Missionary and Mandarin: The Jesuits at the Court of China*. Berkeley and Los Angeles, 1942.

Rowland, Benjamin, Jr., *The Art and Architecture of India: Buddhist, Hindu, Jain*, second edition. Baltimore, 1959.

―――― *Art in East and West*. Boston, 1964.

―――― *The Harvard Outline and Reading Lists for Oriental Art*, third edition. Cambridge, Mass., 1967.

Saddharma Pundarika or the Lotus of the True Law, trans. H. Kern. New York, 1963.

Sagara, Tokuzo, *Japanese Fine Arts*. S.l., 1949.

Sansom, G. B., *Japan: A Short Cultural History*, revised edition. London, 1946.

―――― *The Western World and Japan: A Study in the Interaction of European and Asiatic Cultures*. New York, 1950.

Sarton, George, *Appreciation of Ancient and Medieval Science During the Renaissance*. New York, 1961.

Sastri, K. A. Nilakantha, *A History of South India*. London, 1958.

Schlegel, Frederick von, *The Philosophy of History*, trans. James Burton Robertson. London, 1848.

Schurmann, Franz and Schell, Orville, eds., *Communist China: Revolutionary Reconstruction and International Confrontation, 1949 to the Present*. New York, 1967.

Schweitzer, Albert, *Indian Thought and Its Development*, trans. Mrs. C. E. B. Russell. London, 1936.

Seznec, Jean, *The Survival of the Pagan Gods*, trans. Barbara F. Sessions. New York, 1961.

Sickman, Laurence and Soper, Alexander, *The Art and Architecture of China*. Baltimore, 1956.

Sidhanta, N. K., *The Heroic Age of India: A Comparative Study*. New York and London, 1930.

Simonde de Sismondi, J. C. L., *Political Economy and the Philosophy of Government: Selections from the Writings of J. C. L. Simonde de Sismondi*. New York, 1966.

Sirén, Osvald, *The Chinese on the Art of Painting*. New York, 1963.

―――― *A History of Early Chinese Painting*. London, 1933.

―――― *A History of Later Chinese Painting*. London, 1938.

Smith, Adam, *An Inquiry into the Nature and Causes of the Wealth of Nations*, ed. Ernest Belfort Bax. London, 1899.

Smith, Huston, *The Religions of Man*. New York, 1958.

Smith, Vincent Arthur, *The Early History of India*. Oxford, 1924.

Spear, T. G. P., *India: A Modern History*. Ann Arbor, 1961.

Spengler, Oswald, *The Decline of the West*, trans. C. F. Atkinson. New York, 1926.

Stcherbatsky, F. Th., *Buddhist Logic*. New York, 1962.

Stein, Aurel, *Serindia*. Oxford, 1921.

Sullivan, Michael, *Introduction to Chinese Art*. Berkeley, 1961.
———— *A Short History of Chinese Art*. Berkeley and Los Angeles, 1967.
Suzuki, D. T., *Outlines of Mahayana Buddhism*. New York, 1963.
———— *Zen and Japanese Buddhism*. Tokyo, 1951.
———— *Zen Buddhism*, ed. William Barrett. Garden City, N.Y., 1956.
Swann, Peter C., *The Art of China, Korea, and Japan*. New York, 1963.
Sykes, P. M., *A History of Persia*. Third edition, London, 1930.
Sze, Mai-mai, *The Way of Chinese Painting*. New York, 1959.
The Taiheiki, a Chronicle of Medieval Japan, trans. Helen Craig McCullough. Records of Civilization, Sources and Studies. New York, 1959.
Tarn, W. W., *Hellenistic Civilisation*, third edition, revised. Cleveland and New York, 1966.
Taylor, Henry Osborn, *The Emergence of Christian Culture in the West, The Classical Heritage of the Middle Ages*. New York, 1958.
Terukazu, Akiyama, *Japanese Painting*. Cleveland, 1961.
Thapar, Romila, *A History of India*. Baltimore, 1966.
Thibaut, George, trans., *The Vedanta Sutras of Badarayana*. New York, 1962.
Thomson, Ian, *Changing Patterns in South Asia*. New York, 1962.
The Tibetan Book of the Dead, ed. W. Y. Evans-Wentz. New York, 1960.
Tibetan Yoga and Secret Doctrines, ed. W. Y. Evans-Wentz, second edition. London and New York, 1967.
Tinker, Hugh, *South Asia: A Short History*. New York, 1966.
Tomlin, E. W. F., *The Oriental Philosophers*. New York, 1963.
Townsend, Meredith, *Asia and Europe*, third edition. New York, 1907.
Toynbee, Arnold J., *A Study of History*. London, 1934–1961.
Tuveson, Ernest Lee, *Millennium and Utopia: A Study in the Background of the Idea of Progress*. Berkeley and Los Angeles, 1949.
Underhill, Evelyn, *Mysticism*, tenth edition. London, 1923.
Vivekananda, Swami, *Bhakti-Yoga*, eighth edition. Mayavati, Almora, 1946.
Voltaire, François Marie Arouet de, *Philosophy of History*, in *The Best Known Works of Voltaire*. New York, 1940.
Wach, Joachim, *The Comparative Study of Religions*, ed. Joseph M. Kitagawa. New York, 1958.
Wales, H. G. Quaritch, *The Making of Greater India*. London, 1951.
Waley, Arthur, *An Introduction to the Study of Chinese Painting*. New York, 1958.
———— *Three Ways of Thought in Ancient China*. New York, 1956.
———— *Zen Buddhism and Its Relation to Art*. London, 1922.

Ward, Barbara, *India and the West*, revised edition. New York, 1964.
————— *The Interplay of East and West*. New York, 1962.
Warmington, E. H., *Commerce Between the Roman Empire and India*. Cambridge, England, 1928.
Warner, Langdon, *The Enduring Art of Japan*. New York, 1958.
Watson, William. *Early Civilization in China*. London, 1967.
————— *Sculpture of Japan from the Fifth to the Fifteenth Century*. London, 1959.
Watts, Alan W., *The Way of Zen*. New York, 1962.
Weber, Max, *The Religion of India*, trans. and ed. Hans H. Gerth and Don Martindale. New York, 1958.
Welch, Holmes, *Taoism, The Parting of the Way*, revised edition. Boston, 1966.
White, Lynn, Jr., *Medieval Technology and Social Change*. New York, 1965.
Wilhelm, Hellmut, *Change: Eight Lectures on the "I Ching,"* trans. Cary F. Baynes. New York and Evanston, 1964.
Wilkinson, J. V. S., *Mughal Painting*. Pitman Gallery of Oriental Art. New York and London, 1949.
Willetts, William, *Chinese Art*. New York, 1958.
Williamson, George, *The Senecan Amble*. Chicago, 1951.
Wint, Guy, *The British in Asia*, second edition. New York, 1954.
————— *Spotlight on Asia*. London, 1955.
Wittfogel, Karl A., *Oriental Despotism: A Comparative Study of Total Power*. New Haven and London, 1964.
Wölfflin, Heinrich, *Classic Art: An Introduction to the Italian Renaissance*. Greenwich, Conn., 1961.
————— *Principles of Art History*, trans. M. C. Hottinger. New York, 1950.
Woodward, F. L., trans., *Some Sayings of the Buddha*. London, 1960.
Wright, Arthur F., ed., *Confucianism and Chinese Civilization*. New York, 1964.
————— *Studies in Chinese Thought*. Chicago and London, 1967.
Yang, C. K., *Religion in Chinese Society*. Berkeley and Los Angeles, 1967.
Zaehner, R. C., *The Comparison of Religions, East and West*. Boston, 1962.
————— *Hindu and Muslim Mysticism*. London, 1960.
————— *Mysticism Sacred and Profane*. New York, 1961.
————— *The Teachings of the Magi*. London, 1956.
————— *Zurvan, a Zoroastrian Dilemma*. Oxford, 1955.
Zimmer, Heinrich, *Myths and Symbols in Indian Art and Civilization*, ed. Joseph Campbell. New York, 1962.
Zinkin, Maurice, *Asia and the West*. London, 1953.

INDEX

333

Anukara, 199
Apara vidya, 144. *See also* Brahman; Knowledge
Apelles, 317
Apollo, 315
"Apollonian man," 128, 201
Apollonius of Perga, 118
Apollonius of Tyana, 133
Appleton, William W., 312, 320
Aquinas, Saint Thomas, 105–108, 115, 284, 288
Arabian Nights, 37, 176
Arabs, 24, 115–120, 126–128, 183, 200, 278, 289, 313
Archeology, 235
Archery, 216
Archimedes, 118
Architecture, 18, 41, 44, 58, 85, 119, 127, 166, 172, 177, 186, 190, 207, 209, 216, 226–229, 243, 266
Arcimboldo, Giuseppe, 148
Arhat, 62, 73, 77, 202–204, 207
Ariosto, Lodovico, 37
Aristotle, 37, 68–69, 83, 102–106, 115, 123–127, 132, 180, 195, 262–264, 275
Arjuna, 60, 140–143, 151, 216
Arnold, Thomas, 178
Art, stereotypes of, 168–179
Arthashastra, 312
Asat (nonbeing), 160
al-Ash'ari, 115
Ashoka, 65, 296, 299
Ashvaghosha, 255
Asia and Europe, antithesis of, 15, 17, 87–88, 98, 146, 165, 259
  ambiguity of terms, 23–25, 35
  development of, 45
  differences exaggerated, 15
Asia and Europe, stereotypes of, aesthetics, 165–254
    emotion and reason, 176
    expression and imitation, 168

idealism and naturalism, 40, 214
internal and external representation, 40, 226–230
intuition and theory, 168–170
spirituality and realism, 40, 168, 194, 226–230
spontaneity and science, 168–170, 214
subjective and objective emphasis, 168
two- and three-dimensional emphasis, 214
"mode of production," 271–272
nature, attitudes toward, 51, 215–242
philosophy, 49–162, 243–256
politics, 259–310
religion, 49–162
  Asian influence on Europe, 122–137
  world-affirmation and world-negation, 15, 140–141
temperament and orientation
  "aesthetic" and "theoretic components," 15
  contemplation and action, 26, 51–52, 67–68
  introspection and extroversion, 26
  intuition and reason, 101, 152
  mysticism and science, 15, 138–162
  Nirvana and Utopia, 49–100
  otherworldliness and this-worldliness, 45–100
  religion and humanism, 15
  self-mastery and mastery of nature, 51
  spirituality
    and materialism, 15, 26–27, 49–100, 113–114
    and reason, 15, 131